RESEARCHING CRIME

WITHDRAWN

2 3 APR 2023

York St John University

3 8025 00616178 3

Also by the authors:

Crowther, C. (2000) *Policing Urban Poverty*. Basingstoke: Macmillan.
Crowther, C. (2007) *An Introduction to Criminology and Criminal Justice*. Basingstoke: Palgrave Macmillan.
Senior, P., Crowther-Dowey, C. and Long, M. (2007) *Understanding Modernisation in Criminal Justice*. Milton Keynes: Open University Press.
Silvestri, M. and Crowther-Dowey, C. (2008) *Gender and Crime*. London: Sage.

Fussey, P., Coaffee, J., Armstrong, G. and Hobbs, D. (2011) *Securing and Sustaining the Olympic City*. Aldgate: Ashgate.
Richards, A., Fussey, P. and Silke, A. (eds) (2010) *Terrorism and the Olympics*. London: Routledge.

RESEARCHING CRIME

APPROACHES, METHODS AND APPLICATION

Chris Crowther-Dowey

and

Pete Fussey

YORK ST. JOHN
LIBRARY & INFORMATION
SERVICES

palgrave
macmillan

© Chris Crowther-Dowey and Pete Fussey 2013

All rights reserved. No reproduction, copy or transmission of this publication may be made without written permission.

No portion of this publication may be reproduced, copied or transmitted save with written permission or in accordance with the provisions of the Copyright, Designs and Patents Act 1988, or under the terms of any licence permitting limited copying issued by the Copyright Licensing Agency, Saffron House, 6–10 Kirby Street, London EC1N 8TS.

Any person who does any unauthorized act in relation to this publication may be liable to criminal prosecution and civil claims for damages.

The authors have asserted their rights to be identified as the authors of this work in accordance with the Copyright, Designs and Patents Act 1988.

First published 2013 by
PALGRAVE MACMILLAN

Palgrave Macmillan in the UK is an imprint of Macmillan Publishers Limited, registered in England, company number 785998, of Houndmills, Basingstoke, Hampshire RG21 6XS.

Palgrave Macmillan in the US is a division of St Martin's Press LLC, 175 Fifth Avenue, New York, NY 10010.

Palgrave Macmillan is the global academic imprint of the above companies and has companies and representatives throughout the world.

Palgrave® and Macmillan® are registered trademarks in the United States, the United Kingdom, Europe and other countries.

ISBN: 978–0–230–23019–4   hardback
ISBN: 978–0–230–23020–0   paperback

This book is printed on paper suitable for recycling and made from fully managed and sustained forest sources. Logging, pulping and manufacturing processes are expected to conform to the environmental regulations of the country of origin.

A catalogue record for this book is available from the British Library.

A catalog record for this book is available from the Library of Congress.

Typeset by Aardvark Editorial Limited, Metfield, Suffolk

In memory of Tony Dowey

CONTENTS

LIST OF FIGURES AND TABLES

ACKNOWLEDGEMENTS

We are indebted to many people, both professionally and personally, who have contributed in various ways towards making the publication of this book possible. As always, all errors and omissions are our own.

We are particularly grateful to Palgrave Macmillan for their patience over the past few years, in particular Anna-Marie Reeve (now at Roman & Littlefield) for her constructive advice at all stages of the publication process. Thanks also to Jenny Hindley for her guidance in the final stages and for bringing the book into production. We owe a great many thanks to the work of Linda Norris and the team at Aardvark Editorial, especially to Maggie Lythgoe for possessing such fine editing abilities.

The support and good humour of academic colleagues and friends is always welcome. In particular, Chris would like to thank Natasha Chubbock, James Hunter, Terry Gillespie, Paul Hamilton and Roger Hopkins Burke for the jokes, banter and teamwork. Tony Poyser is a good friend and a reminder that there is a bit more to life than books and that live music still matters. Pete would like to thank his criminologically inclined colleagues at the University of Essex's Department of Sociology – especially Eamonn Carrabine, Nigel South, Dick Hobbs, Darren Thiel, Pam Cox and Jackie Turton – for helping to provide such an enjoyable and intellectually stimulating environment in which to work. Thanks are also due to Jon Coaffee, Dan Sage, Andy Dainty and Paddy Rawlinson, who have all had the dubious pleasure of accompanying Pete in the field, have been generous with their sharp ideas (and sharper advice) and, ultimately, have informed many of the ideas expressed in this book.

Our families are always there too. Pete is especially grateful to his family, both Fussey and Doshi, and particularly to mum and dad, for years of support. Above all, Pete would like to thank Jai, Mia and Mo for their unfailing and unconditional love and encouragement. Chris has dedicated the book to the memory of Tony Dowey, his father-in-law, as a belated thanks for his generosity and now much missed stories about football, antiques and the odd bit of skulduggery. Finally, thanks to Helen for her enduring love and for making sure there is still wonder in the world.

The authors and publisher would like to thank QSR International Pty Ltd for permission to use the NVivo qualitative data analysis software screenshots in Figures 5.1, 5.2, 5.3, 5.4, 5.5, 5.6, 5.7, 5.8, 5.9, 5.10, 5.11 and 5.12, and would also like to thank International Business Machines Corporation for permission to use screenshots of their IBM® SPSS® Statistics software.

INTRODUCTION

OVERVIEW

The aim of this chapter is to:

- Explain the rationale of the book.
- Outline why we need to care about criminological research, not least because the evidence obtained by researchers goes beyond a commonsense understanding of crime and its control.
- Give some examples of what research looks like by focusing on general theoretical and conceptual issues relating to quantitative and qualitative approaches to researching crime.
- Summarize the structure, content and purpose of the book.

THE RATIONALE OF THE BOOK

Researching Crime: Approaches, Methods and Application is, in essence, a handbook aimed at providing guidance on how you can conduct robust criminological research. A key requirement to make sure you do this properly is the ability to ask and attempt to answer questions, potentially about any aspect of crime and its control, by using the most suitable tools or methods available. The methods outlined in this book are:

- Interviews and focus groups
- Surveys and questionnaires
- Ethnographic approaches or observational research
- Secondary research

- Library-based literature reviews
- Content analysis, conversation analysis and discourse analysis.

For each method, we will refer to:

- its purpose and the reasons for doing a particular piece of research
- issues of planning, design and preparation
- the processes and procedures for using the selected research method
- data collection and analysis or attempts to make sense of data
- the relationship between methods, research data and theory
- reviewing, evaluating and assessing research.

An overarching aim is to highlight what a researcher like you needs to know and to identify the skills needed if you are to apply particular methods in your own research project. We cover many different types of research in terms of the size and scale of projects, but the practical guidance provided is intended to be realistic about what you can reasonably be expected to achieve. Although a core objective is to outline the fundamentals of how to do research, for example how to interview, survey or observe, criminological research is not done in isolation from other factors.

Our approach to crime research is underpinned by the assumption that it is a practical activity conducted for a variety reasons. It can be motivated purely by interest in the subject matter and nothing else, but we are more pragmatic and take on board the more instrumental reasons for engaging in this activity. Many of you will be learning about this topic to gain a qualification and probably to enhance your employment prospects. Most crucially, crime is a big social issue and one that not only concerns those of us directly affected by it, but is also a policy issue taken seriously by governments and criminal justice agencies. For instance, what can the police and prison services do to prevent future terrorist attacks such as the attack on the Twin Towers in New York City (9/11) in September 2001, the Madrid train bombings in March 2004, or the suicide bombers who attacked London's transport network (7/7) in July 2005? Research has been carried out by government bodies and universities to look at the causes of these acts and to inform the formulation and application of fitting policy responses. Subsequently, on the back of research evidence, governments across the world have implemented legislation to increase police powers and enhance surveillance, to reduce the threat of similar future attacks. Sometimes, it serves the needs and interests of powerful groups such as policy makers, so it is important that all researchers think critically about such influences.

Another important matter having a bearing on crime research is that criminology is an interdisciplinary enterprise drawing on many bodies of knowledge and approaches to research. Our focus on the application of research methods is explicitly social scientific, drawing mainly on sociology, but also on other disciplines across the social sciences and humanities, for example psychology, social policy, law, geography, cultural studies and history. These disciplines all share an interest in describing and explaining the relationships between individuals and the environment or society they inhabit. However, other disciplines such as the natural sciences, for example biology, genetics, engineering, have made and continue to make a contribution. For all these disciplines and the separate areas of research they address, research methods are core features. In short, criminological research is open to the influence of many disciplinary traditions. This is reflected in the richness and diversity of its content.

There are two other central rationales of this book. The first is to stress how criminological research cannot be seen in isolation from criminological theory, and that the interplay between theory and the methods used is fundamentally important. Theories exist to explain what research data is telling us about crime and social control and, over time, theories are revised, adapted or rejected in light of new research data. Bluntly, criminological theory would not exist without research and vice versa.

Second, we stress the importance of treating criminological research as a process. The book identifies several distinctive stages, which inform the planning and execution of all criminological research. For example, it is necessary to identify a topic and ask a question. The question asked determines the selection of an appropriate research strategy and the method(s) used. The application of these methods faces several constraints, not least that it is not possible to study everything relating to a topic. Important factors that must be taken on board include sampling and gaining access to data and resources, that is, time and money. Different methods generally produce different forms of data, which, in turn, require varying techniques of data analysis. Information and nuances extracted from the data are then used to reflect on existing knowledge, literature and research on the selected topic.

Since the late 1990s, a key item on a researcher's checklist is ethical considerations, especially for projects involving empirical research or fieldwork with human subjects. Research into crime is preoccupied with subject matter that is politically and morally controversial and ethical guidelines lay down safeguards to protect the integrity of everyone involved, particularly by respecting the anonymity and confidentiality of people and data. Due to the vulnerability or potentially harmful behaviour of, and information held by, some of the groups being researched, for example offenders and victims, it is imperative that the physical safety and moral and legal probity of the researcher as well as the research participants are preserved.

We say more about the themes rehearsed above in the summaries of the chapters in Part 2.

THE VALUE OF CRIMINOLOGICAL RESEARCH

To do criminological research, it is not only necessary for you to understand the different research methods used by criminologists, but also to appreciate why this activity is important. Undertaking research into crime allows us to go beyond common sense or our basic assumptions about criminological matters and develop a detailed and sophisticated understanding of these issues. As noted above, criminological research starts with a question about a particular issue or problem related to crime and the activities of the criminal justice system. Think about the following questions:

1. Does addiction to hard drugs, such as heroin, cause people to rob and steal more than people who do not misuse this type of drug?
2. If the police service decides to deploy additional officers on patrol for a few days, does this result in the police catching more criminals?

These are the sort of questions a criminologist might ask and many of us may already hold an opinion on these issues. Two plausible and natural reactions would be to conclude either: 'The answer to this question is definitely yes', or 'Given what I know about this, I think the answer is no'. How can these answers be backed up? Someone may have strong opinions on these topics based on personal experience or might even draw on the second-hand experiences of people they have talked to. Such views may be informed by a television documentary, news item or a website. As a criminological researcher, you should not rely on these as the only or main source of information; you must find other forms of evidence, data or information to support an answer to the question.

This data needs to be acquired by applying particular research methods, such as speaking to or watching the people involved in crime-related activity or by extracting written information and records on particular issues. For the topical examples above, data can be obtained from official agencies, such as government departments, the police, the courts and correctional agencies, that is, prison and probation. Offenders, victims and practitioners working in the field can also provide potentially relevant evidence. It may be that the evidence amassed through research supports an answer of 'yes' or 'no', but the answer arrived at has more credibility than just one person's opinion. If the researcher has used tried and tested research methods, then others should be able to evaluate and assess or understand how the researcher arrived at their conclusion. This means the research findings are more valid and reliable. It may also be possible for others to repeat the research to either support or reject previous research findings. This, and much, much more, is the stuff of criminological research.

FORMS OF CRIMINOLOGICAL RESEARCH

Doing criminological research – and certainly before you can commence with any fieldwork – entails reading a lot of research material from many different sources, including academic lecturers, government researchers and various interest groups. Research appears in many formats including reports, journal articles, monographs and academic books. Compared to 15 years ago, research data is relatively easy to access in printed and electronic formats via the internet. The structure of each piece of published research is similar, in the sense that each study contains a clear methodological and theoretical thread running throughout it and the gathering and analysis of data is preceded by a systematic review of the relevant literature. Despite these commonalities, there is a fundamental division between two distinctive research methodologies – quantitative and qualitative – which may not present you with irreconcilable differences but will certainly generate an ongoing debate about the pros and cons of these distinctive styles. The points made below are central to all criminological research.

Quantitative and qualitative approaches to research

Most books on research methods draw a distinction between qualitative and quantitative data: the former generally refers to words and textual information, and the latter largely concentrates on numerical or statistical information.

Positivist social scientists tend to practise quantitative research and hold to a view that criminological research can produce the type of data obtained by natural scientists such as physicists and chemists. The work undertaken by scholars working in these fields is complex, but a central organizing principle of what they do is an assumption that the natural world is open to measurement through the use of mathematical formulae, especially statistics, and the emphasis is on quantifying phenomenon. There is a view that statistics are what is sometimes called 'hard data' that cannot be reasonably questioned. They are facts about an objective reality.

Qualitative research is more difficult to define than quantitative research. In essence, criminologists whose preference is for qualitative research express scepticism towards the assumptions held by positivists and others, objecting to the presumption held by the latter that the world is amenable to an objective quantification. Interpretivists, as many qualitative researchers are often described, argue that the methods used by positivists are faulty, but, more fundamentally, that quantitative research and data do not capture the complexity of human experience. It is not possible to come to terms with human emotions and subjectivity. As far as statistics go, they are not facts existing independently of human interpretation. Statistics can only be made meaningful as part of an interpretative process. Qualitative data is not produced to quantify human experience and is based on recognition that the universe is not subject to being counted. Human experience cannot be contained in this way and is much more open ended.

THE ORGANIZING STRUCTURE OF THE BOOK

Part 1 (Chapters 1–3) is dedicated to learning about the principles of research and we touch on some key themes of immediate relevance to the crime researcher. As well as outlining some of the practicalities of what research actually involves, it examines the factors that drive and shape it, including social scientific and political values. We have already acknowledged the close relationship between research and theory and Chapter 3 gives some concrete examples that underline the importance of such connections.

The emphasis in Chapter 1 is placed on viewing crime research as an iterative and integrated process, including the collection and analysis of data. The chapter contemplates the many practical elements of research, starting with some observations about integrating theory and research. Every research project, large and small, follows a broadly similar process but student research is, quite understandably, going to be more modest and constrained. For instance, you will not have the same resources to invest in a project. It may also be difficult for you to gain access to organizations and groups of people. There are factors that all criminologists must take into account, such as being realistic about the scope or aims and objectives of a study. Research ethics, and the role of research ethics committees and independent review boards, is a notable development in recent years. An appreciation of and commitment to adhering to ethical guidelines is important and empirical research cannot be done without the approval of such committees. This topic is introduced in Chapter 1 and we elaborate on its importance in Chapters 5, 6, 7 and 9, where we provide anonymized examples of student research projects. On the one hand, this process is sequential, but on the other hand, it is iterative, in the sense that a researcher may move back and forth between the different stages at different times.

Chapter 2 describes some of the complex factors that shape and influence criminological research. We argue that internal and external influences exert themselves on the research process. Taking the former, the selection of a particular research method is based on the assumptions a researcher makes about the nature of the social world. This is reflected by their theoretical preferences and their commitment to either qualitative or quantitative traditions of research. In particular, deeply held beliefs about the requisite standard of evidence and how knowledge is derived exert a significant influence on the design, progression and outcome of criminological research enterprises. At the same time, a number of external factors play a role in shaping criminological research. These may include the source of project funding, whether the research is of an applied nature, and a range of practical factors, such as the availability of time and access to the research population. Other less obvious but still important influences on crime research are the values underpinning government policy and the activities of the state and the media. The government can determine the types of research that receive financial and political support. The media can also be a powerful influence because it draws on crime research in its outputs and can campaign for research into issues it deems important.

Chapter 3 provides a brief and necessarily selective outline of the development of criminological thought and theory since the nineteenth century to the present day, stressing the centrality of research methods to its growth. The tone of this chapter necessarily varies in style from other chapters because discussion of theory is different to the practice of doing research. We appreciate that theory is sometimes quite daunting, but by reading this chapter, you will come to terms with how research and theory inform each other. The chapter starts from the premise that our personal opinions about crime and crime control are limited and clearly defined scientific principles offer us more accurate and plausible accounts of human behaviour. Many different criminological theories attempt to develop systematic explanations of what we claim to know about crime and the choice of methods is vitally important. The chapter includes a basic description of the research methods used by criminologists, representing a diversity of theoretical perspectives, including biological positivism, the Chicago School, social control theory, postmodern and cultural criminologies, realist criminology, feminism and crime science.

Part 2 (Chapters 4–9) focuses on the practicalities of doing research. It details the essential research methods used by criminologists to explore issues such as offending behaviour, victimization, and efforts to reduce crime by the police, courts, prison and probation services, as well as the private and voluntary community sectors. The chapters provide guidelines and suggestions on how to conduct your own research. Each research method is different and therefore the coverage of each one will vary to some extent, which means the chapters sometimes have a slightly different feel. For instance, Chapter 8 includes more than one distinctive approach and some methods are more amenable to quantitative instead of qualitative research. However, to ensure consistency and enhance accessibility, each chapter refers to the general features of a particular research method, highlights examples of research produced by professional researchers, and then shows you what you would need to do if you applied the method in practice.

Chapter 4 concentrates on using other people's data, especially official sources. It examines the wealth of existing data available to you and demonstrates how it can be accessed and drawn on in your research project. The chapter begins by explaining what 'official' data is and how it is created. Since crime recording began, understanding the amount of crime in society has been a problematic endeavour. An essential part of any application of official crime statistics is an appreciation of the many shortcomings and difficulties associated with such data. Next, it looks in more detail at how these official findings may be accessed for reanalysis and explores the role of the internet as a resource for criminological researchers. This is complemented with a comprehensive online research guide in Appendix 1.

Chapter 5 looks at surveys and questionnaires, probably the most easily recognized forms of research method. Most of us have, at some point, been stopped on the street by a researcher with a clipboard, telephoned or emailed by someone asking us to complete a questionnaire. Although surveys are perhaps most widely employed to canvass opinion about consumer preferences or voting intentions, increasingly they have become an important tool for criminologists studying patterns of crime and trends in offending behaviour. However, survey design can be an extremely complex undertaking, with numerous pitfalls you must be aware of in order to avoid devaluing the acquired data. This chapter explores these issues and provides a comprehensive guide for those of you planning on using this method of research. This is broken down into several stages, including types of survey, types of questions, phrasing questions correctly, piloting research, sampling, identifying variables, and understanding types of data. The chapter also demonstrates a number of techniques that can be applied to analyse survey data, and provides an introduction to using the industry-standard quantitative research software package, SPSS®.

Chapter 6 explores the interview, a popular method with criminologists, used to explore almost all issues covered by the discipline. This chapter differentiates interviews from questionnaires and describes four main types of interview – structured, semi-structured, unstructured and what are commonly described as 'focus groups'. We outline some of the reasons given by researchers for choosing to adopt interview methods, which are mainly used to gather qualitative data. We examine the main approaches to interviewing, the context of the research process and show how to develop, design and administer uncomplicated interview schedules. The focus is on a host of practical issues, paying close attention to the negotiation of access to potential interviewees or participants, thinking about the resourcing of interviews, and ethical considerations. The chapter also investigates the topic of sampling or selecting interviewees, with regard to qualitative data and how researchers go about evaluating its reliability and validity.

Throughout are sections dedicated to the analysis of qualitative interview data, referring mainly to paper-based approaches, although there is some acknowledgement of the availability of computer packages to help researchers analyse this material. The relative strengths and weakness of interviews are scrutinized.

Chapter 7 introduces ethnographic and observational research. This approach has been the foundation of a number of studies that have made an immense contribution to knowledge and understanding of many criminological issues. The chapter begins by introducing the ethnographic method and outlines some of its important features. Of particular interest here is the context or environment within which research participants (and researchers) operate. Next, it discusses the process you have to undergo when conducting ethnographic studies. The different stages are delineated, including an account of design, doing the research and data analysis. You are encouraged to think about how you could do some ethnographic research and, crucially, to consider issues of access and ethics. This is followed by examples of student research projects using this method.

Chapter 8 has a dual focus and considers the use of documents either in the context of a library-based study or in relation to methods known as 'content analysis', 'discourse analysis' and 'conversation analysis'. The first part of the chapter tells you how to do a piece of library-based research, including rapid evidence assessments and the systematic preparation and writing up of literature reviews. Literature reviews are, however, an essential element of any piece of research, because they help to define and refine the focus of a piece of research. After taking on board the incentives for doing this type of research, there is a detailed discussion of the skills needed to successfully gather and analyse this type of data. The chapter also introduces a number of methods used to analyse texts. Some advocates of discourse and conversational analysis argue that language plays a key role in shaping social reality. This is a radical view and it stands as an alternative and innovative set of approaches compared to some of the traditional, more established methods described in earlier chapters. Given the constraints you might face, in particular the increased influence of research ethics committees in many universities and colleges, these are useful alternative research methods that are relatively inexpensive to apply and can yield interesting insights into the influence of language on crime and society.

Whereas Chapters 4–8 deal with each method independently, Chapter 9 looks at combining and mixing methods or 'triangulation' in criminological research. The purpose of this relatively short chapter is to advise you that many researchers use several methods and types of data in a single project. Drawing on the important notion of 'triangulation', the chapter aims to show how different methods enable researchers to amass different types of data, resulting in the enhanced validity and reliability of research. Crucially, you are made aware that although it is possible to combine research methods, important epistemological and ontological issues must be taken into account.

The concluding chapter summarizes the key themes relating to researching crime, specifically methods, approaches and application. We provide you with a checklist, which is designed to help you with the intellectual and practical challenges you will face at each stage of the research process.

PART

1

THE PRINCIPLES OF RESEARCH

CHAPTERS

1

RESEARCH AS AN INTEGRATED PROCESS

OVERVIEW

The aim of this chapter is to:

- Describe the things you need to think about before starting your research.
- Explain how to review research literature and ask your own research questions.
- Outline the research design choices.
- Outline the practical things you need to think about when doing your research including resources and access, sampling, research ethics, and analysing and writing up data.

INTRODUCTION

This chapter gives a flavour and broad overview of the processes all researchers move through when tackling a research project, emphasizing that it is an integrated process. Focusing on the pragmatic considerations that researchers confront, it also introduces some of the practical things to think about when planning and doing research. This will be followed up in terms of specific research methods in Part 2. The chapter shows that there are established means to conduct research and several separate but interconnected stages belonging to the research process. The different stages are examined sequentially, but criminologists are aware that the process does not always follow such an ordered sequence, as if one stage – and all its sub-activities – was first completed before proceeding to the next. Rather, what is involved is an iterative process, meaning that later stages, for example resources and ethics, feed back into earlier stages, necessitating further consideration of the appropriateness of the method(s) selected for achieving the aims and objectives of the research.

Appropriateness and achievability are major considerations. Appropriateness concerns the best method, or mix of methods, to investigate the subject area and answer the research question. Achievability (feasibility or 'doability') is essentially about the constraints, the limitations imposed by time, space and access, and – a more prominent concern today than in the past – research ethics and the associated approval procedures. Thus, appropriateness issues could be seen as 'ideal-world' considerations. What would be the most accurate, incisive, enlightening, revealing ways of 'getting at' the topic? Questions of appropriateness range from large philosophical questions, about research values and criminological theory, to the concrete practical decisions involved in thinking through the specific research design for the project. Achievability concerns scale down these ambitions to real-world possibilities. Broadly speaking, the key stages identified here – starting out and designing a research strategy – are about finding an appropriate research approach, while practicalities, as the name suggests, focus on achievability.

In sum, to be a competent and effective practising researcher, it is necessary to be familiar with a range of wider influences on the research process rather than simply the nuts and bolts of applying particular methods. At any one time, you must also be realistic about what can be achieved in a research project and there are a series of reality checks throughout the chapter to ensure this. There are, for example, guiding principles and ideas that govern social scientific research, which we call 'internal drivers' or influences. There are also myriad motivations and drivers or external shapers behind research, not least the influence of the state and politics in general (see Chapter 2). This chapter and Chapter 3 foreground the need for criminological theory to interact with empirical research.

INITIAL CONSIDERATIONS

Integration of theory and research

On the surface, the bulk of this chapter – and book – is very much hands on and is about the physical constraints of doing crime research. Yet, we cannot stress enough that there is a strong connection between research and theory. When studying the complex subject of research methods, it is all too easy to be consumed by the practicalities and technicalities of this process and overlook the fact that all criminologists carry out research to build, develop or reflect on theory.

What is criminological theory? Answering this question is far from straightforward and it is probably more difficult than responding to a question about a particular theoretical approach, such as 'what is social control theory'? A useful way of looking at criminological theory is to see it as a toolkit used by criminologists to offer explanations of the reasons why crime occurs and what can be done to prevent and reduce it. Harrison et al. (2005: 67) offer a helpful definition:

> ❝ In attempting to explain the facts that we know about crime we use theoretical perspectives. Theories are part of that explanation and, according to Vold et al., 'an explanation is a sensible way of relating some particular phenomenon to the ... information, beliefs and attitudes that make up the intellectual atmosphere of a people at a particular time or place'.

A key point is that those 'facts' Harrison et al. (2005) refer to are obtained through research. Theory is dependent on research but at the same time research also depends on theory. Theoretical approaches often heavily influence key elements of the research process, especially the type of questions that are asked and how we attempt to answer them in practice. They also inform fundamental beliefs about the nature of knowledge and how it can be generated, as well as the way in which **research aims** are developed and the selection of methodological tools. In turn, empirical data is often used to reflect on the **validity**, applicability and relevance of such theoretical positions.

Scope of student research: what you can achieve and prove

Before a researcher can even begin to research a project, they must be realistic about what they can deliver, its significance and impact. The research you will be asked to plan and carry out is likely to be more basic than the projects completed by professional criminologists, but doing research involves the negotiation of a steep learning curve and every researcher needs to begin with some basic tasks before advancing to the next stage. Undergraduate and graduate studies will be relatively small scale but it is still possible to make a contribution to knowledge and provide some original insights into an issue. Over several years and with a lot of practice, the work of researchers can impact on crime and public policy and redefine the parameters of theoretical criminology. The aims and objectives of the research you will do will be more modest, reflecting the skills and knowledge you possess. Thus, for various methodological reasons discussed throughout this book, the kind of work you will produce at this level is not going to prove that violent films can trigger a serial killer into action or that poverty is the main cause of rioting. Notably, even established crime researchers do not necessarily prove something, but they will have provided a transparent and explicit account of the different stages of the research process leading to the claims they make. This means it is possible for future researchers to replicate this research, which could actually lend support to the original study or show something else. Despite these comments, all research is significant in the sense that it is being done for a particular reason, even if that is to pass an assessment and graduate with a qualification. The 'doing research for a reason' theme is followed up in Chapter 2.

STARTING OUT ON THE RESEARCH PROCESS

We have indicated that there are various established ways of doing research and that these belong to an integrated process. Next, we refer to each of the different stages, which all researchers need to pass through as part of a 'journey'. Unfortunately, there are no shortcuts and if attempts are made to find them, this can compromise the quality – and possibly the legality – of the research. We have set out these stages in a way that is more or less logical and we suggest you read this chapter for the purpose of familiarization. The sequential framework below will help you to prepare for and plan a piece of research, with most emphasis being placed on the planning. Being organized and approaching problem solving systematically is a key prerequisite for this activity. Because the process is iterative, all researchers necessarily refer back and forth between these stages. For example, after reading the vast literature on sex offending, one of your fellow students may be interested in further exploring the causes of this behaviour by interviewing a group of prisoners serving a prison sentence for committing a sex offence. They may have designed an interview schedule and be ready to commence the research, but the **research ethics committee** or **independent review board** rejects the proposed research because the interview questions are unethical. Your colleague therefore needs to reflect on the aims and objectives of their original research plan, possibly by rewriting the interview schedule, deciding to use a different method or even rethinking the whole project. This is an extreme example, but this continuous cross-referencing and reflection are important.

Conducting a literature review

It is assumed that you will have a general research topic in mind. Before doing any systematic research, it is necessary for you to read around the topic to see what has been written and what we already know about a particular aspect of the topic you wish to research.

What is a literature review?

Put simply, a **literature review** is an overview or summary of what has been written on any given subject, although within certain parameters, not least the research question that is being explored. We elaborate on this point about research questions in the next section. Sometimes, a full overview is not feasible so a review only investigates some of the literature. Reviews of this kind are inconclusive and can include information that is inconsistent and contradictory in terms of content and quality. For some popular themes, the literature is vast and without a generous allocation of time to the project, it is rarely possible to read everything about an issue. Literature reviews are therefore selective and partial, so care must be taken to ensure that the work read and reviewed actually represents the state of play in a research area. There are parallels here with sampling, in particular the emphasis on **representativeness**, and it is necessary to have a rationale for selecting the targeted literature. Any review should be rigorous and based on awareness of publication bias, which is important because some publications tend to focus more on research findings that are positive, that is, a policy to reduce reoffending that works, rather than negative, that is, a policy to reduce reoffending that does not work.

A literature review can be written on any topic so long as there is available literature. The topic may be theoretical, about policy/practice or a combination of both. Because criminological knowledge has been growing for at least three centuries, the chances of there being a topic with no literature is small. From time to time, it may seem that 'there is nothing on a topic', which in nearly all cases is untrue – there are many ways to locate and retrieve information provided a search is systematic and correctly focused (see Chapters 4 and 8). If there is a topic on which nothing has been written, it is possibly because the topic is not regarded as researchable. This is not always the case, though, and just because there is not any easily found body of research, it does not mean research should not be done. For example, a new crime or policy response to it may be discovered.

It is advisable for you to refer to a checklist when producing a literature review:

1. The aim is to identify the available literature relating to the research topic.
2. The methodologies used in the studies, as well as the assumptions underpinning the research, are important.
3. The populations and samples used in the studies being reviewed must be noted. In some instances, this information may not be disclosed, which is important.
4. The key findings and concluding arguments of the study should be summarized.
5. The 'politics' of research and ethical issues. Please note that some older research did not require ethical review and clearance and researchers used their discretion and subjective judgements when deciding what to do. You must obtain ethical approval.
6. Any piece of research has areas where improvements could be made so the limitations of the research should be spelled out.

What counts as literature in criminological research?

Books are an obvious source of information about a subject area. You should be reading academic books rather than texts intended for the general reader, although for those of you interested in populist or media representations of crime about gangsters or serial killers, references to publications of this kind are unavoidable and exceptions can be made. There is not just one type of academic book. Textbooks offer an introductory and hopefully balanced overview of the area it covers but little more than that. Other, more advanced books, such as monographs that are narrowly focused, and edited collections based on particular themes or conference proceedings, are often useful resources for a research project. When referring to a book in a project, check that it covers what it says on the jacket, is relevant to your project and, if a current issue is covered, is up to date.

Journals publish articles, typically 5,000–10,000 words in length. There are many kinds of journal and this type of publication tends to be more specialized and contain more up-to-date, 'cutting-edge' research that stands as an original contribution to knowledge. There are general criminological journals that cover the breadth and depth of the discipline and others that concentrate on key areas of the criminal justice process like the police and correctional or prison and probation services. Others may specialize in theory or a criminological theme such as cultural criminology or topics such as gender. To find the highest quality articles, a search could be focused towards peer reviewed journals, where several experts review an article to judge its quality and whether or not it is publishable. Such journals are widely considered to be the most authoritative. Some articles review the work of others and although these are important, they are not seen to be as prestigious as the research article. Some journals are non-peer reviewed and these must be treated with some caution. To assess the quality of a journal, the Journal Citation Reports database can be accessed, a source that includes information about citations taken from 7,000 journals (speak to your librarian about how to use this database). This shows those journals that are used the most and those that have the highest impact on the discipline and on crime policy.

Grey literature is work that is either in progress or unpublished, such as conference proceedings. The quality of this work could be excellent, although an absence of formal quality control is likely because it is a first draft that has not been through the peer review process. It is vital to judge this work by referring to the authority of the author or organization and the intended audience. In policy-relevant research, the term **grey literature** sometimes refers to a diverse range of crucially important documents that are not 'academic'. If you are aiming to embark on an empirical study of an organization working in the criminal justice

field, documents such as policy statements and strategic plans, relevant legislation, annual reports, minutes of meetings are all significant. Other sources
include diaries and personal letters, especially if the research is historical and
attempting to gain knowledge and understanding of past events through autobiographical materials.

While grey literature can sometimes be difficult to locate, there is no doubt
about the organization or individual responsible for writing it. For policy-relevant
research, the agency commissioning the study will give the researcher access to
those documents central to the research, but the funder of the research determines those texts that they think are significant. Some files may be treated as
confidential or sensitive and not for the eyes of the researcher. In contrast to
academic literature, which adheres to certain scientific principles and protocols, grey literature serves the interests of the author(s). This could be to formulate, implement and evaluate policy or create a personal account of their ways of
seeing the world that is not designed as a dispassionate and value-neutral text.
This is not to say that the information is not important, rather that any potential
bias must be acknowledged and confirmation and verification is dependent on
the use of other sources and methods.

Many web sources are of high quality, especially those belonging to key
criminal justice organizations. This is not always the case, though. The fact that
anyone, anywhere, can create their own website means that some materials
should be treated with caution and scepticism. See Chapter 4 for details of this
source of data.

Why do criminologists conduct and write literature reviews?

The literature review is not optional for any project and must be done. Empirical
research is always informed by previously published research. For example,
an attempt to question, interview or observe burglars to discover their motivations depends on some knowledge about previous research findings in the area.
Criminological knowledge is typically built gradually over time through research
and theory, which can only be achieved by a sound understanding of prior work.
The literature review ultimately enriches a project and is a vital step in the process, because it:

- saves you saying that you are doing something new when you are not
- shows you are familiar with the topic
- helps you to formulate and refine a research question
- enables you to connect analysis to the discipline of criminology.

One alternative to conducting fieldwork, for example trying to access organized criminals, is to undertake a research project that is entirely library based.

This type of research is essentially an extended literature review. Such a project is legitimate and could be the most appropriate approach if:

- Gaining access to do fieldwork proves difficult: but do not assume accessing literature is always easy going. While much may have been written about some topics, this material is not available in all libraries. Many universities have inter-library loan systems for researchers, yet there may be limits on how many sources can be borrowed and processing requests can take up a lot of time.
- The research topic is ethically sensitive and contentious: but library-based studies may require careful thinking about the use of language, such as particularly offensive and derogatory methods of ethnic classification and phrases describing the sexual orientation or social class of a person. Research ethics committees often issue statements on this.
- The proposed empirical work is not going to achieve anything that has not already been achieved: but this reason on its own should never put you off trying.

Beyond these negative considerations is a positive reason for this approach, namely to provide an original and novel synthesis of the existing literature relating to a particular issue. Chapter 8 discusses the practicalities of doing a literature review and document-based research.

So, we have established that a literature review is a key aspect of any proposed and live research project. Like any area of research, it is a good idea to have a clear view about the type of information needed to complete it. What information is it that must be captured to meet the needs of your project? This will depend on the title, aims and objectives of the research, key themes explored next.

Identifying gaps and developing research questions

At the outset of the process, any criminologist will ask themselves a fundamental question: 'What are the aims or objectives of my research?' You must ask yourself this too. When answering this question, you will be identifying a gap in the existing literature. A gap, in this sense, is an issue that has not been examined before, or a question that remains unanswered or needs revisiting in order that it can be updated. This will entail some reflection on theoretical assumptions, such as the relative importance attached to particular views about what causes people to steal, that is, because they are greedy or because they are mentally ill and not in full control of their thoughts and actions. Although setting a question seems like a straightforward task, you need to spend considerable time in getting this absolutely right or your research will never take off and, even if it does, it will, in all likelihood, never be satisfactorily finished. Among other ways of looking at things, there are two types of research question: those that are researchable or doable; and those that are not. In order to ensure your question is in the former category, you must know how to set a research question that is sufficiently clear to enable you to arrive at some answers, however provisional and inconclusive.

To illustrate this part of the process a little more concretely, take the following research question as an example: 'What is the cause of crime?' Put simply, this question is too big and lacking in focus. It would prove difficult to answer without infinite time and resources. More specifically, it is based on an assumption that all crimes have the same cause. Do offences against property, for example theft, have the same causes as crimes against the person, for example assault? Do you look for the cause of crime at the level of the individual or social structure? For example, the causes of rape are likely to be different from the causes of theft. A better, more doable research question needs to be narrower and more specific. Rather than asking: 'What is the cause of crime?', the question could be revised to ask: 'Why do men commit rape?' or 'Why do people commit the act of theft?'

While these examples have a more distinct question, they are not without their problems, mainly because they are still quite broad. This could be improved by adding some related sub-questions. For instance, a traditional criminological approach focusing on the individual level might anticipate that there would be more than one factor accounting for a man raping a woman. Sub-questions have traditionally included drug or alcohol consumption by the perpetrator, but might perhaps consider the age of or educational qualifications held by the men committing this crime, locating this as a more structural factor; that is, something bigger than or external to the individual that enables or constrains what they do. Emphasis on drug/alcohol consumption as a cause of rape is likely to entail explicit or implicit reliance on the theoretical assumption of the lawbreaker as a rational actor and the extent to which his capacity to make rational choices was affected by consuming mind-altering substances. By contrast, a feminist researcher would take a quite different approach, typically focusing on questions of male power, at the structural and individual level, to explain how women are coerced, how this is linked to male pleasure in rape and arguing that, while rape is officially condemned as a crime, it also forms a powerful mechanism of social control (Silvestri and Crowther-Dowey, 2008). There are many – contested – possibilities but researching a specific question is much more manageable and ultimately doable than the big question about the causes of crime in general.

DESIGNING A RESEARCH STRATEGY: CHOOSING THE APPROPRIATE TOOLS TO ANSWER RESEARCH QUESTIONS

Designing the research strategy and selecting the appropriate research tools to address the project's central questions represent key stages of the research process. It is in **research design** that much of the project's theoretical and conceptual elements, which we discuss in later chapters, connect with practical considerations of conducting the research, generating useful data and delivering tangible outputs. To approach these issues, researchers need to be mindful of a number of issues, in particular the relative significance of quantitative and qualitative approaches.

Having analysed the key literature relating to the project's focus and defined the central aims, objectives and questions for the research, we now examine the techniques available to criminologists undertaking empirical research. For any piece of empirical research, it is not only *what* we find that is important, but also *how* we find it. In many respects, selecting the correct method is the main way outside observers can be sure of the quality of our research. A key stage of the research process therefore involves the selection and, crucially, justification of the method and approach to research. Typically, these discussions are captured in the **methodology** section of a research project. There are a number of features that constitute a methodology, including discussion on the selection of method, sampling, access to the research population and ethical considerations. These are now discussed in turn.

Although the different approaches each have their supporters and critics, it is useful to take the view that each method and approach has strengths and weaknesses. Particular research methods are not inherently 'good' or 'bad'; they are merely differently suited to different tasks. Good criminological researchers, then, need to hold two key skills. The first is an understanding and appreciation of the different research methods and strategies. The second is the ability to distinguish which methods are most suited to the area of enquiry at hand. The following approaches set out the tried and tested methods researchers have used, systematically, to answer criminological questions.

Quantitative and qualitative approaches and methods

As stated in the Introduction, many criminologists classify the many available methods of research into two broad categories: quantitative and qualitative research. While these categories should not be seen in isolation – **quantitative methods** can adopt some qualitative principles and vice versa – this classification provides a useful way of initially understanding the different types of method and their general uses. **Quantitative research** attempts to 'quantify' the social world and often presents data in a numerical form. Figures such as '43% of people want more police on the streets', '18% of males aged under 15 have been a victim of crime in the last 12 months' and '28% of males aged 40–50 class themselves as "afraid" or "very afraid" of crime' are all examples of quantitative data. Many quantitative research projects use statistical analyses in a variety of ways to arrive at their conclusions. The examples above refer to the **prevalence** or degree to which something occurs. Other statistical measures seek to identify and put a value on **correlations**, the degree two or more things are related to each other. As such, if a research project is seeking to attach a value on the prevalence of something, or the degree to which different things are related, it is likely that a quantitative approach is appropriate. Quantitative research is not all about extracting numbers and percentages, however. Many quantitative surveys also contain open questions (see Chapter 5), which researchers seek to make sense of by grouping answers together in the data analysis stage of the project. You may notice the significance of some of the language here. Words like 'degree', 'extent', 'prevalence' and 'correlation' are commonly used in connection with quantitative research. This gives us an idea of its purpose. In general, quantitative research is used to help us to understand trends and general tendencies. It normally captures or surveys a large number of participants and gives a broad overall picture of the topic of study. Another common use for quantitative methods is in the area of **evaluation research**, where the effects of criminal justice or crime control interventions are measured. **Surveys** (Chapter 5), **quantitative observation** (Chapter 7) and quantitative **content analysis** (Chapter 8) are all examples of quantitative research methods available to criminologists.

One of the key themes of **qualitative research** is the centrality of interpretation to social life. It seeks to understand research questions in less structured ways, and is concerned with how participants construct and make sense of their social world. For most qualitative researchers, the social world is not seen as something external, objective or necessarily measurable. Instead, it is something that is constructed by people as they experience it. Qualitative research, when conducted among people, normally utilizes methods geared towards collecting data that 'yield[s] rich insights into people's experiences, opinions, aspirations and feelings' (May, 1997: 109). A comparison between qualitative and quantitative interviewing techniques illustrates the key differences between the two perspectives. Quantitative interviews often take the form of a survey, where a large number of respondents are asked a fixed set of questions, many of which have a predetermined choice of answers, that is, being for or against the death penalty by age, that are then analysed via statistical techniques. Qualitative interviewing is normally less structured and has more scope to interact with the participant in unanticipated ways. This can involve a range of techniques, from semi-structured to completely unstructured interviews. One of the aims here is to allow the participant to express and frame their responses in relation to their own experience. Qualitative interviews are different because they are seeking to collect a different type of data. Fewer people may be involved as participants, but their participation with the research process may be more prolonged and substantial. In addition to **semi-structured** and **unstructured interviews** (Chapter 6), **focus groups** (Chapter 6) and ethnographic research (Chapter 7) are both examples of qualitative research.

Two further considerations when choosing between quantitative and **qualitative methods** relate to focus of the research and the cultivation of data. In general, quantitative research projects have a well-defined focus before any substantive research is carried out. This means that quantitative researchers place a lot of emphasis on the design of their research tools. Shortcomings here are difficult to rectify and may only become visible once the research is under way or the data is being analysed. This is why quantitative researchers often **pilot**, or test their research tools before going out into the field. Many forms of qualitative research, such as **ethnography**, involve a more dynamic process where the focus and approach are refined as the research progresses. Such considerations extend to the way in which data is developed and the level of prior understanding around the issue being researched. As such, quantitative research is often characterized as **deductive**. Deductive research means that an idea, hypothesis or assumption is being tested. This supposes that a researcher already holds a good deal of knowledge about the issue they are hoping to research. By contrast, qualitative research regularly adopts an **inductive** approach: research themes are 'induced' or emerge during the course of the research. This can be particularly useful when trying to research a **population** that the researcher knows little about at the outset. These approaches to data are discussed in greater detail in Chapter 2. Next, we look at some of the most important practical elements of the research process.

THE PRACTICALITIES OF DOING RESEARCH

Resources

Resources comprise the time, tools and money required to carry out a research project.

Time

Time is always an issue and must be considered, because at some stage we will be called to account by the person setting the deadline for submitting a piece of work. Some large-scale, centrally funded studies may be spread over several months or even years, whereas some of the mini-projects only take a few hours or days, or at most several months. Big research projects may look and actually are impressive, but in most cases a condition attached to their funding is completion of the project by a date set out in a contract. Failure to meet a deadline may result in a penalty.

Tools

For a quantitative study, it may be necessary to use a program like the Statistical Package for Social Scientists (**SPSS**®), which is used to generate a range of statistical analyses that require a reasonable level of numeracy and sufficient time to input the raw data (see Chapter 5). Most universities hold a licence for SPSS and most students who can access a PC can utilize this resource. Qualitative studies may also use computer packages for analysing interview data, such as **NVivo**, Ethnograph, MAXQDA or ATLAS.ti, so it's worth checking whether your university can provide you with access to these.

Many interviews are recorded, with the consent of the interviewee, using a tape recorder, Dictaphone or digital recorder. Some Interviewers use a transcribing machine to aid them in their analysis of the data they collect from such sound recordings. These machines are there to make the task of writing up the interview more manageable, through the use of various pausing devices, such as a footswitch. It is also worth noting that some qualitative data analysis software, such as NVivo, allows the coding of audio data prior to transcription. Some university departments have audio recorders that it may be possible to borrow, but some training is advisable. Alternatively, most mobile phones now include a microphone, making it possible to record an interview in the same way as a Dictaphone. We'll go into some more detail about this in Chapter 6.

Money

Money is also an essential prerequisite for doing research, but not one that you might immediately plan around. Most of the research activities lecturers and professors are involved in are 'costed' and paid for through research funding or other income streams. The funder might be the government, a research council or agency in the statutory, commercial or voluntary and community sector. When they make available a pot of money for a researcher to submit a bid, the tender or research proposal prepared by the latter often needs to cost each activity. The funder will need to pay the university for the:

- time of the researcher(s)
- activities – seminars, workshops, travel expenses – that are part of the project
- physical resources used – PCs, including their deprecation, stationary, the use of office space.

As a criminology student, you'll also need to budget for your project, considering how much money there is to spend on travel and resources, because this can limit what can be achieved in a research project.

Negotiating access

When researchers talk about **access** to do fieldwork, they're often referring to the ways in which they found a **gatekeeper** or a person to aid their entry into an organization or group. Finding a contact is therefore something for you to think about. We also need to think about access in terms of how to get hold of the various sources of data needed in order to answer a research question. Without data of some kind, it is not possible to do research and it needs to be gathered in a systematic and methodical way, whether its from your desk or from fieldwork. First, we'll talk about access to documents and texts, before going on to discuss gaining access to research subjects when doing fieldwork.

Accessing published material

To do research, it is essential to get hold of literature that is of direct relevance to the research you are undertaking. Most libraries provide access to search engines to obtain traditional academic sources, including books, that is, text-books, edited collections and monographs, and journal articles in both digital and print formats, which means that studying can be desk based. Most libraries also have links to other libraries and some of the city, state or national ones hold more or less every publication in print. It is quite likely that there is a limit to the number of resources that can be requested and, with the exception of obscure topics, this should not present too much of a problem.

In many respects, criminology is a policy-relevant discipline and it is necessary to refer to materials made available by government departments, criminal justice agencies and a disparate group of other organizations located in the private, voluntary and community sectors. Many criminal justice organizations have their own websites, including links to research studies and reports (see Chapter 4) and the internet can be used to accumulate sources usually stored in archives. Across the world, and in the spirit of openness, such organizations also inform the wider public about various aspects of their work. In a sense, there is now a risk of 'information overload', with resources accessible 24/7 from potentially anywhere in the world. Without a clearly defined research question and the application of filtering skills, experienced researchers can soon become overwhelmed.

It is also possible to focus your research on the analysis of secondary data, or the reanalysis and reinterpretation of existing datasets such as the International Crime Victims Survey, which provides datasets to download online (Pakes, 2010) (explained in more detail in Chapter 4).

Bear in mind that you can't always expect to find data that meets your exact requirements. Data is often generated in a format that is user friendly for those working in an organization, but not an outside researcher. Criminal justice is a morally and politically contentious arena, where public access to some information and data is necessarily restricted. Freedom and openness are only partially applied and, due to data protection and legislation protecting human rights, some bits of information are, for good reasons, not accessible. To give two examples:

1. The information and data an organization holds about offending and victimization does not reveal to any academic researcher the identities of the offender or victims.

2. National agencies do not make public details about all their operations, such as covert intelligence-gathering techniques that are used to disrupt organized criminal gangs and terrorist cells.

Increasingly, researchers can also exploit the opportunities presented by the internet and social networking sites, such as Facebook and blog sites, where opinions about criminal justice can easily be obtained. These should be used with caution because, rather like Wikipedia, they lack academic credibility and are unreliable and often inaccurate sources of information.

Accessing people involved in criminal justice

Documentary sources only tell part of the story about crime and many research-ers focus on the first-hand experiences of people who know something about the criminal justice system. Empirical research is quite likely to focus on one of two main groups of people: criminal justice workers, and those at the other end of criminal justice activity, that is, suspects/offenders, victims/witnesses, and, less directly, members of the public.

Gaining access can be difficult, and in some cases impossible, and success is often dependent on finding a gatekeeper or a contact. This observation increas-ingly applies to all researchers, whether you are a student or a professional who has been commissioned by the government. Since the mid- to late 1990s, there have been a growing number of criminological researchers and students taking degrees in the subject. The sheer volume of people out there, doing research, has increased hugely and criminal justice agencies are inundated with requests for help with research projects, and there simply are not enough staff or hours in the day to deal with this level of interest. Demand is so high that some agen-cies no longer consider undergraduates' requests for access to do crime-related research. Fortunately, research still does get done and other agencies may be willing to help out. Indeed, agencies can benefit from research into their activi-ties because the findings can inform future developments in policy. If you have no prior concrete connections with the organization you're interested in, and you think you may have difficulty gaining access to your research subjects, it may be worth including contingency arrangements or alternative research strategies in your research design.

There are still many stages to navigate if access to an agency is to be gained. If, for example, you receive approval permitting research that examines the perceptions of a small number of police officers about the adequacy of police powers in the face of the threat of global terrorism, decisions need to be made over whom to contact. This would partly depend on the sample of officers you planned to survey or speak to. At the outset, there is a need to identify a potential contact, which may be a person in a particular force area or department. If a named individual is found, which will be easier for some topics than others, contacting them is potentially straightforward. If there is no identifiable individual, and such a person is lacking in many cases, it is quite likely you will end up ringing or sending an unsolicited letter/email to a research department or the force as a whole. The likelihood of successfully contacting the right person is limited and a letter or email may be ignored, destroyed or passed on to another person who forwards it to someone else: this cycle is then repeated. If, at first, or later on, the right person is reached, they may or may not agree to help. We do not know what percentage of requests made in this way succeed but the chances are slim, at least for the core organizations – police, courts, prison and probation. Other statutory agencies involved in criminal justice, such as local authorities, housing departments, youth workers, could be approached, although similar difficulties and outcomes should be anticipated.

If you have a criminal justice connection, access is still not a certainty, for many of the reasons listed above. It might be a slight advantage to be employed or know someone working in this sphere. If these scenarios apply, there is potentially access to a population and your colleagues could be persuaded to support the research if they are convinced of its relevance and importance. It is probable that permission will still be needed from a line manager, so do not automatically assume access is ensured.

Over the years, criminological researchers have increasingly concentrated their efforts away from offenders of crime, partly because of agendas set by the government, but also due to the influence of ethical considerations that restrict this type of research. At the same time, the victim has been recognized as an important agent in criminal justice policy. This trend has been mirrored to some extent by research activity and you may be inspired to do some research into victimization, that is, including the perspective of victims. The considerations about gaining access outlined above are also pertinent here, specifically the difficulties arising when trying to identify victims of crime. They may be contactable through a job, like a charity supporting victims, but the practical and ethical dilemmas that arise for offenders apply for victims too. The nature of victimization, in particular the loss and suffering it causes, places the victim in an uncomfortable position and they may experience further harm and anxiety by being drawn into a research study.

Sampling

When planning research, we need to clearly identify who and how many will be researched. The process of selecting participants from the wider population is known as **sampling**, and it is concerned with these broad questions. For example, it is rare that every potential participant (the **research population**) is interviewed, surveyed or otherwise engaged in the research project – this would be a **census**. Instead, a **sample** of key participants is selected based on a range of criteria and considerations. Consider surveys of public opinion you might have heard about, such as retail preferences or voting intentions; these often select a small number of people to question and an assumption is then made that this group represents a wider body of people. This is the notion of **generalization**, the extent to which the findings of a particular piece of research are relevant beyond the immediate context where the research was done. This has implications for the credibility of the conclusions the research project arrives at, so the correct use of sampling techniques is often a critical phase of the research and a criteria on which the quality of the research is often judged, particularly in quantitative studies. A number of sampling techniques available to criminological research-ers are discussed in Chapter 5.

Research ethics and ethical awareness

Research **ethics** is all about the moral principles that underscore research activ-ity – they are there to guide researchers to ensure that no one comes to any phys-ical or emotional harm, including the researcher and the people or organization they are researching. Some of you may be eager to speak to offenders but in the risk-averse environment we inhabit, there are all kinds of potential hazards.

Although academic disciplines, for example criminology, sociology, psychol-ogy and law, have for many years published ethical guidelines to govern social scientific research in general, and criminological research in particular, they have come to the fore in the 2000s and now have a greater impact on research. There are dedicated boards and committees in place that set out guidelines and procedures. For instance, there are independent review boards in the USA. In the UK and the Antipodes, there are research ethics committees, which were heavily influenced by developments in the USA. Basically, anyone doing research, especially empiri-cal research, anywhere in the world – undergraduates and professors alike – must be approved by a research ethics committee. Some lecturers have criticized these on the grounds of what they perceive to be excessive bureaucracy. Many students have complained about the amount of forms they need to fill in and some of the hoops they need to jump through to satisfy the requirements of these committees. It is worth noting that some classic and important criminological studies referred to in Chapter 3 would struggle to gain ethical approval through such committees today. However, the credibility of a piece of research partly depends on it observing ethical principles and guidelines.

Research ethics exists to protect the researcher and researched. This partly comes out of a concern with the health and safety and welfare of both parties, yet it is also an effect of living in an increasingly litigious society where people are not shy about suing and attempting to prosecute organizations for causing harm. The more practical implications of research ethics are discussed below in relation to the stages of a research project and in Part 2 they are considered in the context of each of the main research methods.

To undertake empirical work, research ethics committees will require you to reflect on ethical considerations and complete some paperwork. A standard research ethics form normally starts by asking a number of questions to determine if your research needs ethical approval. In most cases, this will be needed if you are doing any empirical research involving human subjects, especially if it involves sensitive issues, but even a library-based study presents ethical dilemmas, such as the language and terminology being used. If debates about race and crime are explored, certain terms used to classify ethnic groups may cause offence to those being classified.

Thinking about, and anticipating, ethical issues at the planning stage of research project facilitates the identification of potential obstacles that can get in the way of a research project. The following issues are likely to be key considerations for ethical review boards and committees.

A criminal record

If your research involves vulnerable individuals, including children or young people under 18 years of age, adults with learning difficulties and some disabled persons, it is likely that your criminal record will have to be checked out. For those with a criminal record, it may be advisable to study a different group or to choose a topic and method that doesn't require a check in order to avoid your project being stopped before it's even started.

Sensitive issues

Criminological research, by default, explores issues of a sensitive nature and raises politically sensitive questions. For example, you may have an interest in public perceptions about terrorism and decide to canvas the views of a small sample of your fellow students in a focus group, a setting where some of the participants express derogatory views about certain religious faiths. It is worth speaking to a lecturer or your supervisor about the range of sensitive issues that your research question may provoke and try to make contingency plans that will avoid those.

Confidentiality

There are 'limits to confidentiality', particularly in qualitative studies where large chunks of data are presented in a study. For example, you might interview a prison officer and quote what they say, which means that what they say is not confidential because it appears in a report that is read by several people. However, the source of the material will remain anonymous because the identity of the participant will not be known. Because criminal justice research is potentially contentious, participants need to have their identities protected. It is imperative that the data collected from participants is deposited securely and anything that can identify the person and the agency or organization for which they are working needs to be removed. Data needs to be fully anonymized, wherever appropriate, by disidentifying the place where the research takes place, the organization employing the participants, job titles that make participants easily identifiable and so on. Having said this, it is important to know what pieces of data belong to whom, so you will need to use a coding system of letters/numbers (identifiers) to guarantee that nobody else can identify a research participant. Keeping interview scripts in a separate place to the coding system is a recommended course of action.

Consent

When we refer to 'consent', we mean that a research participant needs to be aware of and agree to their involvement in a research study. In the past, some researchers, especially ethnographers, observed people in their own environments without drawing attention to themselves as researchers, so criminal justice workers and criminals were studied and written about without ever knowing or consenting to being watched. These days this would be frowned upon and, with some notable exceptions, all researchers need to give their participants clear written information about the research they are involved in. You should ask your participants to sign a consent form that states that their involvement in the study is voluntary and they have been fully informed about its aims and objectives. Participants must also be informed that they can exercise the right to have their data withdrawn from a project without any repercussions. In practical terms, this is not possible once a study has been finished, that is, a published research report or a submitted assessment/assignment, so the form needs to include a cutoff date.

If your participants are from vulnerable groups, gaining consent can be more complicated and you will need to plan for this. For example, it is difficult to say you've been given informed consent from children and young people aged under 18 years, any person with a learning difficulty, or non-native speakers. Therefore, consideration needs to be given to who is in a position to provide consent, how higher standards of certainty can be employed, and what alternative research strategies or plans could be pursued if ethical approval was declined.

Harm

Harm may be direct – being physically hurt – or indirect, such as a damaged reputation, and it can impact on the researcher and the participant. If you are planning to do any fieldwork, you need to discuss with your supervisor any possible risks and make sure sensible precautions are taken to maximize personal safety and security. For instance, when administering an interview, do not invite participants to your own home or agree to interview them at their own home; instead, meet in a public space at the university or, if the participant is a practitioner, at their workplace. It is also good practice to observe other personal safety precautions, such as informing a friend/family member of your intended whereabouts and how long the meeting is likely to last. These precautions are obvious yet can easily be overlooked.

Disclosure of harm or crime

If a participant makes a declaration of current criminal activity or something that is planned in the immediate future, you will need to report this. When planning the research, you should also assess whether there is any risk that participants may disclose evidence they have committed or are about to commit a criminal offence. This deliberation is especially important if children or vulnerable adults are at risk. To avoid being put in a difficult position like this, the respondent should be informed before the research starts that they should not disclose such information and of any consequences if they ignore this piece of advice.

Analysing and writing up data

Data analysis is one of the most important stages of the research process, yet it is also one that is regularly overlooked during the early stages of research planning. The analysis of data is a crucial part of generating 'findings'. Analysis underpins the data and informs the conclusions presented to those reading your work. In addition, data analysis methods are the area that often attracts critical commentary. It is therefore extremely important to adopt a robust approach to data analysis that is based on tried and tested principles. This book provides details on specific ways to analyse different types of data generated through the use of different methodological techniques in the relevant chapters of Part 2. For now, we will highlight some initial considerations to bear in mind when planning your research.

One of the first steps when analysing data is to consider what kind of information the selected research methods will yield, and what kinds of questions the wider project is seeking to answer.

Having understood the type of data that the selected method will yield, and considered how this relates to the aims and questions of the research, one of the next steps involves the organizing, cataloguing and categorizing of data. There are some similarities, as well as significant differences, in the ways quantitative and qualitative data are analysed and presented. Key to the analysis process for both quantitative and qualitative studies is the activity of coding.

If you are involved in quantitative analyses, **coding** often involves placing a value on one of the research **variables**. A variable is normally a theme of the research or something the researcher wishes to measure or otherwise analyse. Themes such as age, class, ethnicity, length of time in prison, attitudes and beliefs are all examples of variables. For example, if a researcher wishes to understand the relationship between age and attitudes to punishment, age is one variable and attitudes to punishment is another. Therefore, the analysis of many quantitative research projects involves establishing what the variables are, attaching a value to them (coding), and then performing the desired analysis (such as measuring their relationship). Quantitative data is presented numerically using graphs, charts, tables and other means of rendering statistical data.

Qualitative data analysis can also involve a process of coding. This process also aims to identify and coherently catalogue key themes within the data, but is carried out in a different manner. One of the key differences is that during quantitative studies, the themes and often the types of measurement are normally known in advance. This is less often the case for qualitative research as the themes normally emerge inductively during the processes of research and analysis. As such, qualitative coding, of which one of the most regularly used techniques is known as **thematic coding**, involves the identification of important themes by systematically reviewing the data. This could involve reading through an interview transcript, or ethnographic field notes, and tagging seemingly important statements or events as they are encountered in the data. These tags are then refined in subsequent readings of the data. These tags are also variously called **nodes** or themes. There are many ways to further analyse these once they have been identified and refined. For example, a researcher may wish to analyse how one theme, such as a response to criminal victimization, is experienced by different research participants. Qualitative data analysis may involve more complex processes and activities than those listed above and is often presented as quotes or a **thick description** of events, circumstances or beliefs. These are discussed and developed in Part 2.

For both research traditions, software packages exist that are specifically designed to assist with the data analysis process. However, such computer assistance does not replace the analytical expertise the individual researcher needs to apply before the computer reviews the data, and the use of computers is not appropriate for all research projects. Some researchers prefer not to use computer analysis packages at all, fearing that it makes it more difficult to get 'close to the data'. This applies particularly in relation to qualitative research, where analytical skills and an eye for detail are often required to identify and tease out some of the key research themes from the recorded data.

CONCLUSIONS

This chapter has offered a broad outline of the process of research alongside some of the key practical and theoretical concerns accompanying criminological research. One of the most important themes here relates to the interconnectivity of the practical and theoretical realms and the different stages of the research process. Moreover, we have highlighted the role of tried and tested strategies that have shaped the ways in which we think about crime and the approaches we take towards its study and analysis. Understanding these core approaches and principles provides criminological researchers with a good basis to develop robust and valuable research.

Of particular importance here is the interconnection of theory and research. As this chapter has shown, some theoretical positions privilege the individual as a site of analysis, whereas others focus on institutions, organizations and individuals belonging to large social groups, for example women, the elderly. In turn, these positions often influence the assumptions we make when commencing research. Theoretical perspectives are not the only influence. As Chapter 2 demonstrates, there are certain internal drivers or principles and beliefs concerning how knowledge is generated and external shapers such as political and other external pressures, which exert themselves on the research process. While it could be claimed that we are able to conduct truly objective, value-free research, in reality this is almost never the case. Criminological researchers must therefore be aware of such influences and recognize the impact they may have.

Regarding the practicalities of research, it is helpful to view criminological research as a process. In this sense, the process comprises distinct as well as integrated parts that, as researchers, we engage with as we progress through our projects. It is important to remember that this process is not entirely linear. One aspect of the sequence is not necessarily finished and forgotten as we progress to the next. Instead, the sections of research must link together, inform each other and, in many respects, become refined and further conditioned throughout the process. The checklist in the Conclusion provides some helpful questions for researchers to ask themselves when carrying out criminological research.

REVIEW QUESTIONS

- Think of a research question, then outline and discuss the key stages of the research process.

- Design a brief outline of a research project to assess the level of fear of crime among students and to understand the ways police officers view suspects.

- Critically assess the importance of treating criminological research as an iterative and integrated process.

FURTHER READING

If you were to read one book, our recommendation would be:

Davies, M.B. (2007) *Doing a Successful Research Project: Using Quantitative or Qualitative Methods*. Basingstoke: Palgrave Macmillan.

In addition to this, we suggest you refer to:

Black, T. (1999) *Doing Quantitative Research in the Social Sciences: An Integrated Approach to Research Design, Measurement and Statistics*. London: Sage.

Harrison, J., Simpson, M., Harrison, O. and Martin, E. (2005) *Study Skills for Criminology*. London: Sage.

Noaks, L. and Wincup, E. (2004) *Criminological Research: Understanding Qualitative Methods*. London: Sage.

2

CONNECTING RESEARCH AND THEORY: INFLUENCES ON CRIMINOLOGICAL RESEARCH

OVERVIEW

The aim of this chapter is to:

- Explain the important connections between theory and research.
- Introduce the main qualitative and quantitative traditions of, and inductive and deductive approaches to, research.
- Introduce basic theoretical arguments concerning epistemology and ontology.
- Understand the adoption and application of different styles and approaches to criminological research, for example research done for its own sake and research done for a reason.
- Consider how external factors, such as the media, values and politics, impact on crime research.

INTRODUCTION

This chapter explores the way criminological research is shaped and influenced by various factors. Behind the practicalities of doing research are some complex ideas and processes at work. As a prospective researcher, you will make decisions over your approach to research, which, in turn, shape the data and influence the analysis that follows. While good practice normally involves the selection of an appropriate method to investigate a particular issue, the decisions we take as researchers are often far from neutral. Instead, a range of deeply held beliefs over the way in which knowledge is created and how the social world may be observed often influence our choice of method. Hence, research and theory are related in important ways. Not only does research data help us to construct theory (see Chapter 3), but, often, theory also informs our overall approach to research.

At the same time, other equally vital factors, such as external shapers, drive and motivate criminological research. In contrast to the view that it is an activity that exists simply to extend our knowledge of the possibilities of tackling myriad crime-related problems, crime research is animated by passions, personal beliefs and commitments, as well as politics. For example, a number of key influences – including professional preferences and resources, values, political perspectives and mechanisms for disseminating findings, that is, the media – may all exert themselves on the research process.

A FRAMEWORK FOR UNDERSTANDING KEY INFLUENCES ON RESEARCH

To capture these influences and describe the way they shape the research process, this chapter is divided into two main parts. The first explores the internal drivers affecting the research process in relation to how we select particular methodologies and approach data collection. It begins by discussing the main styles of criminological research. Offered here is a basic description of the different ways you can generate data and knowledge, drawing particular attention to deductive and inductive approaches to research. It demonstrates how deductive methodological approaches are employed to test existing hypotheses, while inductive methods are used to generate new information. Such discussions connect with, and build upon, the initial examination of qualitative and quantitative strategies discussed in Chapter 1. Also key here is the analysis and assessment of the epistemological and ontological assumptions that underpin criminological research. Your choice of methods and data is also connected to deeper theoretical beliefs about the nature and scope of knowledge itself. Here, we introduce the rationales for both approaches, outlining the types of data each approach is likely to yield, its most suitable application, and the various qualitative and quantitative methods that are commonly used.

The second part examines the external shapers that impact on the research process. It discusses some of the key styles and approaches used by criminological researchers, stressing that the choice of approach is based on the personal and/or professional preferences of the researcher. For instance, there is research that can be done by a lone researcher who has a passion for knowledge and learning, with nothing more than a pen and paper or a laptop. By contrast, there are individuals and groups of researchers who are working for or funded by big organizations like government departments or multinational corporations. Different pressures bear on each of these forms of research.

There is also a complex and ambivalent relationship between crime research and the media and there are a few points we need to make here about this connection. The mass media disseminates a lot of information about crime, some of it factual, for example news items, and some of it fictional, for example films and video games. As such, it potentially shapes public knowledge and understanding of a range of criminological issues relating to offending behaviour, victimization and how the criminal justice system operates. Your choice of a research topic could be influenced by or based on a news item or television drama. Sometimes, the words and images produced by the media are informed by criminological research and this can be seen as a positive thing by researchers. However, the media sometimes ignores research and some criminologists are critical of some media representations because they are based on common sense, opinions or stereotypes instead of research evidence. Because of this, it is argued that the media can oversimplify often complex debates. The solution to oversimplification is to carry out academic research to show that the media can create a false impression of crime and its control. Crime research is therefore also a means of debunking myths.

This is followed by a brief assessment of the influence of values and politics on the research process. Values shape research in terms of the nature of questions asked and the methods used to come up with answers. Some researchers view offenders as damaged people in need of help, while others view offending in terms of individual responsibility. There are researchers who consider the criminal justice system to be too tough (too many offenders are sent to prison), whereas others say it is too soft (not enough criminals are sent to prison). Such assumptions will have at least some influence on how they approach their research. Politics also influences crime research, and the ideological orientation of the state and government determines the nature of the type of research that is funded and gets done. Thus, research is inevitably linked with the workings of state power and its ability to influence other people and organizations conducting research.

INTERNAL DRIVERS

Approaches to data and knowledge

One of the key messages of Part 1 is that there is a strong relationship between theory and method. Our ideas about crime should not come from mere opinion. Instead, robust knowledge is acquired by a careful understanding of the field of enquiry and, crucially, a systematic and justifiable method of collecting information. There are many ways to collect information about crime and then construct an informed opinion or argument from it. Fortunately, there are a number of tried and tested approaches that help researchers to navigate this complex process.

There are many ways of cataloguing and understanding the different methods of social research. As we noted in Chapter 1, it is generally accepted that most of the available methods fall into one of two categories: quantitative methods and qualitative methods. It is important to note that, while each tradition may have its supporters and critics, they are not necessarily mutually exclusive. Increasingly, researchers are seeking to combine, or **triangulate**, different methods (see Chapter 9), and it is therefore important for new researchers to become familiar with and able to apply methods from both traditions.

What are the key differences between quantitative and qualitative approaches? Generally speaking, the clue is in the name. Quantitative approaches normally deal in quantities. Large-scale surveys, interviewing tens of thousands of participants, such as the Crime Survey for England and Wales or the US National Crime Victimization Survey, are examples of quantitative research. Large-scale studies of this kind are immensely valuable and tell us a great deal about overall trends and tendencies. Not all quantitative criminological research operates on this scale, however. A number of criminologists have drawn on statistical data to analyse a specific issue within criminology, such as lethal violence (Zimring and Hawkins, 1997) or reasons for the growth in the prison population in many modern societies (Wacquant, 2009). Chapters 4 and 5 provide detailed discussions on the use of quantitative research in criminology.

Qualitative research often focuses on the meaning – the 'quality' of experience – participants attribute to various social phenomena. Qualitative approaches often deploy different research tools, aimed at capturing nuance and details at the expense of generalizability, and normally favour approaches that help capture the ways in which social reality is constructed by its participants. Examples of such research include the way in which door staff construct and perceive masculine identities (Winlow, 2001), the viewpoints of crack dealers (Bourgeois, 2003) and the perspectives of actors within informal and criminal economies (Hobbs, 1995). It is important to note that just as quantitative research is not necessarily solely preoccupied with numbers, qualitative research is not only confined to words (Neuman and Wiegand, 2000). A rule of thumb is that quantitative research generally focuses on numbers and overall tendencies, while qualitative approaches stress the detailed meaning, description and, normally, words.

Another difference concerns how these methods generally approach theory and knowledge differently. Quantitative methods often perform deductive 'theory testing' functions. A clearly defined research question or prior understanding of the research population is often a prerequisite for this kind of approach. While qualitative research may also adopt a deductive focus, it is more commonly used in an inductive way, where key research themes and theoretical inferences emerge during the course of the fieldwork. Inductive research has been fruitful when researching active criminals. Here, the researcher may have insufficient initial knowledge of, say, formations or values of particular groups of people or the way in which serious criminals operate. In such circumstances, it would be difficult to adopt a deductive approach because the researcher doesn't have sufficient prior knowledge that can be tested. Inductive approaches are also particularly useful when researching policy communities, and when seeking to understand the reasons behind specific decisions or courses of action. What these diverse groups, such as active criminals or criminal justice policy makers, have in common is that they may be 'closed' to many outsiders. Thus, a substantial part of the research process revolves around gaining access to these communities and understanding what counts as important research issues.

Inductive research, then, is a process where key themes emerge as the fieldwork progresses. Because of its more flexible structure, qualitative tools may be modified during the period of research. This could occur within a single interview or over the course of a project spanning many months. Regarding the former, for example, qualitative semi-structured interviews would allow you to prompt the participant in various ways and allow the participant to expand on an interesting topic that may at first appear to be of limited relevance. In other respects, qualitative research may be subtly modified over a long period of time, for example in an ethnographic study (see Chapter 7) that takes place over many months or even years. This flexibility comes at a price, however, in that it places additional pressures on the researcher to identify and capitalize on emerging themes during the period of fieldwork.

Overall, then, deductive research is normally used to test knowledge, while inductive research enables key themes to emerge during the period of fieldwork.

The development of theory from the data is closely connected to the (contested) concept of **grounded theory**, which was founded by Glaser and Strauss (1967) and has been used in the social sciences for over 40 years. It has been interpreted in many ways and inspired much debate among its followers and detractors alike. Bryman (2008: 541) provides a helpful definition here by suggesting that 'grounded theory is not a theory – it is an approach to the gener-ation of theory out of data'. In its simplest form, grounded theory refers to a process of inductive research. Data is collected and then analysed and tagged with codes. These codes signify relevant issues or themes in the research. The codes are grouped into concepts and then into larger categories and, finally, into theories. The way in which codes, concepts, categories and theory are derived has been the source of many debates, most notably those occurring between Glaser and Strauss, the founders of the theory. The development and popular-ity of grounded theory demonstrates the breadth of established social science research methods and that it is equally valid to engage in unstructured inductive research as it is to develop sophisticated and statistically informed quantitative research, provided the methods are applied to the tasks to which they are suited.

Epistemology and ontology

This discussion leads us to consider questions that lie at the very foundations of the social sciences, the issue of what constitutes knowledge and how we understand and characterize the social world. Respectively, these are questions of epistemology and ontology.

Epistemology is concerned with 'how we know what we know' (Baille, 2003: 94). In cultivating knowledge about the social world, researchers normally hold a set of assumptions. You could argue that the social world can be understood objectively in a similar way to the natural sciences. Other social scientists reject this view and, like them, you could argue that the social world is entirely different from the natural world; people influence the social world in multiple ways, and they interpret and construct meaning from their surroundings. In effect, these are different epistemological positions.

The former position, which seeks to identify the social world with the natural sciences, is known as **positivism**. In criminology, those holding the view that the drivers of criminal behaviour can be objectively identified and categorized, often through the application of the methods and principles belonging to the natural sciences, are known as positivists. Many positivists, then, use similar methodological and conceptual tools to those employed by natural scientists. Crucially for them, there are clearly observable processes that impact on various social phenomena. For example, where an astrophysicist may calculate the way gravitational forces affect the orbit of the planets, or a chemist may measure the outcome of combining different elements together, a positivist social scientist may consider the measurable outcome of particular social processes on crime. In many (but by no means all) forms of positivist research, there is an expectation of an outcome or relationship, which is then tested. Such underlying epistemological perspectives tend to favour deductive research, lend themselves to hypothesis-testing exercises, and are therefore more present in quantitative research projects.

The second position, **interpretivism**, stresses the difference between the natural and social worlds and claims that it is people who make sense of the latter. More importance is attached to the capacity of human actors to interpret. Interpretivists acknowledge the subjective and value-laden character of social action, people's beliefs, and the researcher. Interpretivists are less likely to consider themselves as objective and detached observers of society, being more likely to focus on the ways people subjectively experience and create their own social realities.

However, like all epistemological positions, interpretivism is a disputed field. For example, from these Weberian origins, the field has diversified into **phenomenological**, **symbolic interactionist** and **ethnomethodological** approaches. Despite these differences of opinion, these approaches appreciate both the individualized and impressionistic interpretations of the social world and the short-lived nature of relationships, and therefore lend themselves to qualitative methodologies.

Between these opposing perspectives lies an intermediate epistemological position, that of **realism**. Like the other positions, realism is further subdivided but basically posits that external, identifiable and measurable structures exist (as argued by positivists). However, **critical realism** (one of the major strands of realist epistemology) argues that these structures do not necessarily and completely direct, determine or govern social action. Instead, these external structures are conceptualized as asserting a constraining effect, while also facilitating opportunities for subjective social action to flourish. Structure and action are thus regarded as distinct, yet interconnected phenomena (Bhaskar, 1989). This approach therefore allows an awareness of structural impositions while retaining the importance of agents' subjectivity. Roy Bhaskar (1998), one of the main proponents of critical realism, has also conceptualized this approach as a 'relational model of society' that emphasizes how social relationships between actors generate structures. According to Bhaskar (1998: 30), this contrasts with both positivist (and Durkheimian) notions of collective action and interpretivist emphases on individualism.

Ontological issues are closely related to those of epistemology. Both epistemology and ontology are concerned with questions about the cultivation of knowledge and understanding, but **ontology** is specifically concerned with the question of how we can observe and understand the social world. At its heart is a debate over whether the social world is something that exists *externally to* its actors, or whether it is something that is *constructed by* them. Ontological debates broadly fall into two categories. On one hand is **objectivism**, the perspective that social reality is something that operates separately from social actors. The alternative position is that of **constructivism**, which posits that the social world and its realities are socially generated and, crucially, constructed by its participants. With specific reference to criminological research, these positions can be demonstrated in the way in which we view the operation of social control. From an objectivist perspective, social control would be something that exists externally yet asserts an influence on individuals and groups. Constructivists, by contrast, would contest that order and control are not necessarily received by their subjects, but are negotiated and constructed.

In this context, it is possible to see the value of the constructivist perspective in some of the classic sociological analyses of the prison. While there are clear rules and regulations within prisons, qualitative research shows that order in this setting is changeable. Gresham Sykes' (1958) landmark study *The Society of Captives*, for example, shows how numerically inferior prison guards continually engage in an informal negotiation of control with prisoners. The guards tolerate the rule breaking by some inmates as a concession, enabling them to secure more general compliance. Elsewhere, Sparks et al. (1996) draw attention to the competition and contestation surrounding the organizations, affiliations and value systems within a prison. Similar notions of negotiation are present in more recent works too, such as Carrabine's (2004) study of prison riots and Crewe's (2009) ethnography of prison life.

Overall, like epistemological positions, ontological perspectives tend to be associated with particular methodologies. While this is by no means a fixed relationship, there are clear conceptual and methodological consistencies between quantitative methods, positivist epistemologies and objectivist ontologies on the one hand, and qualitative methods, interpretivist epistemologies and constructivist ontologies on the other.

Evaluating and selecting methodological approaches

So far, this chapter has explored links between theory and empirical research and then discussed the broad methodological approaches available to researchers. We now examine how you can make an informed choice when selecting the appropriate tools for your empirical projects. For instance, how would you decide whether to use qualitative or quantitative approaches? The simple answer is that it depends on what you are researching. You now know that qualitative and quantitative research strategies generate different forms of data, so, if your research project is seeking to understand the percentages or categories of people, for example women or men, holding particular opinions about the death penalty, for example, then a quantitative approach is normally required. If your study aims to understand the meaning that people give to certain social phenomena and seeks to understand things from the perspective and outlook of participants, using their own language and frames of reference, then qualitative approaches are often appropriate.

There are several other considerations you should take account of, particularly to understand the strengths and weaknesses of each approach. You will be aware that no method is perfect, nor is a particular approach to research fundamentally good or bad. Instead, social science research is often about applying the correct method(s) to the appropriate circumstances.

The examples below discuss the application of research methods in various criminological studies and draw out the key considerations relating to the application of each method and for the design of research projects. You need to read them carefully because one of the review questions at the end of the chapter asks you to assess the strengths and weaknesses of their respective methodologies. The focus of these examples is on issues of research design, validity, bias and the processes of quantifying criminological phenomena. It is extremely important that all researchers, including yourself, try to fully explain and justify the criteria they use to quantify social phenomena and categorize their data. At the heart of this discussion are debates connected with the conflicting ontological and epistemological approaches discussed earlier.

The above considerations are not only important in order to protect the research from criticism; assumptions and biases have a substantial impact on the quality of the data and researchers' ability to draw conclusions from it. Let us look at an actual example of criminological research that illustrates these concerns, specifically the early criminological work of Cesare Lombroso (1835–1909). He was an Italian criminologist who attempted to use scientific methods, that is, positivist epistemology, objectivist ontology, to study a range of factors that may determine whether individuals become criminals. Lombroso made claims in his early work about the physiognomic differences between offenders and non-offenders (see Chapter 3 for another account of Lombroso's work). While such a classic historical study does not reflect modern approaches to research, it demonstrates the interplay of epistemological and ontological approaches with the selection of method and development of theory.

Although rooted in the seemingly robust methods of 'hard' science, generations of criminologists have found Lombroso's findings difficult to accept because they worry about the way he collected, catalogued, interpreted and presented his data. Having become convinced that criminals displayed observable physical features that differentiated them from non-criminals, it appears that Lombroso ([1876] 2006) sought and presented examples that supported his theory at the expense of a more objective form of measurement. He collected a great deal of information but, in the process, he selected examples to fit his assumptions and failed to critically examine his data in an objective or systematic way. As Hooton (1939, cited in Wolfgang, 1972) noted, Lombroso used single examples and anecdotes as a way to 'prove' a much wider general theory of criminality. This approach not only neglects information that contradicts his theory but is also unscientific. The lack of methodological rigour in this area contradicts and undermines Lombroso's claim that his theory was based on objective scientific principles.

Perhaps the most serious criticism levelled at Lombroso's method is the absence of adequate sampling and the failure to use appropriate control groups in much of his work. Many critics (and supporters) have noted that Lombroso failed to ensure that his samples were representative of the larger population they were drawn from. For example, his deduction that criminals had small 'cranial capacity' could equally be explained by the possibility that he was simply examining the skulls of younger offenders. Unless attempts are made to demonstrate that the specimens are samples of a range of different age groups, it is difficult to accept the findings as genuinely representative of the wider populations of both criminals and non-criminals. In addition, Lombroso rarely compared his findings with examinations of non-offenders (a control group), which makes it difficult to identify the differences between criminals and non-criminals. Although later work, particularly that examining criminality among women, did make some attempt to address these shortcomings, these important methodological considerations are largely underdeveloped in Lombroso's work.

You can learn many methodological issues here. The first is the question of generalizability. How many cases does the researcher need in order to generalize their findings to a wider population? To what extent are the findings likely to be representative of the wider population? Clearly, when using single examples, as Lombroso did, it is difficult to justify that the findings apply more widely. It is important to note that research does not have to be generalizable to a wider population. Indeed, much qualitative research makes no claim to apply more broadly than the particular focus of empirical study.

Second, consistency of approach is an important consideration for researchers. The Lombroso example reveals a conflict between inductive and deductive approaches. Deductive approaches are designed to test the strength or weakness of an existing **hypothesis** and Lombroso looked for data that 'proved' the strength of his assumption. By forming his theoretical assumptions very early on without a sufficient understanding of the many possible influences on criminality, Lombroso had to continually revise his theory in new and inconsistent ways. Further problems are apparent within his deductive process. For example, Lombroso claimed to have found associations and similarities between the physiology of epileptics and criminals. However, even if we agree with this position, an association does not necessarily mean **causation**.

Another difficulty with Lombroso's method is in the categories (or codes) he used to define key variables. When Lombroso defined what made a 'criminal man', he often gave physical features rather subjective and value-laden labels. This included descriptions of different types of criminals having 'mobile, restless, frequently oblique eyes' and 'brilliant eyes', 'delicate faces' and 'cold, glassy eyes'. It would be difficult to quantify many of these adjectives or assume that there was universal agreement on what 'delicate faces' or 'cold eyes' looked like. Such adjectives are highly subjective descriptions that are not appropriate tools of quantitative classification. If you were to consider labelling categories, this should be done in a way that is both clear and likely to be understood and accepted by as many people as possible.

As we have seen, a key challenge for criminological research is the difficulty in attributing specific quantifiable values to continually changing social phenomena. This is something that has continued to affect crime-related research since Lombroso's time and remains as important today as it was in the nineteenth century.

In one relatively recent piece of 'crime science' research, Farrell et al. (2005) undertook the laudable yet difficult task of trying to create a cost–benefit analysis of the impact of various crimes. This was to allow an assessment of the efficiency of responses and the related allocation of resources. Yet, the outcomes of such research are controversial. For example, Farrell et al. (2005: 66) claimed that, in their calculation, rape is considered to cost 62 times that of burglary, a view that leads some criminologists (for example Haggerty, 2008) to question the subjectivity on which these decisions are based. While some subjectivity is acknowledged by Farrell et al., it is grossly underplayed and, arguably, critically undermines the research. Why are some criteria included as the costs of these crimes, yet others ignored? Who decides what constitutes victim 'pain'? How can they be objectively quantified? Is it on the basis of visibility? On this basis, it could be argued that 'a rape could just as easily be costed at 120 or 73.5 times the cost of a burglary' (Haggerty, 2008: 87). Ultimately, are the impacts of different crimes really comparable or amenable to statistical quantities? Single offences will impact different people in different ways. Moreover, the authors of this textbook, having been the victims of domestic burglary on seven different occasions, can attest that, from a victim's perspective, the same offence, if repeated, may also affect the same individual in different ways. Some burglaries impact more heavily than others. Had Farrell et al. (2005) employed qualitative research to speak to any victims of crime and understand how they make sense of their experiences, they may have reached the same conclusion.

The above discussion shows that one of the important tasks facing quantitative researchers is how certain social factors are categorized and quantified. This often entails difficult decisions over which factors are selected as significant and which are not. It also relates to the risk of claiming that the research explains more than it actually does. These issues are particularly apparent in other areas of crime science (and wider criminological) research. One example here is the use of computer modelling of crime reduction strategies in order to assess their effectiveness (Groff and Birks, 2008). Here, attempts are made at generating computer 'simulations [that] create artificial worlds and populate them with virtual beings' (Groff and Birks, 2008: 176), or using software modelling to imitate how offenders make their choices. In developing simulated models of human behaviour to 'assess which factors might be important in offender decision making', Groff and Birks (2008: 176) note that 'reality must be simplified and only the most important aspects represented in the model'. Selective decisions need to be taken as to which elements of reality remain in the model, which are *simplified* and which are excluded, if they can be quantified at all. Compounding this is the way in which qualitative research has demonstrated how criminal actors may act in entirely unforeseen, contradictory and unpredictable ways, such as in relation to organized crime (Rawlinson and Fussey, 2010) or terrorism (Fussey, 2011). Others may take risks that may not be in their rationally conceived best interests as part of a chaotic lifestyle or an attempt to cultivate status. For example, as Katz (1988: 312) observed:

> the careers of persistent robbers show us, not the increasingly precise calculations and hedged risks of 'professionals', but men for whom gambling and other vices are a way of life, who are 'wise' in the cynical sense of the term, and who take pride in a defiant reputation as 'bad'.

Such unpredictable behaviour may be difficult to anticipate and build into a comprehensive model of criminal action. Attempts to construct such models at a distance or far away from the lived reality of the crime and the claim that the explanation is objective have been critiqued in recent years, leading Young (2004) to deride such attempts as 'voodoo criminology'. Yet, as Haggerty (2008) correctly notes in his review of one of crime science's key texts, distanced quantitative methodologies have an important role in criminological research, but they are often less able to easily access the worlds and experiences of 'hard-to-reach' groups that much groundbreaking qualitative work has entered. Moreover, reflecting the limitations of terrorism research, models such as these risk examining offending without acknowledging the offender. Indeed, many criminologists have pointed out the difficulties of abstracting crime control as a subject and examining it independently from a detailed analysis of criminality. As Hobbs (1988: 14) notes:

> in attempting to improve our knowledge of crime and the relative performance of the criminal justice system we must not isolate criminality and control, but must locate their origins and enacted environment.

To do so would require the use of a range of quantitative and qualitative methodologies – both of which have strong traditions within criminological research.

Overall, these examples of real criminological research raise a number of issues that concern both our approach to research – including the selection of method and techniques of analysis – and our deeply held beliefs and philosophies of how the social world can be observed and knowledge captured. These latter considerations are the issues of ontology and epistemology and, while often underacknowledged by criminological researchers, they have a profound effect on the outcomes of such research. Yet these are not the only influence on the research process. As the next section demonstrates, criminological research is also subjected to and conditioned by a range of external processes.

EXTERNAL SHAPERS

Motivations behind criminological research

Whenever we think about and do criminological research, there is a danger that many different things are lumped together, such as tools and techniques, and we can quite easily lose sight of other factors that impact on the research process. For example, there are different styles of criminological research, of which there are two main kinds:

1. pure research or research that is done for its own sake
2. research that is done for a reason.

All research is, to varying degrees, like the latter and driven by instrumental concerns, mainly because someone has an interest in an issue such as elder abuse or the impact of police patrols on street prostitution. The motivations behind that interest will diverge in individual cases, as some research is done simply because someone wants to find something out and that acquiring more knowledge about a topic is the only goal – this 'pure research' is also known as curiosity-driven or blue-skies research.

The main difference between these styles is the freedom the researcher has to pursue their own interests. In other words, to what extent should a researcher be able to do the research they want or are they undertaking research that someone else expects them to do because payment is involved? The distinctions between these styles of research are not always hard and fast, yet this is a useful way of showing the differences between the research you will read and be asked to explain and understand, and the research you will actually do.

Pure research: curiosity-driven/blue-skies research

Curiosity-driven/blue-skies research is research done purely for its own sake. There are no predetermined outcomes for such curiosity-driven studies and there are no great expectations about what can be achieved. Sometimes, great things will happen following this research, possibly a decade or so after it was done, but this is something that cannot be predicted. It may be theoretical as well as of some practical use but if it is the latter, this is often not the main goal of a study.

With curiosity-driven research, the boundaries are potentially limitless – notwithstanding the resource considerations rehearsed in Chapter 1 – so long as a researcher has the time and energy. Because in many cases there is no money explicitly invested in the research by a third party, no immediate, tangible return is anticipated. The main requirement is a healthy sense of curiosity about the world, albeit one which needs to be balanced by a sense of perspective. But without blue-skies research, some of the important criminological ideas and theories that are now taken for granted would not have come into being, possibly because it would not have been funded. Perhaps one of the most well-known scientific discoveries that has major criminological significance is the work of Sir Alec Jeffreys, a professor of genetics, responsible for the discovery of DNA (deoxyribonucleic acid) profiling. His contribution is an exemplar of blue-skies research, as well as a piece of research that is of practical use in many areas of social life, not just the field of criminal justice.

Corbyn (2009) tells us that at 9.05 am on 10 September 1985 at the University of Leicester in the UK, Sir Alec made a major scientific breakthrough: the discovery of 'idiosyncratic southern blot mini-satellite hybridization profiles'. Fortunately, this finding was given the more memorable name – DNA profiling. This pattern tells us our genetic makeup and where we come from – our mother and father, and their and previous generations' ancestry – also giving us our individual identity. The study yielding the vitally important discovery of DNA was not funded for the purpose of catching killers and was discovered as a result of Sir Alec and his research assistant exploring other lines of enquiry. Jeffreys has said that if he was doing this research in 2009 instead of the mid-1980s, the funder, the Medical Research Council (MRC), may have ignored this finding because it was not part of the remit for the research that was funded and DNA profiling would not have come to light. But the consequences of this research for criminology are many, most notably in helping the police solve serious crimes. We now know that DNA, in the form of traces of blood, tissue fibres and strands of hair, can be left at a crime scene. In other words, a criminal can leave a part of themselves at a crime scene and this source of forensic evidence can incriminate them. However, in the USA, it has raised a moral dilemma because DNA profiling has shown that a significant number of offenders sentenced to death were in fact innocent (Pakes, 2010: 140).

Applied research

Criminological research is often driven by economic and political motives as it can make a clear contribution to policy evaluation and policy formation. For example, the government or a criminal justice organization may pay for a research project that evaluates or assesses the impact of a policy, for example mandatory drug testing in prisons, or a piece of legislation, for example anti-terrorist legislation. This type of work, described as **applied research** and 'policy evaluation', shows just how important research can be to the wider world. To give a few examples, it can show if a particular policy is working, what needs to be done to reduce crime and victimization, or how the criminal justice system could be made to work more effectively.

Examples of this style of research can be found by looking at the websites of various government departments in the field of criminal justice (see Chapter 4). Because this research is funded by the taxpayer, there is a view that the research must be relevant, of practical use, and provide value for money. A belief in progressive change based on scientific evidence in the form of **evidence-based policy** has dominated criminal justice policy making in the late twentieth and early twenty-first centuries (Wiles, 1999; Davies et al., 2000; Hough, 2004). Policy makers base this on understanding a specific problem, its causes and the likely impact of any policy interventions. This approach to policy making is dependent on evaluations of interventions to find out which policies are effective, or 'what works', and under what circumstances (Tilley, 2005a). The findings of these evaluations are then fed back into the policy-making process as examples of good and best practice. It is important that the evaluations are appropriate assessments of specific interventions.

Evidence-based or evidence-led policy has changed the relationship between governments, research, evaluation and policy making (Senior et al., 2007). Before the mid-1990s, it was unusual for government to refer to evidence obtained from scientific evaluations of existing policy and practice. Instead, it often acted 'on the hoof' by prioritizing short-term political goals, such as maintaining a lead in the opinion polls, instead of sound policy based on research evidence. Various wars on crime, increasingly punitive penal policies and rising prison populations across most parts of the world are examples of this (Waquant, 2009), as is the global appeal of tough, coercive approaches to the policing of antisocial behaviour, crime and disorder through the implementation of zero-tolerance policing (Hopkins Burke, 2004).

The main aim of the evidence-based approach is to strengthen the relationship between policy interventions and the evaluations of such strategies and initiatives. In particular, evidence is not just used to introduce a programme but is also gathered and evaluated as part of its development. Thus, policy formulation and its implementation and the ideas and knowledge derived from research or evaluations are inseparable.

The media as a driver of criminological research

Earlier we spoke about the ambivalent relationship between the media and crime research. It is true that the mass media is an invaluable source of information about crime and deviance for researchers, although we must exercise caution when treating articles, tweets or blogs as 'facts' in our work. But the media is also an important site of research and a motivating factor for researchers to ask particular questions about crime. This is especially so because you may be motivated to research a topic that has attracted media attention. Why is this? Reports in the media have the power to shape public understanding of particular forms of crime or specific events. They can simply reflect cultural attitudes towards crime and disorder, but it could be argued that media accounts of criminality shape and create norms and values in our society, by defining and maintaining moral boundaries that identify behaviours as normal and consistent with the prevailing status quo. Media agents and organizations also play a part in shaping what is thought and said about crime control policy, and in some instances their actions help to generate 'moral panics', whereby they exaggerate the extent and prevalence of a type of crime (Cohen, 1972). Researchers may be determined to find out if these widespread perceptions of crime are valid, justified and appropriate, or fabricated by media outlets for the sake of an entertaining story.

The media also has less direct influences on the research process. Media stories and campaigns often only make visible specific subjects. The media also plays a significant role in generating or reflecting the topicality of an issue. These factors may, in turn, influence which criminological issues appear attractive for you to research. While the influence of the media on society is one of the most heavily researched and thus debated issues in the social sciences (Carrabine, 2008), it is important to recognize the role of the media in framing the way certain crime issues are portrayed.

For example, in the 1970s, Hall et al. (1978) carried out a well-known study of a 'moral panic' around street crime in the UK. The popular press had homed in on several atypical examples of mugging, including one where the victim died, to stir up fear in the community. Newspapers published stories where the perceived race of the muggers was African Caribbean. It did not take long to disseminate a view that mugging was a black crime and that black men were most likely to be the perpetrators of this offence. Hall et al. (1978) did not deny the involvement of some black men in street crimes but on the basis of alternative forms of research evidence, they argued that it was grossly distorted and overexaggerated by the media. One of their conclusions was that the criminalization of ethnic minority communities gave the state an opportunity to divert criticism away from an economic and social crisis. The research study showed that the widespread 'commonsense' view, which had been perpetuated by the media, was not necessarily accurate or fully explored, and the media had become involved in the politics of crime control.

Values and politics as shapers of criminological research

Values and ideology

Values and beliefs are central to criminal justice and although some commentators suggest that research is a value-free activity, this is arguably a simplistic view. The Introduction showed how common sense is of crucial importance for making sense of our attitudes to crime and antisocial behaviour, but now consider these popular debates:

- Are paedophiles evil, nasty, manipulative monsters, who should be castrated, or individuals in need of care and treatment?
- Is the street robber a drug-addicted bully, who picks on the weak to feed their habit and buy expensive designer training shoes, or a damaged individual trying desperately to make ends meet and make sure they are 'respected'?
- Should the police force be given more powers to deal with anti-capitalist protesters or is the death of an innocent protester at the hands of the police a sign that things have gone too far?
- Money is tight. When hospitals and schools are being closed, should we really be spending more money on prisons?

To design a piece of research exploring such themes would be influenced by personal and political values, as well as involving a decision to do quantitative or qualitative research, to distribute a survey or watch people in their own environment. The factors motivating the completion of a piece of research – to improve something in the 'real world' or to study purely for the sake of studying – reflect values, big ideas and philosophical questions, like justice, fairness and equality, which may or may not be deemed important by the researcher.

As well as our personal values, political ideologies are important to informing decisions of what and how to research. Debate between left- and rightwing political values spills over into criminological research where there is conflict and argument, attested to by the tensions existing between two criminological theories, such as left and right realism (see Chapter 3). Criminology is a fragmented discipline, as is criminological theory, and there is a lack of consensus in responding to all the key research questions. It is unlikely that criminologists are ever going to agree about why people commit crime. For example, radical and critical criminologists, who challenge existing power structures and relations, are not likely to be asked by government to conduct research into strengthening police powers, unless government is thinking about being presented with an anti-state polemic. Psychologists with an interest in crime will tend to concentrate on the human psyche and cognitive processes as factors predisposing people to fight and steal, whereas sociologists look to social structural explanations, such as the influence of economic factors on criminality. Social psychologists will go some way towards bridging the gap between these two positions, but in the last analysis, researchers will choose to look at the mind or brain or at society or conceivably the interaction between them. These illustrations are, of course, caricatures but the values and politics of criminological researchers will resemble the political ideologies and social values existing in wider society, especially at the level of the government and state.

State, government and the politics of research

Government or state organizations use research findings to inform their decisions around policy or legislation and/or to evaluate their impact and effectiveness. For example, research can:

* measure and describe a criminological phenomenon that requires tackling
* provide explanations and predictions of activities, which can be used to inform policies to respond to social problems
* explore changes in wider society and the economy, to see if they are likely to lead to more crime, for example a global recession
* identify factors, such as values, that may be used to influence behaviour.

The nature of the relationship between research and policy will vary from government to government according to their values and the circumstances in the external world, that is, the social structure, the economy, but inevitably government can control or influence the kinds of questions researchers can ask, the research topics that are funded and the styles of research methods that are afforded a higher status. So, the power of government should never be understated when it comes to crime and public policy because government not only sets the agenda, it also controls finances and the budget.

CONCLUSIONS

This chapter discussed the nature of criminological research, stressing that criminologists are just one group involved in the production of knowledge about the reality of crime. Whenever we concentrate on any aspect of crime and disorder, there are multiple realities and what is said about these issues is tied up with the values and politics of the researcher, which interact with an underlying reality, for example there are offenders, victims and workers dealing with various aspects of crime and its control. On the whole, our personal politics and values should be treated with some doubt and scepticism because they offer an incomplete, distorted view of the world. It can contribute towards phenomena such as 'moral panics', prejudice and discrimination. As criminological researchers, we should aspire to offer a more balanced, less value-laden account of the world and, to a point, we can deliver this. There are methodological rules and frameworks that govern criminologists – note we refer to rules not a rule and frameworks not a framework. However, research agendas are influenced by a range of factors, not least powerful people and groups who shape criminological research and theory.

By now, the contested status of criminological research and knowledge can be appreciated, which forms the background noise to the design and administration of all research projects and this cannot be ignored. It is essential that all researchers reflect on the consequences of these factors at each stage of the research process. Connecting with these issues, Chapter 3, which offers an overview of criminological theory, shows the interplay of social scientific principles, political and personal values with the practicalities of doing research.

REVIEW QUESTIONS

- Outline the main epistemological and ontological standpoints and discuss the main differences between them.

- Using two examples of criminological research referred to in this chapter, evaluate the strengths and weakness of the methodological approaches they adopted.

- Critically assess the extent to which research can ever be 'value free' due to the influence of politics and the media.

FURTHER READING

If you were to read one book, our recommendation would be:

> Benton, T. and Craib, I. (2010) *Philosophy of Social Science: The Philosophical Foundations of Social Thought.* Basingstoke: Palgrave Macmillan.

In addition to this, we suggest you refer to:

> Hollis, M. (1994) *The Philosophy of Social Science: An Introduction.* Cambridge: Cambridge University Press.

> Little, D. (1990) *Varieties of Social Explanation: An Introduction to the Philosophy of Social Science.* Boulder, CO: Westview Press.

> Matthews, R. and Young, J. (eds) (2003) *The New Politics of Crime and Punishment.* Cullompton: Willan.

CHAPTER 3

3

CRIME RESEARCH AND CRIMINOLOGICAL THEORY

OVERVIEW

The aim of this chapter is to:

- Illustrate the centrality of research to the development of criminological thought and theory since the nineteenth century to the present day.
- Describe the relationship between crime research and criminological theory, using a diversity of theoretical perspectives, including biological positivism, the Chicago School, social control theory, postmodern and cultural criminologies, realist criminology, feminism and crime science.

INTRODUCTION

This chapter focuses on criminological theory. You will see that the key ideas and concepts discussed are the end product or outcome of research. At the same time, as Chapter 2 shows, the findings of research may also be influenced by the methods and values adopted by researchers. So, in this chapter, we show that criminological theory is closely related to research in terms of the questions criminologists ask and the practical approaches and tools they use in a particular research project to answer these questions. To remind you of the quotation taken from Harrison et al. (2005: 6) cited in Chapter 1, theory exists in order to offer a *sensible explanation* of the significance of what we think we know about various aspects of crime and crime control.

The following overview of the rich and varied history of criminological theory over the past 200 years shows you the importance of the historical and socioeconomic context in which these ideas were developed. In other words, the research undertaken by criminologists is often a product of a particular time and place. Our choice of theoretical perspectives is necessarily selective, but the examples we use reflect the diversity of criminological theory and method, taking on board the influence of the natural and social sciences. It is not a complete history and on one occasion we jump from the nineteenth to the twentieth century. Instead, it is an attempt to consider the main currents of criminological thought and illustrate their connection to the research process. Many of the ideas discussed below also continue to resonate today. There are examples of quantitative and qualitative research, research that embraces politics and other research that is dismissed as being non-scientific.

Research has been the cornerstone of criminological theory for over 200 years and will be a core element of any research you do. What separates modern criminology from its more value-laden and 'superstitious' predecessors, for example saying that criminality is caused by demonic possession (see Pfol, 1985), is the grounding of argument in facts and observable data that is developed through research. Both the theoretical explanations of crime and the policies implemented to ameliorate it have often sought to justify themselves by referring to research studies. Many of these theories stand and fall on the strengths and weaknesses of the research methods they use.

CRIMINOLOGY AND THE NATURAL SCIENCES

Throughout the history of criminology, some researchers have claimed that crime and criminals can be studied by applying the methods and techniques of the **natural sciences** – the 'hard' or physical sciences such as biology. This chapter starts and ends with examples where researchers have made claims that their work is scientific and, by implication, value free and objective. Such research includes claims that criminals are somehow biologically or psychologically different from non-offenders and, more recently, that objective scientific methodologies can be applied to the study of crime and its control. Cesare Lombroso, perhaps the most famous of the early criminologists, is known for applying the natural sciences and the principles of positivism in an attempt to identify the biological components of a 'born criminal'. If you've read Chapter 2, you will be at ease with this thinker, but here we give you another example. Lombroso ([1876] 2006: 51) observed that:

> while offenders might not look fierce, there is nearly always something strange about their appearance. It can even be said that each type of crime is committed by men with particular physiognomic characteristics, such as a lack of a beard or an abundance of hair; this may explain why the overall appearance is neither delicate nor pleasant.

This scientific approach drew heavily on biology, what Lombroso called 'criminal anthropology', and throughout his career he conducted thousands of postmortems on the bodies of dead convicted criminals in an attempt to provide evidence for his theories.

Before examining his research and findings in more detail, it is important to note that when you assess the work of Lombroso, there are a number of important lessons for criminological research. First, it is one of the most famous examples of attempts to differentiate criminal and non-criminal populations. Despite being written in the nineteenth century, his main arguments are still important today. For example, journalists, academics, politicians and police officers commonly make claims that criminals are somehow 'born evil' or hold particular psychological or physical characteristics that distinguish them from non-criminals – something that has never been proved convincingly.

Lombroso's primary focus was on human biological features and, in studying these, drew on the established traditions of his time. Less than 50 years before, the practice of phrenology – the notion that an individual's personality can be deciphered from the shape of their head – had been developed. Overlapping the period of Lombroso's research was the publication of Charles Darwin's hugely influential *The Origin of the Species* ([1859]1998) and *The Descent of Man* ([1871]2004), the latter arguing that certain character traits emerged due to an incomplete evolutionary process. Both these themes can be seen in Lombroso's work and, to some extent, it can be argued that his ideas were a product of his time.

Approach and findings

Like all the criminological theories outlined in this chapter, you will see that Lombroso's ideas are connected to the research methods he used to obtain his results. Using clinical methods, he found that criminals harboured physical characteristics that were tangible, observable and could be subjected to statistical analysis. In doing so, he therefore adopted the position that 'evidence' of criminal intent or predisposition is something that could be quantified. He did this by taking measurements from thousands of postmortems, examinations of donated skulls and observations of living subjects. Describing his work in retrospect, Lombroso (cited in Ferrero-Lombroso, 1911: xiii) describes how he

> Examin[ed] ... cases of mental alienation [via] the study of the skull, with measurements and weights, by means of esthesiometer and craniometer. Reassured by the result of these first studies, I sought to apply this method to the study of criminals.

In Chapter 1, we emphasized that a factor affecting the scope of any research is the availability of or access to information. Lombroso was aided significantly by the Italian government's practice of compiling statistics on diverse issues, including military recruitment and convict populations during the last three decades of the 1800s (Wolfgang, 1972). This availability of 'hard data' combined with his meticulous attention to detailed clinical examinations led Lombroso to call himself a 'slave to facts'.

An illustration of his approach to 'criminal anthropology' can be seen if we look at one of his first studies, a postmortem on an Italian criminal named Vilella, famed for his strength. On examining the skull, Lombroso claims to have found, at the spot where the spine joins the 'normal' skull, 'a distinct depression which I named *median occipital fossa*, because of its situation precisely in the middle of the occiput as in inferior animals, especially rodents' (cited in Ferrero-Lombroso, 1911: xiv). He used this observation to generate a theory that connects criminality to the idea of atavism – that certain physical elements of criminals were less evolved than in non-criminals and, as such, were closer to their evolutionary ancestors. This observation (cited in Ferrero-Lombroso, 1911: xiv–xv)

> **❝** explained anatomically the enormous jaws, high cheek bones, prominent supercilliary arches, solitary lines in the palms, extreme size of the orbits, handle-shaped or sessile ears found in criminals, savages and apes.

Other early studies aimed to find out the statistical degree of abnormality among criminals. For example, one study of the skulls of 66 offenders led Lombroso ([1876]2006: 48–9) to conclude that among criminals:

> **❝** 61 percent exhibit fusion of the cranial bones; 92 percent ... an ape-like forward thrust of the lower face ... 20 percent, a large jawbone ... 59 per cent small cranial capacity.

This approach was then developed to consider the physiological differences between those committing different types of offence. A study of 832 living criminals led Lombroso to the conclusion that criminals, in general, were above average height, and robbers and murderers were taller than rapists, forgers and thieves. Lombroso (cited in Wolfgang, 1972: 251) added that thieves had 'mobile, restless, frequently oblique eyes' and 'thin beards', rapists had 'brilliant eyes, delicate faces and tumid lips', and murderers had 'cold, glassy eyes', strong jaws and hair that was 'curly, dark and abundant'.

Regarding Lombroso's methodology, if you read his work you will notice that the more participants (criminals) he studied, the more diverse his theory became. This occurred fairly early on in his work when trying to account for the actions of a young soldier called Misdea who, with no prior history of violence, suddenly attacked eight superior officers and comrades. On finding that Misdea's cranial formations did not display any atavistic resemblance nor notable abnormalities, Lombroso was forced to look for another explanation, albeit one rooted in his original outlook. In doing so, he designated the missing link to be epilepsy, claiming that 'the greatest criminals showed themselves to be epileptics, and, on the other hand, epileptics manifested the same anomalies as criminals' (cited in Ferrero-Lombroso, 1911: xvi). This was then developed into a cohesive model detailing five different 'criminal types': born criminals, epileptics, insane criminals, occasional criminals, and criminals of passion.

This incorporation of other elements into Lombroso's theory was typical of the diversification and modification of his approach throughout later editions of *The Criminal Man* and is often overlooked in many accounts of his work. Many criminologists often fail to acknowledge that Lombroso's later work also moved beyond purely biological explanations of criminality and attempted to account for a raft of environmental influences that even included climatic changes. Although flawed, one could consider such multicausal explanations of criminality to be groundbreaking for their time.

You might be thinking that the more Lombroso generated data, the more his findings failed to fit into his narrow positivistic theory of criminality and atavism. To accommodate the many variations in findings, the theory becomes unwieldy and unworkable as a coherent explanation of crime. This represents a fatal flaw in his methodological approach that has attracted much criticism and, ultimately, led to his research being found deficient.

CRIMINOLOGY AND THE SOCIAL SCIENCES

We now move on into the twentieth century to consider another tradition in criminology, particularly the influence of sociology that was characterized in the nineteenth century as a 'science of society'. One of the most influential 'schools' in criminology derives from the work of the University of Chicago's Department of Sociology. Although a vast and not entirely cohesive body of work, the key theoretical and methodological innovations, particularly those initiated between the 1920s and the 1950s, have had a lasting impact on criminology that can be clearly felt to this day and it is possible that you will already be acquainted with some of them.

The Chicago School: the city as laboratory

Marking a clear break from many earlier attempts that examined the individual, the Chicago School looked towards the environment, specifically the life of the city, as a key determinant of offending behaviour. The continual expansion of the city and the movement of populations within it were seen to foster particular social formations and, crucially, internally distinct subcommunities. To understand the work of the Chicago School, it is important to recognize how the rapid growth of the city provided the context for much of the methodological and theoretical work that was to take place.

Between the 1830s and the 1930s, Chicago experienced a phenomenal rate of growth, attracting migrants from inside the USA and from overseas. In doing so, the population of the city expanded from around 4,000 inhabitants in the 1830s to over 3 million people a century later. This growth triggered many social processes, including a heightened competition for space, overcrowding of low-rent areas, and an unprecedented strain on the city's physical and social institutions. In this turbulent environment it was reasonable to view crime as a product of social, rather than individual, factors. This realization led to the development and refinement of methodological approaches that allowed the city and its impact on criminality to be assessed.

The founder of the Chicago School was Robert Park, a journalist who had studied the city's social conditions for several decades. He arrived at a number of conclusions about how the city evolves and impacts on its inhabitants. Perhaps the most important here is his idea that the location and growth of urban communities was not random. Instead, borrowing from the scientific principles of plant ecology, Park claimed that these social processes mirror the way natural organisms, such as plants, intersect and arrange themselves in relation to each other. So, for Park (1928, cited in Downes and Rock, 1998: 69), 'the city is not merely an artefact, but an organism'. In fact, the city was characterized as a 'superorganism', one that grew according to the three-stage model of 'invasion, dominance and succession' that governed the expansion of plant life. Importantly, Park viewed this process as a metaphor for development rather than a strictly binding deterministic principle. What is crucial from a research methods point of view is that these relationships and processes could only be fully understood through attentive observation and engagement with the lives of those experiencing them. This encouraged researchers to develop, refine and adopt a range of methodologies that became one of the Chicago School's major contributions to the study of crime.

Approach and findings

Chicago School sociologists argued that if we are to understand the tides and currents that shape community life in the city, researchers need to access the practical, everyday experiences of its inhabitants. To achieve this deeper level of understanding, qualitative research techniques were developed, which could access the world of deviants and those on the margins of society and, crucially, interpret how these actors create meaning and make sense of their own world. In many studies, attempts were made to combine these qualitative innovations with quantitative approaches to validate and triangulate (see Chapter 9) the data (see below). This emphasized the role of experience and led to a reliance on methods that involved **participant observations**, life histories and extended interviews. The words of Park (quoted in Downes and Rock, 1998: 39) may help us to appreciate this:

> ❮❮ people had to get out and if they wanted to study opium addicts they went to the opium dens and even smoked a little opium maybe, they went out and lived with the gangs and the ... hobos and so on.

The research process often involved prolonged periods of fieldwork consisting of close engagement with the research population. Among others, research projects sought to understand *The Hobo* (Anderson, 1923), *The Gang* (Thrasher, 1925) and, later, *The Professional Thief* (Sutherland, 1937). The city had effectively become the sociologists' laboratory.

The Chicago School is perhaps most famous for Ernst Burgess's (1925) characterization of the city's social division into distinct concentric 'zones'. Rather than urban spaces growing at the edges as they absorbed larger populations, new arrivals instead chose to live in other, perhaps more affordable areas and then move away once they had attained the means to do so. These areas remained in continual transition and lacked the stability to maintain a universally shared set of values and understandings across communities. This resulted in weak social controls and environments where crime could flourish. In Chicago, these neighbourhoods were concentrated around the central business area of the city and dubbed 'zones of transition'. As you might expect, the perceived criminogenic characteristics of such spaces influenced the choice of location for the fieldwork that was to follow.

One of the earliest examples of such work was Thrasher's (1925) study of the city's gangs. You might be surprised to learn that Thrasher spent seven years collecting and preparing data gathered from the streets, youth groups, juvenile detention facilities, charities, schools, welfare organizations and parent associations, among other sources, in order to build an accurate understanding of what he claimed were 1,313 active gangs in the city. This information was then analysed and used to form the basis of a number of conclusions. Among these, Thrasher concluded that gangs were extremely diverse in their formations and were most likely to prosper in deteriorating communities. In particular, communities experiencing a high degree of transition, where large numbers of people were continually moving into and out of the area, would generate a type of disorganization that favoured gangs prospering. Thrasher also asserted that solidarity within these gangs strengthened as conflicts between groups (a consequence of disorganization) escalated.

In addition to the groundbreaking, detailed data on Chicago's gangs, Thrasher's work raises a number of methodological points you must consider. Most notably, to gather robust data and detailed understandings of the research population, a researcher needs patience and must be prepared to spend a great deal of time in the field. As Thrasher's work demonstrates, such research becomes extremely focused over time, and so the findings become increasingly tied to the environment being studied. As such, valid research doesn't necessarily require that the findings are generalizable or transferable to other environments.

A later, but similarly influential study also connected Burgess's theory with empirical work in the city. Shaw and McKay (1942) developed an understanding of the relationship between urban environments and criminality by statistically analysing the spatial distributions of delinquency. As Shaw and McKay note, statistical enquiry into urban delinquency has a rich history, from early ecological studies conducted by Guerry in France (1833), Mayhew's (1862) exhaustive study of crime and delinquency in London, to Burt's (1925) mapping of delinquency in London. These studies attempted to locate deviancy in their urban geographical contexts. Shaw and McKay extended this analysis through a detailed study of how the environment may generate conditions for deviancy. They concluded that delinquents were 'normal', no different from the rest of the population, and that illegal activities were intrinsically related to the environment one resided within. To verify this, they attempted to statistically test the assumption that crime was greater in socially disorganized zones of transition than elsewhere in the city.

According to Burgess (1942), Shaw and McKay spent 20 years preparing, collecting and analysing data gathered from 20 cities across the USA. During this time, they used various measures to understand the locations of delinquent behaviour in the city, including 'spot maps, statistical tables showing the rates of delinquents and economic and social variables computed for large zones and classes of area' (Shaw and McKay, 1942: 13–14). This formed part of the method Shaw and McKay (1942: 3) used to identify the distribution of home addresses for over 60,000 male individuals in Chicago dealt with by the school authorities, police and courts as 'actual or alleged truants, delinquents, or criminals'. This comprehensive capture of statistical data was then used as a guide from which more detailed qualitative investigations (such as life histories) were conducted.

Based on these methods and the data they yielded, Shaw and McKay developed a multifaceted theory to explain delinquency in the city. First, they argued that deviancy is not randomly distributed but is concentrated in specific locations. Second, these locations host deviant activity because of particular features within those communities, or, as they put it, 'delinquency ... has its roots in the dynamic life of the community' (Shaw and McKay, 1942: 435). We can see, then, that certain communities provide the 'appropriate setting for delinquency careers' (Shaw and McKay, 1942: 446). More specifically, these 'settings' contained physical problems, such as close proximity to industrial premises and a high number of condemned buildings, and socioeconomic problems, including high proportions of residents receiving welfare payments, few homeowners, poor incomes and high levels of infant mortality, all of which were seen as 'causes' of crime. Perhaps most important for Shaw and McKay was the issue of 'population transience' – the continual flow of individuals into and out of these areas. This made such places disorganized, with populations that were always temporary and thus struggled to maintain an organized community or impose any dominant set of values. In turn, this cultural fragmentation allowed delinquency to thrive, to the extent that it formed a social tradition or way of life for particular communities.

It may have occurred to you that what was particularly novel about Shaw and McKay's approach was the theory that delinquency was attached to the geographies of an area, not the people who lived within it. Thus, despite the social or ethnic composition of communities residing in these particular areas changing, levels of delinquency would remain stable. This is because the instability of the area would continue regardless of who lived there. This idea was then developed into what you might recognize as one of the most influential theories to emanate from the Chicago School – the coupling of social disorganization with the cultural transmission of delinquency. Here, the idea is that not only are these areas conducive to delinquent activity, but this deviant behaviour is transmitted over time and across the different generations that live in these places. Delinquent behaviour cannot be attributed to a particular social or ethnic group, but is a result of social and geographical features. Such features include the instability and mobility of the populations residing in specific areas.

Overall, while the Chicago School had a big influence on criminological thought, many of its studies have been criticized on methodological grounds. Although some theoretical positions remain controversial – including the argument that much Chicagoan theorizing overdetermines and overplays the role of the environment, known as the 'ecological fallacy' – the emphasis given to the way delinquency may be transmitted through disorganized spaces has provided a major contribution to the study of urban life and its impact on deviancy. Above all, we should acknowledge the innovative application of qualitative research methods to understand how people make sense of their own environments, socially interact and mediate their desires.

Theorizing control

Another development in criminology you might be familiar with that continues to resonate today, and where theory and method are closely linked, is the body of work labelled 'social control theories'. Instead of attempting to identify which factors were likely to cause an individual to offend, as had been the emphasis of much criminological work up to this point, social control theories aim to explain why people *refrained* from criminal behaviour. According to Hirschi (1969: 99), one reason is that 'the child attached to his father is less likely to commit delin-quent acts'. Such theories suggest a rather different view of human behaviour. Instead of seeing offending behaviour as something that is inherently wrong with an individual or their environment, social control theorists argued that people are largely motivated by greed and self-interest. To acquire the things we want and satisfy our desires, it is perhaps in our interests to offend. Deviance is seen as an expression of our natural desires rather than a pathological condition, something offenders are compelled or predestined towards. To prevent people committing crime to satisfy these desires, social control theorists explored the mechanisms that kept people in a state of conformity – an idea that draws on Thomas Hobbes's ([1651]2002) philosophical view that human choices are regu-lated by consensual social arrangements.

One of the most prominent social control theorists is Travis Hirschi, whose *Causes of Delinquency* (1969) was one of the most influential criminological studies of the 1960s. Of particular interest in Hirschi's work is the way these abstract philosophical concepts of human desire and the regulation of choices are examined through transparent research methods. Hirschi designed a quan-titative apparatus to understand the emotional attachments and social bonds affecting a large sample of young males. This was then cross-referenced with local police statistics in an attempt to discern whether the answers of young people who did offend differed from those who did not.

Approach and findings

Because Hirschi wanted to discover generalized patterns across large numbers of young people, he adopted a quantitative methodology. Hirschi first identified a research population of 17,500 students attending eleven schools in a region of California. From these, he selected a sample of 5,545 students to participate in his research and secured agreements from schools to distribute and oversee the completion of the questionnaires he had designed. These questionnaires were extremely detailed and consisted of hundreds of questions designed to generate a comprehensive understanding of participants' everyday lives and uncover a range of deeply held beliefs. These included questions on topics as diverse as whether participants shared their mealtimes with parents to whether they believed in life after death. It could be claimed that Hirschi was attempting to measure the impact of **independent variables** (such as parenting, family attachments, edu-cation and beliefs) on the **dependent variable** of crime (variables are discussed in greater detail in Chapter 5). Owing to a range of factors, including a lack of parental consent, students being absent or transferring to other schools during the research period, and errors in completion, Hirschi received 4,077 completed questionnaires, which he then cross-referenced with the police records of 3,605 boys held by local sheriffs' departments. The collective data was then analysed and used to inform a general understanding of the factors that prevent young people from engaging in delinquency – the theory of 'social bonds'.

From his data, Hirschi theorized that there were four 'social bonds' which kept non-delinquents in a state of conformity. These are:

1. *Attachment:* the bond with a role model or guardian figure, usually a parent
2. *Commitment:* the commitment to a conventional lifestyle. The individual has more to lose, such as their reputation or employment, by engaging in delinquency
3. *Involvement:* the time spent engaged in conventional activities
4. *Belief:* those with a strong belief in the validity of laws and conventional values are less likely to become delinquent.

A loosening of any of these four bonds would increase the likelihood of delinquent behaviour. In sum, Hirschi's theory of social bonds has become extremely influential in crime research. Most notably, perhaps, it has been seen by many policy makers as an important site of intervention, where attention is placed on issues such as parenting rather than more structural factors such as unemployment, and has informed many of the strategies currently used to tackle crime. Hirschi and his followers often claimed that because his work was based on a strong empirical foundation, the theory was robust and universal. However, while Hirschi is correct to link the strengths of a theory with the strengths of its empirical basis, it is also true that the weaknesses of his research design manifest in theoretical shortcomings. We outline these methodological problems in greater detail in Chapter 5, where you are introduced to survey methods and quantitative research.

Postmodern and cultural criminologies

The idea of postmodernism has provoked debate across a range of academic disciplines, including philosophy, sociology, cultural studies and literary criticism, and has also been used in the arts, especially in painting, architecture, cinema and literature. It is via these areas of study that postmodern and poststructuralist theories have influenced criminological research agendas, although sometimes in indirect ways.

Before continuing, it is necessary to explain the term 'postmodern'. The first and perhaps obvious point is that the word 'post' means after and beyond, so we are discussing after modernity and after the modern. Modernity is a product of the Enlightenment, a period in history when scientific ideas replaced religious beliefs. Modernity was characterized by industrialization, economic growth and a general commitment to social progress. For some commentators, such as Giddens (2007), human societies are still a part of modernity, albeit late modernity. Others have argued instead that by the last third of the twentieth century, there was a move beyond modernity towards a condition of postmodernity (Lyotard, 1984). If this is the case, what are the theoretical implications? If we have moved beyond the period of modernity, how do we make sense of our world when doing research? Do the ideas of modernity still apply or are they now redundant?

Postmodernism is a powerful critique, which subjected to criticism traditional Enlightenment values such as reason and progress. Lyotard described reason as a metanarrative – a single explanation for everything – and the postmodern as 'incredulity towards narratives'. Taking this further, we can see positivism and interpretivism as metanarratives. Thus, postmodernism is an attack on traditional values and the view that there are universally relevant value frameworks. It is argued that there is no set of higher rational principles to judge what research and knowledge can tell us and all that remains is a plurality, or many different but equally legitimate sets, of values. It is no longer possible to appeal to the overarching principles of justice and truth because they do not exist, and, if they did, we would all have different views of what they were. Anyone who speaks of 'truth' and a notion of 'reality' can only do so in a particular, local context, but beyond that, what is said is not necessarily transferable to other contexts. This leads to fragmentation, individualization and diversification.

It could be argued that this diversification, the acknowledgement of multiple discourses and rejection of single explanations of crime, has informed one of the most prominent schools of recent criminological research: cultural criminology. This perspective owes much to Jack Katz's (1988) exploration of the 'seductions and repulsions' of crime. Perhaps more influential now than when it was first published 25 years ago, Katz's work is seen by many as a landmark event in criminology. Drawing on subjective first-hand perspectives and experiences of those perpetrating violence, murder, shoplifting, burglary, vandalism, joyriding and armed robbery, Katz's research views the world through offenders' eyes to explore the sensual and live 'attractions' of crime. He actually compares crime to eating, illustrated by his statement that: 'It is not the taste for pizza that leads to the crime; the crime makes the pizza tasty' (Katz, 1988: 52). In seeing things in this way, his central thesis is that our emotions, such as excitement, pride or humiliation, are the most important feature of criminal behaviour. Indeed, 'the closer one looks at crime ... the more vividly relevant become the moral emotions' (Katz, 1988: 312).

In contrast to his emphasis on emotions, Katz argues that social science and state-led understandings of criminality have been rather sterile, because we are insulated from 'the slaps and curses ... the pushes and shoves, or feel the humiliation and rage that may build toward the attack', the 'thrilling experience' and 'attraction' of robbery (1988: 3), and the meanings and significance the labels of deviance have. In Katz's view, such traditional accounts have attempted to account for criminal behaviour in one of three ways:

1. An illegal pursuit of conventional goals, such as material possessions.
2. A response or reaction to an individual's social, economic or environmental location.
3. Some physical, psychological, pathological difference (Fenwick and Hayward, 2001).

All these explanations encounter significant limitations, as they ignore what are called the 'experiential facts of crime' (Katz, 1988: 314). In sum, Katz characterizes these sensual emotions governing criminality as 'foreground', while representing social, economic, cultural or pathological factors as 'background'.

To capture a detailed understanding of how people experience emotion and invest their actions with meaning, it would be essential for you to employ qualitative research methodologies. Following this tradition, Katz applied a number of strategies to accumulate data for his study that utilized different primary and secondary sources. For example, to analyse shoplifting, burglary and vandalism, he spent three years soliciting first-hand accounts from university students. Mostly, Katz drew on previously published materials, largely comprising ethnographies and life histories, written by professional social scientists, academics and the police, and the autobiographies and biographies of criminals. This information was supplemented by data collected from his ethnographic fieldwork in Los Angeles.

Together, this strategy represents an inductive approach to research, where themes are developed as the research progresses, as opposed to deductive approaches, where ideas are formulated and then tested by the research (see Chapter 2). In effect, the search for evidence and the development of theory operate in tandem. Katz (1988: 11) argued that this allows the continual revision of his theoretical position when negative cases arise, and also generates data 'which does not produce abstract, summary forms of evidence (sampling designs, statistics of association, tests of agreement among coders, and the like)'. Those who prefer quantitative research may argue that Katz's approach provides less structure and transferability to the findings and he adopts vague, opaque and barely replicable research methods. However, such critiques miss the point that Katz offers a detailed understanding of criminal action from a perpetrator's perspective and allows the reader closer access to this phenomenon.

This proximity to the experiences of the research subjects enabled Katz to develop a more detailed understanding of the personal and deeply held emotional motivations driving criminal activity. Katz (1988: 9) summed up this phenomenon by arguing that:

> Central to all these experiences in deviance [are] moral emotions: humiliation, righteousness, arrogance, ridicule, cynicism, defilement and vengeance. In each, the attraction that proves to be most fundamentally compelling is that of overcoming a personal challenge to moral – not material – existence.

This emphasis on 'moral' (emotional) over 'material' factors can only be gleaned from research methodologies that allow the researcher close access to their subjects. Overall, Katz's attempt to reduce the gap between the researcher and the participant to allow actors to articulate their experiences from their own perspectives clearly has much to offer the study of crime and deviance.

'Realist' criminology

Increasingly, criminological research informs policy responses to crime (see Chapter 2). Particularly influential here have been the various 'realist' responses to criminality. There are two main types of 'realist' criminology – left realism and right realism. As their names suggest, these respective approaches echo the traditional (simplified here for the purposes of explanation) political views of the left –emphasizing social and 'structural' explanations for crime – and the right – viewing crime in 'conservative' terms of individual and moral responsibility.

A powerful criticism levelled at criminological theory is that it has done little to reduce crime. Since the 1970s, many have come to believe that liberal crime policies, most notably rehabilitation, have resulted in policy interventions where 'nothing works' (Martinson, 1974). Research evidence confirms that, until the mid-1990s, crime did rise to unprecedented levels. This escalation of crime occurred during a time of relative affluence when people had disposable income and there was decent welfare provision, improved housing, educational standards and employment levels. This provided a challenge to leftwing criminologists who had placed the blame for crime squarely at the door of the state's inequitable socioeconomic policies and deployment of a repressive criminal justice system (see Taylor et al., 1973) – the 'left idealist' position. At the same time, there was a growing realization that the 'Robin Hood' (a mythical figure who stole from the rich to feed the poor) model of criminality simply did not exist. Conventional crime, instead of being perpetrated by the poor against the rich, was largely perpetrated by the poor against the poor. This led both the political left and right to review and renew their focus on criminality.

Right realism

Disillusionment with left idealism allowed rightwing criminologists, particularly from the USA, to take the initiative. Rather than being a cohesive perspective in its own right, right realism is perhaps better characterized as 'an overall conservative view of crime' (Jones, 2006: 262). Yet a common feature is an emphasis on individualistic (rather than socioeconomic and structural) explanations of crime. The individual is seen as a responsible actor who chooses to become involved in crime rather than being compelled by their environment or circumstances. Consistent with rightwing notions of small government, responsibility for preventing crime was shifted from the state onto the individual. At the same time, the 'realist' component of right realists said research evidence should be applied in practice so we can claim to be 'doing something about crime'.

You might be aware of the 'broken windows' thesis (Wilson and Kelling, 1982), which is a good example of right realist approaches. This became a staple of crime prevention strategies across the world and has been applied in environments as diverse as the deprived housing estates of Middlesbrough (a town in northeast England) and the 2008 Beijing Olympics. In brief, the 'broken windows' thesis calls for the tackling of 'low-level disorder', such as littering, loitering youths, public drunkenness, visible homelessness and vandalism, to prevent an escalation into more serious criminality. If a window is broken and left unrepaired, then, over time, all the remaining windows will be broken. In sum, the argument is this:

> A piece of property is abandoned, weeds grow up, a window is smashed. Adults stop scolding rowdy children; the children, emboldened, become more rowdy. Families move out, unattached adults move in. Teenagers gather in front of the corner store. The merchant asks them to move; they refuse. Fights occur. Litter accumulates. People start drinking in front of the grocery; in time, an inebriate slumps to the sidewalk and is allowed to sleep it off. Pedestrians are approached by panhandlers.
>
> *Wilson and Kelling, 1982: 32*

To prevent this spiral of decline occurring, right realists argue that visible disorder needs to be tackled early and strongly. Although James Wilson, the co-originator of the broken windows thesis, has since attempted to distance himself from it, this idea has become the premise for zero-tolerance policing initiatives – police intervention in the most minor incidents of disorder even if they do not constitute criminal acts. Most famously, these measures were applied to the Lower Manhattan district of New York during the early/mid-1990s and credited by its supporters, such as Mayor Rudolph Giuliani and Police Chief Bratton, as responsible for the subsequent decline of murder in New York. Critics of these approaches claim that there is a lack of empirically proven linkages between such minor disorders and more serious crimes (Matthews,

1992). Moreover, crime was proved to have fallen more rapidly in many US cities that did not employ such zero-tolerance approaches and, separately, such
falls have been linked to the changes in drugs markets rather than isolated
policing initiatives (Bowling, 1999).

Left realism

These developments led some key leftwing criminologists to create a new and
influential explanation of criminality that we now see as being central to the
control of crime in communities. Although different to left idealism, left realism retains a number of features of idealism, especially the explanation of crime
in relation to its social environment. This is achieved via the notion of 'relative
deprivation', the idea that while poverty is rarely 'absolute', for example very
few people starve to death in the Global North and Australasia, it is often 'relative'. Those with the least are acutely aware of their circumstances in relation
to others and, as a result, will feel discontented. The concept of relative deprivation thus refers to the material and experiential nature of poverty. Left realists recognize that deprivation does not necessarily directly lead to crime. But
consumer-oriented societies like our own tend to be unequal and have high
crime rates, where crime impacts the most on poor people. Like left idealists,
the left realist accepts that there are social factors influencing crime, but the
latter do not deny the suffering crime causes to victims. Left 'realism' diverges
from the 'idealist' position, in that it calls for practical interventions to reduce
crime. This notion is perhaps most famously encapsulated by Tony Blair's 1992
pledge to be 'tough on crime, tough on the causes of crime'.

This new 'realist' emphasis on the impact of and response to crime has
several research-related implications. If we take the impact of crime first, left
realists have placed considerable attention on the 'fear of crime'. In the past,
many policy-oriented criminologists (and, interestingly, the radical left) pointed
out the 'irrationality' of fear, where people are unnecessarily anxious about the
chances of being victimized (Hough and Mayhew, 1983). For example, national
crime victimization surveys often reported young males as having the lowest
level of fear of crime, yet they were the most likely to become victims. Elderly
females, by contrast, were least likely to become victims, yet articulated the
highest levels of fear (Hough, 1995). This was easily characterized as an 'irrational fear'. Left realists argue that this idea of 'irrational fear' was empirically
false, portrayed certain fears as excessive, such as those of women and the
elderly, and, above all, ignored people's everyday 'lived experiences' of crime
(Young, 1987; Sparks, 1992). From a methodological perspective, critics argued
that complex emotional and cognitive concepts such as 'fear of crime' could not
be quantified into easily measurable criteria (see Ditton and Farrell, 2000). More

influentially, left realists argued that these nationwide surveys overlooked what actually happens in local communities, which could impact on levels of fear in particular places. It is possible for us to ignore the potentially genuine fears of, say, the elderly as 'irrational'. Instead, left realists argued for and undertook localized surveys of crime (Jones et al., 1986), in an attempt to uncover those issues affecting specific neighbourhoods. This localized focus for quantitative crime surveys has now been adopted as standard practice by many researchers.

Perhaps the greatest contribution of left realist research is the notion of the multiple aetiologies of crime, characterized in Young's (1994) 'square of crime'. This theory asserts that crime is shaped by the interplay of four related elements – the state, society, offenders and their victims – each occupying a corner of a metaphorical square. This allows us to produce multicausal explanations of criminality that account for the complex and dynamic interaction between any of these four variables. By implication, these multiple causes are seen to require multiple interventions, which, for left realists, are most constructively addressed by 'multiagency partnerships', involving practitioners and agencies drawn from a diverse range of public, private and voluntary sectors, thus moving beyond crime control being the exclusive preserve of the police. A major practical application of this blend of research and theory is that we now see the police as just one, and not the only, actor who can reduce crime.

Feminist research

Feminist research is an example of a radical or critical perspective in criminological theory. Among the most significant observations made by feminist research is that criminological research is dominated by men and, as such, tends to serve male interests – both in terms of academic theory and criminal justice policy and practice (Walklate, 2004; Silvestri and Crowther-Dowey, 2008). Various feminist perspectives in the social sciences refer to the influence of political, economic and social factors, sharing a view that men or, more precisely, male power oppresses, subordinates and disadvantages women. We are often told that all humans are born equal but in all spheres of social life, women, compared to men, are treated in a discriminatory manner resulting in inequality and injustice. Feminists want to give a voice to women and the necessary knowledge and tools to effectively challenge male control and ultimately create a society where 'all things are equal' for both genders. This may emerge as a result of women living apart from men, through piecemeal changes to society, or through a transformation of the social structure (Wykes and Welsh, 2008). To consider the impact these general developments have had on criminology, it is necessary to acknowledge feminism's contribution to the study of crime. This will be followed by some examples of how feminist research has contributed to the redefinition of criminological agendas.

Although the origins of feminist thought can be traced back at least to the nineteenth century, it did not have any bearing on criminology until the latter half of the twentieth century. From the late 1960s onwards, we can see the emergence of several feminist critiques of so-called 'malestream' criminology, which highlight three points relating to different levels and types of offending, how male and female offenders are perceived differently, as well epistemological and ontological assumptions (Heidensohn, 1968; Smart, 1976). We say a little bit more about these below.

First, most criminological theories are based on research focusing on male offenders. This observation applies to the theories covered earlier as well as criminological knowledge more widely (Hopkins Burke, 2009). This, by itself, is not necessarily a problem because, over time, research confirms that men and boys are responsible for most offending behaviour, especially crimes of violence (Ministry of Justice, 2009). However, the statistical evidence underpinning this 'social fact' doesn't treat the gender of most offenders as a cause for concern. Feminist scholars have argued that this is a problem and that criminology is 'gender blind' or that gender is invisible and needs to be made an explicit issue item for researchers. Some key questions asked by feminists have been:

• Why have criminologists neglected to acknowledge and explain the basic fact that most crimes are committed by males?
• What exactly is it that is wrong with men that makes them steal, fight and kill much more frequently?

Of particular relevance to feminists is the problem of male violence against women, specifically rape and domestic violence – both crimes where the victims are overwhelmingly female (Silvestri and Crowther-Dowey, 2008).

Second, because women who offend are, statistically speaking, more exceptional, they are treated as abnormal. Criminological theories that emphasize biological (Lombroso and Ferrerro, 1895), psychological (Freud, 1961) and sociological (Parsons, 1937) influences on behaviour – including those arguing, on the one hand, that such behaviour is predestined or, on the other hand, that it is a case of individual autonomy and free will – all tend to assume that criminality is a masculine phenomenon. Women who do deviate from social roles and legal norms are described as lacking feminine characteristics and they tend to be treated as if they are sick or described as 'doubly deviant' and/or evil, and, in some instances, as lacking humanity.

Third, at least since the nineteenth century, most knowledge produced by the social sciences is underpinned by epistemological and ontological assumptions that are based on the natural sciences. The natural sciences and positivism reflect androcentric or male-centred assumptions about what we know about

the world. Men represent the culture of a society, which is based on the principles of rationality, reason and objectivity. Women, by contrast, are associated
with nature and expressing their own subjective views and emotions. According to early scientific thought, this meant that in the context of modern, civilized
societies, women were inferior. What we would now call 'sexist thinking' was
carried over into criminological thought and influenced criminological research.

How have these insights influenced criminological research? Although
feminists have questioned the androcentric bias of criminological research
and theory, this has not resulted in them rejecting the research methods that
are still in use. Indeed, early feminist work was empirical in focus, aiming to
measure the extent and prevalence of female offending and victimization. The
main change brought about by feminist social scientists is the introduction of
awareness about the influence of gendered assumptions on research agendas
and, ultimately, a recognition of the relevance of politics to criminological
research (see Chapter 2).

Most nineteenth- and twentieth-century criminology has concentrated on
crimes committed in public spaces or on the streets, an observation supported
by the above sections and the focus on property crimes and the violence of
subcultural groups like gangs. These are the crimes of predominantly young
men on the streets of lower working and 'underclass' communities or in those
places where they spend their leisure time. What is missing from these accounts
is the existence of another type of male crime, namely violence against women
in private spaces such as the home. Feminist researchers did not discover these
offences, rather they exposed the lack of attention given to them by criminologists, as well as criminal justice agencies, principally the police, prosecutors and
the courts.

Since the 1970s, feminists have utilized the full range of research methods
to reveal the underpolicing of rape and domestic violence. Initially, in the words
of C. Wright Mills (1959), these crimes were viewed as 'personal trouble' shared
by a small group of feminists. Gradually, this became a 'public issue' attracting the interest of not only activists and academics but also central government.
There are studies of violence against women based on qualitative interviews
with female victims (Walby and Allen, 2004; Finney, 2006), desk-based reviews
of police and criminal justice system case files (Temkin, 2002), as well as interviews with and observational studies of criminal justice practitioners (Lees,
2002). Violence against women is no longer a personal trouble but an issue of
wider social concern. The government and the media – not just feminist activists – now say they are committed to making better the police response to rape,
demonstrated by the number of reported rapes ending with a successful conviction. In some countries, the figure is in the region of 6 per cent, which means that

94 per cent of men accused of raping a woman are not convicted. This is called the 'attrition rate' (HMCPSI, 2007). For one critic, this gives men the impression that they virtually have a 'licence to rape' (Rake, 2005).

As well as concentrating on women as victims, feminist researchers have also studied female offenders. This shows existing criminological theories to be deficient: for not recognizing female crime and failing to note the different motivational and structural influences on their behaviour. Such research shows us that females do offend but less often than males and that their offending is less serious (Silvestri and Crowther-Dowey, 2008). This observation stands despite sensationalist, often media-led accounts, which, as part of a 'feminist backlash', have attempted to expose a high volume of unreported and unrecorded female criminality. Two examples of this are the idea of the 'mean girl' who belongs to feral girl gangs and the female perpetrator of domestic violence (Miller, 2001; Ringrose, 2006).

Feminist research and its theoretical insights have led to changes in criminal justice policy and practice. For instance, feminists have combined research with their political activism, bringing about changes in the way female victims of male violence are treated by the police. This work has also been instrumental in creating refuges for the victims of rape, domestic violence and human trafficking, which provide support to women that is not available through statutory services. Feminist criminology has gone a long way towards highlighting the inequalities between men and women in the sphere of criminal justice. Criminological research agendas have not been totally transformed, but you will now see that gender is on the radar of the discipline, something you could not have said before the late 1960s.

Crime science: full circle?

Another area of criminological theory that has recently gained attention is 'crime science', which claims to have facilitated 'the application of science to the control of crime' (Laycock, 2008: 149; see also Clarke, 2004; Laycock, 2005; Pease, 2008). According to these authors, this is considered to depart from modern criminology because of its emphasis on the natural sciences to address the immediate problems of crime. For others, many of the central themes of crime science, such as routine activity and rational choice theories of crime prevention (Newburn, 2007) or the 'criminologies of everyday life' (Garland, 1996; Haggerty, 2008), have been argued to have existed as subdisciplines of criminology for some time. From a research methods' perspective, one of the interesting features of crime science is its preoccupation with 'scientific' methodologies over and above the theoretical concerns of other forms of criminology. In effect, we could argue that methodology has become the theory. This discussion now looks at the origins of crime science and its key methodological concerns before examining some of the critiques of this approach.

For its enthusiasts, crime science is founded on the perception that existing criminological research has largely failed to adequately explain and, crucially, reduce crime. For example, Laycock (2008) points out that crime rates fluctuated extensively throughout the twentieth century, but have not been sufficiently explained by the discipline of criminology. It must be added, however, that criminologists have consistently pointed out the unreliability of indicators of crime rates. Here, it is argued that most existing attempts are post hoc, inconclusive and of little relevance to policy, whereas scientific approaches are more suited to anticipate, intervene and reduce criminality. Pease (2008: 154) puts this more strongly, arguing that criminological enquiry has been 'disappointing' and that 'something akin to a paradigm shift should be considered'. We can see that crime scientists have argued that while their ideas have some connection with criminology, their discipline is also distinct from criminology. Smith and Tilley (2005a) liken this relationship to that between medicine and the sociology of medicine, with crime scientists (the clinicians) adopting the (presumably more prestigious) role of applying their curative powers to reduce (heal?) crime, and criminologists adopting the (presumably more subservient) role of abstract theorizing and critiquing of existing policy. Rather than putting forward a new and transformative approach, such statements reflect an old debate within criminology and the wider social sciences. An example of this debate is Becker's (1967) question of 'whose side are we on?' in relation to the unlikelihood of value-free research.

So what is crime science? It is billed as a practical discipline that seeks to apply scientific methodologies and technology to inform attempts to tackle crime. Natural sciences, such as engineering, chemistry and biology, are employed to develop predominantly environmental, situational and/or disruptive approaches to reduce offending. Its successes are then generally measured in relation to what are deemed tangible outcomes. Laycock (2005) elaborates on this relationship by asserting that science can inform the control of crime in four main ways:

1. How science can inform us about the nature of crime
2. How science can contribute to prevention
3. How science can enhance detection
4. How scientific method can apply to crime reduction.

In practice, much work in the area deals with the long-established field of crime reduction – a focus that reflects the various hues of routine activity theory (Felson, 2002), crime pattern analysis (Brantingham and Brantingham, 1993) and rational choice theory (Cornish and Clarke, 1986). Issues of criminal motivation are present, yet largely explained in terms of the relationship between criminal opportunities and the absence of deterrence measures, therefore emphasizing the more traditional concerns of 'crime reduction'.

If we consider the methodologies adopted in these analyses, crime science draws on the approaches of the natural sciences to examine social phenomena. As Laycock (2005: 9) states:

> perhaps most importantly ... crime science is about applying established scientific approaches and technologies to crime control. This means using data, logic, evidence and rational thought. It specifically involves formulating and testing hypotheses and, through that process, building a body of knowledge upon which our existing theories about the proximal causes of crime can be further developed.

Thus, quantitative strategies involving statistical modelling where hypotheses are transparently tested are favoured. Although the use of such approaches is far from new in criminology – and emphasis on 'data, logic, evidence' has been a key component of criminological enquiry over the centuries – the methodological (and epistemological) approach is not just elevated *above* the theory, it could be argued to *be* the theory. This is perhaps what Pease (2008: 155, 156) has in mind in his criticism that theoretical criminology 'seems not much constrained' by empirical work and his view that established criminological research has value when 'good empirical criminologists [act as] as *bona fide* scientists'.

In undertaking this approach, a number of studies have examined a range of different aspects of crime reduction. These include evaluations of mechanisms to reduce bullying and violence in prisons (Wortley and Summers, 2005), reducing crime at motorway service areas (Tilley, 2005b), assessment of vehicle excise duty evasion (Smith and Webb, 2005), crime mapping (Chainey, 2008), DNA profiling (Webb et al., 2005), cost–benefit analysis of crimes (Farrell et al., 2005), the use of econometrics to explain repeat burglary victimization (Tseloni and Pease, 2003), the application of mathematics and physics to understanding crime (Johnson, 2008) and the use of computer simulations to assess the likely effectiveness of crime reduction strategies (Groff and Birks, 2008).

In sum, crime scientists, who prefer quantitative methodologies, have presented their position as an objective application of the natural sciences to inform our understanding of – and, particularly, our responses to – crime. These have yielded a number of valuable and policy-relevant studies to improve our resilience to the impact of offending behaviour. However, crime science approaches have also been seen as controversial and have attracted criticism from criminologists and scientists alike, critiqued on methodological and theoretical grounds. It has been argued by some that crime science is neither criminological (Haggerty, 2008) nor scientific (Goldacre, 2009a). Many of these objections have centred on the calculations and assumptions researchers make when quantifying their parameters of research prior to the application of statistical enquiry. These debates are explored in greater detail in relation to quantitative research in Chapter 5.

Overall, this discussion on the way criminological thought has changed over time shows that there is a strong interdependence between method and theory. Theories stand and fall on the strength and robustness of their research methodologies. Theories that do not have a strong empirical background may become speculative and disconnected from the world they attempt to explain. They may also have less practical use, although this is not always their aim. Conversely, empirical approaches that readily ignore theoretical concepts, debates and innovations run the risk of engaging in narrow investigations and repeating the mistakes and partialities of the past.

CONCLUSIONS

This chapter has rehearsed a short, highly selective review of some key developments in criminological theory, focusing in particular on the centrality of empirical research for these different perspectives. Since its origins in the nineteenth century, but especially from the 1970s onwards, criminological theory and research have expanded exponentially. This chapter has examined a few landmarks belonging to these developments in order to show that the discipline would not be what it is today without the application of research methods. Throughout history, researchers have used methods that are, in part, a reflection of the time when and place where the research was done. We know that early studies of offending behaviour were based on the methods used by natural scientists such as biologists because these were deemed to be the most appropriate for explaining the differential involvement of certain social groups in offending behaviour. More recent studies have also held the belief that crime is best studied through scientific approaches, not least because science allows practitioners to isolate and quantify particular problems and develop solutions accordingly. Other research traditions, such as postmodernism and feminism, have questioned the belief that scientific values are the most appropriate way of coming to terms with the lived reality of offending, victimization and social control. These perspectives, along with right and left realism, also draw attention to the centrality of power and politics in criminological research. The main point is that you have many theories that can inform and be informed by any research you do. Part 2 now moves on to consider the key methods that can be applied in criminological research.

REVIEW QUESTIONS

- Select two of the theories considered in this chapter and discuss the significance of the different methods they used.

- Assess the extent to which the methodological approaches of early criminologists are still relevant today.

- Critically consider the relative significance of science and politics in coming to terms with the relationship between theory and methods.

FURTHER READING

If you were to read one book, our recommendation would be:

Hopkins Burke, R. (2009) *An Introduction to Criminological Theory* (3rd edn). Cullompton: Willan.

In addition to this, we suggest you refer to:

Hopkins Burke, R. (2011) *Criminal Justice Theory: An Introduction.* London: Routledge. Chapters 1 and 2.

McLaughlin, E. and Muncie, J. (eds) (2006) *The Sage Dictionary of Criminology.* London: Sage.

Rock, P. (2012) 'Sociological theories of crime', in M. Maguire, R. Morgan and R. Reiner (eds) *The Oxford Handbook of Criminology.* Oxford: Oxford University Press.

PART

2

THE PRACTICALITIES OF RESEARCH

CHAPTER

4

USING OTHER PEOPLE'S DATA: SECONDARY RESEARCH AND THE ANALYSIS OF OFFICIAL DATA

OVERVIEW

The aim of this chapter is to:

- Introduce some of the secondary data sources used by criminologists.
- Demonstrate how to use such materials in a research project.
- Provide guidance on using the internet to access criminological resources and data for secondary analysis.

INTRODUCTION

This chapter is the first of the more practical explanations of how to conduct criminological research. You are introduced to **secondary data** and shown how it can be used in your research projects. Put simply, **secondary research** involves the analysis of data that has been collected previously. For example, governments, charities and large commercial organizations often commission research into issues of crime and justice. In many cases, their original data is made available to researchers to reanalyse in new and different ways. This original **data collection**, for example the government's research, is known as **primary research**. The subsequent analysis of the data for a different project is secondary research. Many researchers also combine primary and secondary research. A project that interviewed residents about their domestic crime prevention measures (primary research) and compared this to official statistics of crime rates within the participants' neighbourhood (secondary data) would be an example of this. What is particularly helpful for criminological researchers is there is a large amount of data on a wide range of issues available for secondary analysis. This chapter will introduce many of the main sources of existing data, discuss their **reliability** and provide guidance on how you can access them.

While different to primary data collection, secondary research constitutes a valid form of research in its own right and is set to gain importance in the coming years. Another feature of secondary research is that it abbreviates and bypasses many steps of the research process outlined in Chapter 1. For example, access issues are resolved very quickly, generally fewer resources are required, and sampling is usually much more straightforward – and sometimes not applicable at all. While ethical issues may still apply, for example some participants may have only consented to being involved in the original research, they are normally less numerous or complex. The secondary researcher commonly faces fewer immediate ethical dilemmas in their work. Of course, those producing the original primary research (if it is of reasonable quality) would have needed to follow tried and tested principles and practices such as those outlined in the research process in Chapter 1.

This chapter links the two parts of the book together by looking at the way in which criminological knowledge is generated by governments and other agen-cies, and demonstrating the ways this can be used as a resource in your research. To explore these dimensions, the chapter is divided into three main parts. First, we identify 'official' forms of data, including recorded crime and national victimi-zation surveys, such as the Crime Survey for England and Wales (CSEW, formerly the British Crime Survey, BCS) and the US National Crime Victimization Survey (NCVS). Existing official and recorded crime statistics is the first port of call in many media and populist descriptions of crime. Being available and amenable to secondary analysis, this data is easy to access and extremely informative when developing your research projects around crime and justice. Then, we examine how the analysis of official data may count as a form of research in its own right. The ways in which large organizations have exploited these data sources is considered, before exploring how you can access these resources to do your own research. Lastly, we include an example of an anonymized student project that makes use of secondary data, which highlights some of the issues and complexi-ties that emerge in practice when carrying out secondary data analysis.

'OFFICIAL' DATA

We now consider how official data is created, what it looks like, and the ways it can be used, with particular emphasis on 'official' and other government audits of crime. So, what is 'official' crime data? The answer to this is complex and requires us to look at an ever-increasing quantity of data. In the recent past, 'official' crime data largely consisted of statistics relating to the prevalence of offences. Here, 'prevalence' largely means crimes that were recorded by the police or other official criminal justice agencies. Today, what counts as 'official' crime data not only includes recorded and reported crime but may also include:

- predictions of national rates of victimization
- perspectives of offenders, for example so-called 'self-report studies'
- the analysis of the performance of particular criminal justice policies.

As well as extending into new areas of analysis, official crime data now adopts a broader range of methodological approaches. Although largely quantitative, there has been an increasing use of qualitative strategies, as well as the use of mixed methods or triangulation (see Chapter 9).

For our purposes, 'official' data is defined as that produced by state agencies, such as the UK Home Office and the US Bureau of Justice Statistics, and their clients, such as research commissioned by central government, in order to describe the nature of crime and the reasons why it is committed. We will focus on what are perhaps the most important, useful and available forms of official crime statistics. These are studies assessing the extent and prevalence of crime rates in general and specific types of offences. This data is normally generated by measuring recorded crime, reported crime and rates of victimization. Although these three measures sound similar, there are distinct differences between them, which have significant implications for our understanding of crime.

Official statistics are not just concerned with who the offenders and victims are. They are increasingly used to understand *where* offences take place. This is done for practical purposes, so that specific crime control strategies can be targeted where the crime problems are most prevalent.

Reported and recorded crime

Since crime recording began more than 100 years ago, understanding the amount of crime in society has been difficult. Although it might appear relatively straightforward to convey the amount and type of crimes reported to and recorded by official criminal justice agencies, such 'official' statistics have significant shortcomings and, as such, do not give an accurate reflection of the extent of offending behaviour. An essential part of any study of official crime statistics is an appreciation of their deficiencies.

Many of the influences on criminological knowledge, such as the role of politics and the media (Chapter 2), play a significant part in shaping how crime statistics are expressed. It comes as a surprise to many that over the past decade, overall rates of crime appear to have been decreasing in a number of countries, including the UK and the USA. Yet, these general trends mask important fluctuations. Politicians from all sides and the media have made much of the fact that while overall crime has reduced, violent offences – the form of criminality we all tend to be most afraid of – have increased. Because violence occurs much less frequently than 'high-volume' offences, such as property and vehicle crimes, any increases may be buried within the overall trend of crime reduction. Statistical information like this makes it possible for competing newspapers to publish headlines that are both right, in saying that 'crime is down' at the same time as 'violence is up'.

Many critics have pointed to the failure of recorded and reported crime rates to accurately represent rates of offending, particularly in relation to violent and sexual offences. There are a number of reasons for this.

First, these statistics largely include offences that come to the attention of the police and other criminal justice agencies. Because some crimes are more likely to be reported than others, the statistics overrepresent some crimes and underrepresent others. For example, if a property is burgled or a vehicle is stolen, the victim often requires a 'crime number' issued by the police in order to make an insurance claim. Victims of these types of crime are more likely to report them and so these types of offences are well represented in the 'official' crime statistics. By contrast, enormous complexities surround the reporting of sexual and violent offences, particularly when they take place a domestic setting and when the victim knows their assailant. Victims may not wish to report the offence through fear of reprisal from someone who was or still is close to them. Complex feelings of shame and vulnerability often afflict those affected by sexual or violent offences. Feminists and others have also pointed out that most victims of domestic violence are female and that economic dependency on abusive male partners will limit the reporting of such offences. It could also be that the victims might not want their assailant to get into trouble. Others may not necessarily define themselves as victims. Such issues mean that these types of offences are significantly underrepresented in 'official' crime statistics.

A second limitation on recorded and reported crime statistics relates to the perception of victimization. This can work in a number of ways. In some circumstances, individuals may not necessarily know they have been victimized; a phenomenon sometimes associated with fraud and other forms of financial crime. In other respects, some crimes have been labelled as 'victimless'. It is illegal to gamble in licensed premises in some countries, yet those consenting to such activities are unlikely to self-define as offenders or victims. In other countries, such as Australia, organized gambling is permitted in public houses, demonstrating the difficulties of comparing crime rates between different countries. In another example, two 15-year-olds consenting to sexual activity may not define themselves as victims, yet in many countries they could end up being criminalized and placed on a register or list of known sex offenders.

Third, trends in the reporting of crimes also have an impact on 'official' crime statistics, which are independent of any actual changes in the rate of offences. You might have noticed that from time to time the police and other criminal justice agencies launch campaigns to encourage the public to report certain crimes. In many parts of the world, campaigns have been launched to portray a more positive image of the way in which the police investigate reported rapes and violence against women, leading to increased reporting of the offence. This meant that official crime levels for rape increased, regardless of whether there were any actual increases or not. There are often important rationales for such campaigns – including the attempt to uncover serious yet 'hidden' crimes and gain a better idea of the prevalence and location of offences – but they have an impact on official rates of crime.

A fourth factor affecting official crime rates is the classification and recording of crime. There are many aspects of this debate of which you might be aware. At the most fundamental level, there are questions over the numbers of crimes committed and the numbers of victims. One good example is the July 2005 London bombings. On 7 July 2005, four suicide bombers detonated explosive devices on London's mass transit network. How are such crimes classified? There were four attackers, so does this mean that four crimes were perpetrated? There were 52 people killed, so does this represent 52 murders? More than 700 people were injured. Does this increase the number of crimes further still? As a general rule, crime statistics are now organized around the number of victims: an individual who punches five people is normally seen to have committed five assaults. However, this has not always been the case and the victim-focused nature of crime statistics only became established fairly recently. Such developments make it difficult to compare crime rates over long periods of time.

Fifth, changes of categorization have inflated the statistical prevalence of particular forms of crime, without necessarily documenting a change in the 'actual' number of offences committed. Alterations have also occurred in the way violent crime has been catalogued and categorized. As Levi et al. (2007) note, in one year, more minor offences, including common assault, harassment and assaulting a police officer, which may have inflicted no injury whatsoever, were included in the official statistics on violent crime. This change led to an 'artificial' increase in recorded amounts of 'violent crime' by over 250,000 offences in a single year (Levi et al., 2007: 693). Another aspect of this debate concerns the ways in which crimes are categorized (and thus 'recorded') by law enforcement agencies after they have been reported. Criminological enquiry has consistently revealed local, regional, national and international variations in such practices, rendering geographical comparisons problematic (Maguire, 2002; Reiner, 2007). You will see that such nuances and complex processes affect levels of recorded crime and are not always reflected in popular and media discussions of the phenomena.

Lastly, other influences on recorded crime statistics relate to the processes of targeting and criminalization. An often-quoted statistic is that in the UK, the former New Labour government (1997–2010) introduced legislation that established over 3,000 criminal offences (Jewkes, 2007). Perhaps the most well known of these relates to the legislation surrounding 'antisocial behaviour'. If 3,000 new offences are created, it is inevitable that official rates of crime will increase as more activities are criminalized. In addition to the creation of new offences and the reclassification of old ones, another issue concerns the practices of the police and other enforcement agencies. For example, if the police launch an operation to 'crack down' on a particular type of crime in a particular place, it is likely that this intensified policing activity will increase the amount of crime that is 'discovered'. Intensified police activity targeting low-level offences under 'zero-tolerance' policing initiatives, such as those adopted in New York in the 1990s or Sydney in 2000, will inevitably lead to an increase in the statistics for those kinds of offences (Bowling, 1999). Similarly, concentrated police targeting of one particular demographic group, for example under stop and search strategies (see Bowling and Phillips, 2002), inevitably reveals larger numbers of offences within the targeted population.

Thus, if you think that 'official' statistics may appear to be a simple and objective assessment of crime that is reported to the police and other criminal justice agencies, it is necessary to think again. They are, in fact, processed through a number of filters that are planned and unplanned. As such, and with particular emphasis on the processes of criminalization and the targeting practices, official statistics are partial and potentially prejudicial, in part because they are shaped by political considerations. Other critiques of official crime statistics exist (see Maguire, 2002; Reiner, 2007 for comprehensive discussions on this point) and could fill many volumes of criminological literature. The key point here is that there is a disconnection between what is represented in 'official' reported and recorded statistics and the 'real' levels of crime in society. These concerns connect with a number of the theoretical issues introduced in Chapter 2, in particular notions of epistemology and ontology. For example, many criminologists responding to this issue dispute the possibilities of ever ascertaining a 'real' indication of crime levels. There are numerous dimensions to this debate. From a methodological perspective, there is the criticism that social science research is not able to adequately capture such complex and hidden events. From a theoretical perspective, others question whether there is such a thing as 'real' crime at all, given that criminality is a socially or legally constructed phenomenon (see Sumner, 1994 for discussion on this latter point). Indeed, some commentators have estimated that less than 3 per cent of all crimes result in a conviction (Barclay and Taveres, 1999). This assertion is based on the argument that many crimes never come to the attention of law enforcement agencies, of those that are reported, a smaller amount are actually recorded as crimes, fewer still are investigated and subsequently cleared up, and then only a fraction of those result in a caution or conviction (Barclay and Taveres, 1999). Criminologists often call this disparity between known and unknown crimes the **dark figure of crime**.

It is therefore important for you to recognize that recorded and reported crime statistics should be handled with care in your research projects. The overreliance on official statistics by those developing concepts of criminal action has been routinely criticized and has undermined some of theories discussed in Chapter 3. Despite the pioneering and influential theoretical advances, such as those outlined in Chapter 3, it is important to recognize that theories and assertions are only as strong as the methods used to develop them. Taking as an example the work of the Chicago School, and Shaw and McKay (1942) in particular, despite the many years spent gathering data on delinquency from a variety of sources, their work has been repeatedly criticized on the grounds that is was overly reliant on official court statistics. In this instance, it has been argued that crime statistics gained from the courts may indicate more about the activities of criminal justice agencies than an objective measure of offending. If the police choose to focus their resources and activity on one particular area (perhaps because they share the researchers' view that zones in transition harbour more criminals), they are likely to 'discover' more crime in those areas (see Reiner, 2007). If they were to concentrate on alternative areas, they may discover more crime in those areas. Tierney (2005) argues that this use of official statistics overpredicts the crimes of the poor and the young, while underplaying the crimes of the powerful, for example slum landlords, that may take place in these same areas. Another statistical-related problem concerns how Shaw and McKay (1942) chose to map delinquency. In this study, they elected to record the addresses of (actual and alleged) delinquents and not the location where the offences happened. Although there is a strong possibility that these individuals lived and offended in the same areas, as many offenders do (see Bottoms, 2007), this is by no means clear. If the offences were committed in other areas, this would radically alter Shaw and McKay's theory of why crime occurs in particular communities.

Recognition of these shortcomings is not restricted to specialist criminologists. Since the early 1980s, there has been a strong awareness in official circles of the need to adopt alternative measures of crime rates. In response, a number of initiatives have been developed.

Victimization surveys

To overcome many of these limitations, in the USA, crime statistics are derived from two sources. Recorded statistics, of the type discussed above, are collected by the Federal Bureau of Investigation, which collates incidences of crime reported to law enforcement agencies across the country. These are compiled into monthly Uniform Crime Reports, and are divided into two major groups, Part I and Part II offences; Part I crimes are known as index crimes, and are subdivided into four crimes against the person and four crimes against property. These official recorded crime statistics, complete with all the aforementioned problems, are then complemented by an alternative measure of crime prevalence: the National Crime Victimization Survey (NCVS), developed by the US Bureau of Justice Statistics. As the name suggests, this survey seeks to understand rates of *victimization*, thus attempting to uncover crimes that individuals may have been subjected to, but may not have reported to the authorities. This survey has been in operation since 1972, demonstrating an early awareness of the limitations of recorded and reported statistics, and has since reached high levels of sophistication. The use of **victimization surveys** has since become a more standardized feature of data collection strategies for understanding the prevalence of crime in society.

The victimization survey was established a little later in England and Wales. The most well-known, robust and frequently cited victimization survey is the **British Crime Survey** (BCS), which was first conducted in 1982, later becoming the Crime Survey of England and Wales in April 2012. The rationale here, as in the USA, was the ambition to generate a better idea of the levels of crime, but also to identify demographic and geographical indices of risk and, crucially, to understand how the population perceives fears and responds to criminality. The BCS was initially conducted on an infrequent basis – with later iterations conducted in 1984, 1988, 1992, 1994, 1996 and 1998 – and was complemented by more focused academic victimization surveys such as the Islington Crime Survey in the mid-1980s. Since 2000, the British Crime Survey has been conducted annually and from 2001 onwards has been published alongside police recorded crime figures. This means that a more detailed and comprehensive set of crime data is now published annually and is presented in the annual statistical bulletin 'Crime in England and Wales'. As such, victimization surveys are now an embedded feature of 'official' crime data.

The research process connected to the BCS is a considerable undertaking. In 1982, the first 11,000 BCS participants were recruited. Before changing its name, the BCS involved over 47,000 participants. Research on this scale means that interviews are conducted on a continuous basis and data is thus broken down into each financial year. In addition to the large numbers of participants, the BCS enjoys a high response rate of between 73 and 83 per cent (Jannson, 2007). This not only represents high levels of participation for such surveys, it also reduces the impact of **non-response bias** (see Chapter 5) and thus enhances the validity of the data.

An interesting exercise is for us to compare how crime victimization data, and particularly its general trends over time, relates to levels of police recorded crime. As Figure 4.1, which compares the trends of both forms of data, demonstrates, victimization surveys reveal a high number of additional offences. However, if we were to undertake further analysis of the data, it would reveal that a large percentage of these are relatively minor crimes (Maguire, 2002). With the exception of the mid-1990s, victimization surveys generally reflect the overall tendencies and trends of recorded crime statistics, both in terms of general prevalence and with regard to most specific forms of crime. You could also conclude that many of the traditionally 'hidden' offences, such as domestic and sexual crime, remain beyond the reach of victimization surveys.

So, similarities exist but there are also significant variations between the datasets. As Maguire (2002) notes, overall crime has reduced every year since

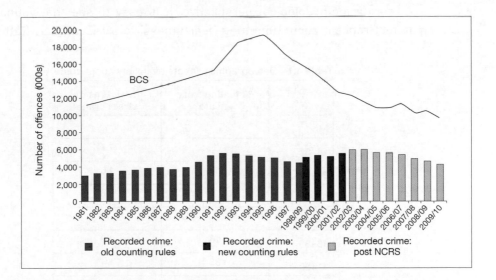

Figure 4.1   *Comparison of BCS and recorded crime data for overall levels of offences*

Note: NCRS = national crime recording standard, introduced in all police forces in April 2002 to make crime recording more consistent.

Source: Home Office, 2010

1995, yet it appears to fall more steeply in the BCS data. At the same time as this overall reduction, there is an important contradictory process occurring with regard to violent crime. The police statistics show substantial increases in violence, while the BCS documents overall reductions. To some extent, this could be explained by shifts in reporting trends, but it also highlights the difficulties associated with both auditing techniques.

An added feature of the BCS is the attention given to broader crime-related issues on an occasional basis. Special themes, such as attitudes towards the police, fear of crime, and more recent issues such as 'technocrime', are embedded into the research design for particular years. In 1994, for example, special focus was placed on public anxieties around crime, an issue that was important in political and academic circles at that time (see, for example, Hale, 1996). To explore this issue, researchers looked at the demographic groupings of those professing to feel unsafe and at risk of street crime. Table 4.1 tells you that young males between the ages of 16 and 30 are the least likely to express feelings of anxiety, yet, paradoxically, this is the demographic group most likely to become victims of crime. Conversely, females over the age of 61 are least likely to become victims (1.2 per cent), but this demographic group expresses the highest levels of anxiety. A straightforward conclusion, you might think, is that those who fear crime the most do so 'irrationally', although a number of methodological and conceptual issues can be drawn on to challenge such assumptions.

From a methodological perspective, it is easy to see that young males may feel reticent about admitting 'fearfulness' to a researcher. Rather than

Table 4.1   Demographic aspects of anxiety about crime

	% feeling 'very unsafe'	% victims of 'street crime'
Men		
16–30	1	7.7
31–60	4	1.6
61+	7	0.6
Women		
16–30	16	2.8
31–60	35	1.4
61+	37	1.2

Source: Adapted from Hough, 1995

providing an objective 'snapshot' of society, issues of gender identity are at play and necessarily influence the findings. Incidents where the researcher influences the environment they are studying are sometimes referred to as **reactivity** (see Chapters 6 and 7). In other respects, such findings make no account of the extent to which these different demographic groups use public spaces. It is likely that far fewer women over 61 years old used the streets as compared with young males, hence the former are less likely to be victims of 'street crime'. Such differentials challenge the extent to which the '% victims of "street crime"' can be used as an objective category. If we refer to fear of crime surveys more generally, other methodological concerns relate to the subjectivity of categories of answers and the way in which participants may interpret the question in different ways. For example, there is considerable debate over the differences between 'anxiety' and 'fear'. Both are emotive states that are difficult to measure in a meaningful way. In addition, a survey that hypothetically asks participants how safe they feel and offers the answer categories 'a bit unsafe' or 'fairly safe' may risk having these categories interpreted as the same thing by different participants.

On a theoretical and conceptual basis, left realist (see Chapter 3) and other criminologists have challenged the way in which 'irrational' fears have been characterized. The argument is that a patronizing tone is adopted towards those fearful of crime without accounting for a range of important factors that both inform fear and question whether it can be measured at all. Among others, Young (1987) has argued that critics who discuss 'irrational' fears of crime never articulate what a 'rational' fear is. At the same time, there are many other factors that inform our unease and feelings of insecurity. Social and environmental factors, for example, play a particularly prominent role in shaping the fears and anxieties we hold (Girling et al., 1999). Controversies and debates over the use of survey data again illustrate the important interconnections between theory and method.

In recent years, there have been attempts to develop crime and victimization surveys that transcend national boundaries. One example of this is the European Union International Crime Survey (EU ICS), a household survey of residents above the age of 16 in 18 (of 27) EU member countries. When we compare it to large-scale national victimization surveys, the sample sizes for the EU ICS, typically around 2,000 per nation, are small. There is little adjustment for differential sizes of countries. The same numbers of participants are canvassed in Northern Ireland as in France, for example. Here, Poland constitutes a particular outlier, with over 5,000 respondents (among a population of 38 million) when compared to Italy's 2,023 respondents (among a population of 60 million), raising questions over generalizability (see Chapter 5).

Further afield, and perhaps more ambitious in scope, is the International Crime Victims Survey (ICVS). The first survey, conducted in 1989, estimated and then compared rates of victimization across nationalities. Perhaps owing to its scale, thus far there have only been five iterations of the ICVS: 1989, 1992, 1996, 2000 and 2004/2005. Nevertheless, 78 different countries and over 320,000 individuals have been surveyed so far under its auspices. The ambition and international scope of this survey is important and interesting on many levels. Criminology is a discipline often criticized for restricting its focus to the English-speaking world. Although the ICVS does lean towards a Eurocentric position, because it connects its findings with the EU ICS, there is genuine engagement with a number of geographical regions commonly over-looked by mainstream criminology. The latest version of the ICVS also reveals interesting data over comparative levels of criminality. It estimates that 16 per cent of the population in the 30 countries participating in the 2004/2005 ICVS were victimized in the course of the previous 12 months. People in Ireland, England and Wales, New Zealand and Iceland experienced relatively high levels of victimization, while offences against Spanish, Hungarian and Portu-guese nationals were among the lowest (van Dijk et al., 2007). If we were to drill down into specific urban settings, the ICVS claims that those resid-ing in the main cities of developed countries had a slightly increased level of victimization by 'common crimes' (19.9 per cent) than those in developing countries. Regarding the latter, urban citizens of the Global South experienc-ing the highest levels of victimization resided in Phnom Penh and Maputo, for example (van Dijk et al., 2007). Another positive feature of this survey is the free availability of its core data, making it accessible for you to reinterpret for other research projects. See below and Appendix 1 for more details of how you can access this data.

Alternative methodologies

You will note the above examples demonstrate that official research into crime and criminality has tended to prefer quantitative methodologies. In recent years, there has been an acknowledgement of the utility of qualitative techniques, par-ticularly when attempting to understand 'hard-to-research' and 'hidden' forms of offending when studying a variety of criminal acts. One notable example is a study into the market and use of illegal firearms (Hales et al., 2006). When compared to the USA, UK firearms incidents are comparatively rare, but are an area of increasing prevalence and growing public, political and media concern. If you wanted to research this issue, it is difficult to imagine that those in pos-session of, or convicted of, firearms offences would be willing to be surveyed or interviewed, and that a large enough sample could be accessed. Hales et al.

(2006), by contrast, conducted in-depth interviews with 80 males aged 18–30 recently convicted of a firearms offence. The use of qualitative methods allowed the researchers to penetrate a number of important dimensions of the offence. These included an understanding of the different social formations that offenders engaged with. In turn, the researchers created nuanced understandings of small group activities that went beyond simplistic (and overused) stereotypes of 'gangs'. Other social phenomena surrounding firearms offenders are also revealing. The use of in-depth qualitative interviews also allowed the often-stereotyped notion of 'gun culture' to be understood in greater depth. Hales et al. (2006) identified different 'ideal types' of 'gun cultures': those who use firearms in an instrumental capacity to assist criminal endeavours, for example as a coercive tool during robberies, in addition to more complex sociological features centring on theoretical debates about the symbolic utility of guns.

Overall, official and administrative approaches to crime research have largely gravitated towards quantitative approaches and, for reasons often related to policy and politics, have tended to focus on evaluations of crime strategies and understanding the prevalence of crime. More recently, this brand of research has engaged with a broader range of issues and, in doing so, has drawn on a more diverse set of methodologies. In addition to the qualitative and quantitative traditions outlined above, there has been some movement towards the 'triangulation' of methods in recent years. Principally, 'triangulation' refers to a blend of different methodological techniques or mixed methods. This can mean a combination of different qualitative approaches, different quantitative approaches, and a blend of both qualitative and quantitative as a means of crosschecking, reinforcing and validating the findings of each method. This technique can, although by no means always, require substantial resources and is therefore more likely to be available to 'official' and government-led research projects. Triangulation is explored in detail in Chapter 9 where we demonstrate how you can use this approach.

It is important to note that official research, like all others, is shaped by its political context (see Chapter 2) and, despite appearances, is not neutral. For example, research is conducted at specific times, sometimes relating to political or broader societal pressures. The terms of reference for these projects are selectively defined and are therefore embedded with assumptions about what is worthy of measurement and what is not. These issues are common to all forms of research and many criminologists and critical sociologists would argue that it is impossible to achieve absolute objectivity when researching complex phenomena, such as crime, that are situated within messy social realities. What is particularly interesting about official forms of research, however, is the access to raw data it affords to other researchers. This provides an invaluable dataset, which can be re-examined in a variety of ways.

ACCESSING AND USING OFFICIAL DATA

We now examine how this wealth of existing resources may be accessed. In recent years, this task has been made easier by the huge quantities of material placed online. The rest of this chapter provides guidance on the mechanics of working with this existing data. Here, data repositories holding information from a range of national and international research exercises are explored and guidance on how to access this information is provided. To make the most of these and other online resources for criminologists, you can read this alongside the internet guide in Appendix 1.

Although there is an abundance of online information available to criminological researchers, there is a drawback: judgements need to be made over the quality and integrity of the research on offer. We know that the internet is full of opinion pieces, blogs and selective interpretations of many issues, particularly emotive ones such as crime. This raises the question: How do we know what is authoritative and robust information? To address this, we are guided by a few general principles and ask questions such as:

• What is the reputation of the institution or individual producing the research?
• How transparent are the methods?
• Are the methods appropriate to the aims of the project?

For example, in the natural sciences, a number of pharmaceutical companies have been accused of using research to 'prove' their product works without supplying the data for independent scrutiny (see Goldacre, 2009b). In these circumstances, valid questions are raised over the robustness of the positive research findings. The same principles apply to much social science research. While this approach does have its drawbacks, and is far from foolproof, it provides a useful barometer of the quality of research on offer. To assist you, the internet guide (Appendix 1) refers you to the most robust sources, which are appropriate for your research projects.

Accessing data for secondary analysis

Although not traditionally seen as an 'empirical study' in the same sense as survey-based projects, qualitative interviewing or ethnographic methods, **secondary analysis** is equally credible and constitutes a viable method for your research projects. Secondary analysis takes many forms. Large government agencies, for example, often undertake this form of research. An example of this is when governments commission meta-analyses (or 'systematic reviews') into the effectiveness of various crime prevention initiatives, such as improved street lighting (Farrington and Welsh, 2002) and surveillance cameras (Welsh and Farrington, 2002). Instead of conducting their own evaluation, they harvest the findings from other studies, selecting them on the basis of distinct criteria such as methodological rigour or geographical relevance. Smaller organizations, such as nongovernmental organizations, also employ secondary analysis techniques of research.

Although it is often large and well-funded organizations that take advantage of secondary research, it provides an interesting and viable method for conducting university-level research projects. Projects can take many forms, including the reinterpretation of 'raw data' collected for previous research studies, such as the official statistical projects discussed above, or the consolidation, integration and review of different research projects covering the same theme – a **meta-analysis**. Taking the reinterpretation of existing data as an example, there is often considerable opportunity to develop new areas of analyses from these datasets. An added advantage of this kind of study is that you can easily define the parameters and scale of the research at an early stage and avoid some of the uncertainties associated with other forms of data collection.

Sources of existing data

The UK Data Archive at the University of Essex hosts a large and diverse set of raw data that has been collected via a range of quantitative and qualitative methodologies and serves as a valuable resource for researchers. Of particular use to researchers is the organization of data into categories of analysis. The home page (www.data-archive.ac.uk) provides a number of useful links and tutorials for accessing the data. Selecting the 'find data' and then 'major studies' links will provide you with a list of the range of datasets available at www.esds.ac.uk/findingData/majorStudies.asp.

These include large UK government-funded research initiatives such as:

- British Crime Survey and the Crime Survey of England and Wales
- Scottish Crime Survey
- British Social Attitudes Survey
- British Household Panel Survey
- Labour Force Survey.

Also included are large international surveys, including those commissioned by the OECD, the UN and the World Bank:

- Eurobarometer
- The European Quality of Life Survey
- The European Social Survey
- OECD International Migration Statistics

- World Bank Africa Development Indicators (including statistics on crime and the impact of perceptions of crime on business in Africa).

Clicking on the 'find data' and then 'search our catalogue' section of the UK Data Archive website will take you to the search area of the Economic and Social Data Service (ESDS) website, which can also be accessed at www.esds.ac.uk/Lucene/Search.aspx.

From the ESDS home page (www.esds.ac.uk), it is also possible to search within categories of research type. This includes large-scale government research, international projects, longitudinal research and qualitative data sources. Qualitative and other data may also be sourced from the UK Data Service, http://ukdataservice.ac.uk. For example, the Economic and Social Research Council – a body that funds a large proportion of internationally recognized social science research in the UK – requests that many of its grantholders share their data with this service.

An online search function allowing researchers to retrieve data relating to specific themes is available at www.esds.ac.uk/qualidata/Lucene/Search.aspx.

Finally, ESDS is in the process of developing dedicated webpages for specific areas of social science research. Those relating to crime and social control have already been constructed and provide an extremely valuable resource for researchers: www.esds.ac.uk/themes/crime/introduction.asp.

In order to download and reanalyse these datasets, users must register with the service at www.esds.ac.uk/aandp/access/access.asp. Further assistance is also provided under the 'access and support' options of the ESDS homepage.

While the UK Data Archive houses data from a range of international research exercises, there are a number of other options for researchers attempting to analyse datasets within and across different countries. For criminologists, a particularly useful resource is the Data Archiving and Networked Services (DANS), hosted by the Royal Netherlands Academy of Arts and Sciences and the Netherlands Organization for Scientific Research. This initiative also serves as a repository for data collected in the course of Dutch and internationally focused research exercises. Similar to the UK Data Archive, DANS hosts a reasonably straightforward search facility, https://easy.dans.knaw.nl/ui/home, which also allows users to deposit their own datasets, although see the cautionary note below. For criminologists, this is a particularly useful resource as it holds the raw data from the ICVS discussed earlier. These ICVS datafiles are available for free by going to the above webpage, entering 'International Crime Victims Survey' into the search field box and then clicking on the appropriate result. Selecting the 'Data Files' tab will then provide access to the specific data in .pdf or .sav (SPSS compatible, see Chapter 5) formats.

Finally, the Council of Europe funds a long-running project that analyses crime and criminal justice statistics across Europe called the European Source-book of Crime and Criminal Justice Statistics (www.europeansourcebook.org/). This is a valuable resource for criminological researchers wishing to look at data from this research initiative.

A note of caution

While these data repositories provide an extremely valuable resource for all researchers, there are a number of limitations that prospective users should be aware of:

1. The scale of the data on offer. This, along with the potential unfamiliarity of the online portals through which they are accessed, may appear intimidating at first. So, it is important to allow time to acquaint yourself with these processes when planning research projects.
2. The distance between the data and researcher created in secondary research means that it is more difficult to become familiar with the variables and the ways in which they are created (Bryman, 2008).
3. Post hoc analysis means there is less control over the quality of the data supplied (Bryman, 2008). As we said earlier, in criminology, there are a number of question marks over the reliability of crime statistics and, indeed, much criminological analysis is concerned with critiquing the institutional practices and political factors that influence the generation of 'official data'.
4. Although data may describe broadly similar things in different countries, such as levels of violence, in most cases they are not measuring exactly the same thing, for example violence is defined differently in different countries. Thus, for data to be comparable, or comparative, attention needs to be placed on the similarity of what exactly is being measured.

USING SECONDARY DATA ANALYSIS TECHNIQUES IN RESEARCH PROJECTS

This chapter concludes with an anonymized student research project, which highlights some of the practical issues facing researchers using existing data-sets to undertake small-scale research projects.

Comparing perceptions of risk of crime across Europe

Mia was interested in the way crime was experienced in different countries and wanted to research issues around crime victimization in Europe. She had initially planned to undertake two surveys, one in her home country and another in the country her university was situated. Common to many projects with a more quantitative approach, Mia's first step involved giving careful consideration to the specific focus of the work. After some initial discussion with her supervisor, she gave some serious thought to what was meant by 'crime victimization', and set about listing and categorizing the different questions and issues covered by this notion. This included issues such as the prevalence of crime, type of crime experienced, people's reaction to crime, and their perception of how likely they were to be victimized. There were a number of ethical considerations here too. For example, Mia would have to ensure that examining participants' prior experiences of crime would not cause any distress to them. She would also have to seek ethical approval for this research through her university. Mia then had to select who was going to be included in the survey. In doing so, Mia had to clarify a few issues, including what steps needed to be taken to ensure her sample would be representative of the wider population, whether participants had to be citizens of the respective countries or if they could be visitors, and where she would do the survey and at what times.

Planning and design

After some serious thought, Mia decided her work would focus on the perceptions people had of their likelihood of being a victim of crime and whether this changed in different countries. Much more difficult was deciding on how to select (sample) participants in a way that represented the wider population. After consultation with her supervisor, it became clear that a survey purporting to represent the populations of two separate countries would be very labour intensive and difficult to achieve within the time and money constraints of a student project. Mia decided it was time to rethink the scope of her project and began to explore the possibilities of using data that had previously been collected for other, much larger, research projects. As discussed earlier, research on criminal victimization is conducted in (and across) a number of countries and the **raw data** (in this case, survey responses) is often made available for other researchers to reinterpret.

Her aim was to then use this data to inform the analysis of a much smaller survey. In doing so, Mia developed a project idea where she would interview students of different nationalities studying at her university and compare perceived risks of victimization with the level of crime in their own countries. This would also address some of the ethical concerns associated with her previous project idea. To carry out this project, Mia conducted a simple survey and interviewed students from specific nationalities, accessed through international student societies at the university. She then accessed raw data on crime rates downloaded from the European Sourcebook project website (www.europeansourcebook.org) and began to analyse what she considered were relationships between perceptions of crime and their actual prevalence in participants' countries of origin.

Gathering and analysing data

Although Mia generated some interesting findings, she encountered a number of difficulties when writing up her results. First, she began to wonder whether perceptions of likely victimization could be influenced by a range of factors not related to issues in their home country, including previous victimization or their current place of residence. Other concerns related to the numbers of those interviewed from each country and whether the results could be said to be representative of a wider group. These and similar issues relating to conducting surveys are explored in detail in Chapter 5.

With specific regard to the secondary data, Mia obtained detailed breakdowns of levels of crime in each country. Yet, these were largely based on official recorded crime statistics and, as noted above, need to be treated with extreme caution. Further difficulties arose when she tried to make comparisons across countries. Types of crime are often coded and classified differently in different places. In Malta, for example, an offence committed by more than one person is counted as multiple offences, whereas in most European countries, it is recorded as a single offence. Thus, comparative research is difficult unless the same standards are applied across areas, issues and variables. In essence, steps need to be taken to ensure the same thing is measured in each place.

There are many ways of resolving these issues with good research planning at the outset. In the first instance, engagement with the wider literature and theory at the outset would tease out some of these issues early on and provide opportunities for them to be rectified. For example, the academic commentary on crime statistics and a review of the literature on the way police operate and investigate crime would reveal many of the issues surrounding the recording and reporting of crime outlined above, and how processes change over different countries. Reference to theoretical debates in criminology may have also helped to guide the research, such as the objections to viewing the fear of crime as 'irrational' raised by left realists (see Chapter 3). For greater reliability, Mia could have focused on nationalities where established victimization surveys are conducted. In addition, steps could have been taken to select countries that define crimes in similar ways. This task is made much easier by referring to the many studies that have attempted to do this, including the European Sourcebook.

Finally, many of the above issues could be addressed by understanding the scope and limitations of secondary data (see Table 4.2). While a number of difficulties emerge when it is used for comparisons that it may not have been originally intended for, secondary data is immensely useful when used in a focused way. For example, if Mia were to choose a single country as a case study, then one or, potentially, a combination of existing datasets – including victimization surveys, arrest statistics and various opinion studies – could have been used for reanalysis.

Table 4.2 Selected strengths and weaknesses of secondary research

Strengths	Weaknesses
Availability of large swathes of data	Constrained by previous methodology choices
Allows the researcher to develop key transferable skills, such as sourcing information and analysing and summarizing existing reports and data	Constrained by research questions potentially set for other purposes
Overcomes a number of difficulties associated with empirical fieldwork, such as access	Data collection may reflect official institutional biases
Addresses many (although not all) ethical issues associated with more traditional forms of fieldwork, for example interviews	Limited control over the initial quality of the data collection method
	Need to understand how to access and retrieve large and often complex datasets
	Need to build in significant time to understand how to use such data

REVIEW QUESTIONS

- Outline three sources of 'official' data that can be used in criminological research projects.

- Examine the main ethical considerations associated with secondary research.

- Critically assess the main strengths and weaknesses of using official statistics and existing datasets to understand one of the following:

  - the fear of crime
  - the risk of victimization in different age groups of the population
  - levels of crime in society
  - another criminological issue of your choice.

FURTHER READING

If you were to read one book, our recommendation would be:

> Riedel, M. (2000) *Research Strategies for Secondary Data: A Perspective for Criminology and Criminal Justice*. London: Sage.

In addition to this, we suggest you refer to:

> Reiner, R. (2007) *Law and Order: An Honest Citizen's Guide to Crime and Control*. Cambridge: Polity Press. Chapter 3.

> Smith, E. (2008) *Using Secondary Data in Educational and Social Research*. Milton Keynes: Open University Press.

CHAPTER 5

ASKING QUESTIONS ABOUT CRIME: SURVEYS AND QUESTIONNAIRES

OVERVIEW

The aim of this chapter is to:

- Describe the ways in which surveys are used in criminological research.
- Introduce a number of key sampling strategies.
- Explore and explain the collection and analysis of quantitative data using SPSS.
- Explain how to design, administer and analyse a survey.

INTRODUCTION

Surveys are perhaps the best-known method of collecting data. While the image of a researcher on the high street with a clipboard is perhaps the first that springs to mind when you think about this method, there are, in fact, many types of survey. These include, among others, postal surveys, face-to-face interviews and telephone questionnaires. If you have been involved in research, either as an investigator or participant, you have probably come into contact with surveys in some form.

Part of the reason for this is that surveys are used by many individuals and organizations for many different purposes. They are seen as exceptionally important across diverse fields for business and marketing researchers, political strategists, local councils, charities and more. Although surveys are perhaps most widely employed to canvass opinion about consumer preferences or voting intentions, they have become an increasingly important tool for criminologists studying patterns of crime and tendencies among offenders. Most notable perhaps is the use of survey methods to understand patterns of crime victimization (such as the Crime Survey for England and Wales and the US National Crime Victimization Survey, see Chapter 4) in a more detailed way than can be achieved by examining recorded crime statistics.

Common to all methods of research in criminology, surveys are suited to achieving specific research aims. Surveys yield quantitative data. They are well suited for capturing trends and general tendencies (see Chapter 2). It is too simplistic to state that surveys will tell you 'what' people think, while in-depth interviews inform us 'why' they think that, but surveys are generally more geared towards finding answers to the 'what', 'where' and 'how many' types of question.

Despite their popularity, and sometimes apparent simplicity, survey design can be a complex undertaking with numerous pitfalls that you must be aware of in order to avoid devaluing your data. But this shouldn't put you off doing survey research. You do not necessarily need to be gifted at maths to produce and analyse survey data. Indeed, there are many software packages that will do the statistical calculations for you. Instead, it is important that some key principles are followed, the right questions are asked of the right people and that surveys are well designed. This chapter will explain these issues and outline some steps that should enable anyone to conduct robust surveys.

To explore these issues in more detail and give guidance on how to carry out surveys, this chapter looks at four areas. It begins by introducing some of the ways in which surveys have been used by government and academic researchers to illustrate their uses, benefits and related difficulties. The main part of the chapter outlines the key considerations and stages in survey-based projects. Particular attention is given to the design of surveys. Next, we show you how to analyse quantitative data, referring to the 'industry standard' software used for this purpose: Statistical Package for the Social Science (SPSS). Finally, we examine some potential student projects and some of the key considerations and lessons that may apply to your research.

PROFESSIONAL, GOVERNMENT AND ACADEMIC SURVEY-BASED RESEARCH

Government research makes strong use of quantitative survey methods. Perhaps the best examples of this are government-led victimization surveys, such as the annual Crime Survey for England and Wales (CSEW) or the US National Crime Victimization Survey (NCVS) (see Chapter 4). As well as focusing on similar subjects (victims of crime), what these and similar studies share is a broadly objectivist ontological position. This is the view that the social world is something that operates separately and externally to its social actors. From this perspective, social phenomena, such as victimization, can be objectively 'captured' and measured.

A more recent government initiative and one that shares the epistemological position of the CSEW and NCVS has been the attempt to understand the levels of crime perpetration. An example of this is the Offending, Crime and Justice Survey (OCJS), conducted over four consecutive years between 2003 and 2006. The original 2003 survey contacted a sample of 12,000 people from the age of 10 (the age of criminal responsibility in England and Wales) to 65. Subsequent versions narrowed the focus to young people aged 10–25. These latest surveys contained a much smaller sample size of 5,000 people. Another technique involved the retention of the same participants throughout each sweep of the survey and, when particular people dropped out of the exercise, they were replaced by people from the same demographic grouping. This approach allowed researchers to examine participants' progression into, and desistance from, offending behaviour over time. This type of 'self-report' study also has the added advantage of 'capturing' more offenders than are present in the official criminal justice statistics. Because many offenders are not caught, charged, or prosecuted, they are absent from these official audits.

Another feature of the OCJS was the use of computer-assisted personal interviewing and computer-assisted self-interviewing methods. These are designed so that respondents can answer questions in privacy in front of a computer and are given time to listen to and digest the survey questions fully. The study also utilized **multivariate analysis**, a technique that allows researchers to analyse several variables at the same time. This multivariate analysis was used in an attempt to understand which combination of factors may contribute towards young people's offending behaviour.

The OCJSs have revealed a number of interesting insights concerning young people's offending behaviour. In 2006, the survey illustrated that 22 per cent of young people aged 10–25 had committed one or more crimes during a 12-month period (Roe and Ashe, 2008). If you look at the OCJSs together, this figure rises to 49 per cent of participants having committed at least one offence. Those who did offend often engaged in criminal behaviour from a young age. For instance, those who stole from school normally began their criminal activities between the ages of 13 and 15 (Hales et al., 2009). Those labelled 'prolific offenders' appeared to start their criminal careers at a much younger age than most other groups of offenders. **Longitudinal analysis** of the four iterations of the survey also revealed the 'progression' of offences, that is, a minor offence leading on to a more serious one. In 2003, just over a quarter of young people who had committed antisocial behaviour or used drugs went on to offend (Hales et al., 2009).

Such research offers fascinating insights into offending behaviour across the wider population, but it is important to remember that projects of this kind are never perfect. In this case, and in common with much research into offending behaviour, there are issues over the reliability of data and the extent to which the data represents the level and types of offending behaviour in society as a whole, that is, its generalizability. Good researchers are aware of these shortcomings and, in the case of the OCJSs, the authors highlight these limitations in Table 5.1, which provides a checklist of problems with many quantitative projects. It

Table 5.1 Methodological problems with the 2006 Offending, Crime and Justice Survey

The OCJS was designed to take on board lessons from previous self-report offending surveys and incorporates some innovative techniques to improve the quality of the data collected. However, it is subject to the following design and methodological issues which should be considered when interpreting the findings.

Sampling variability. A sample, as used in the OCJS, is a small-scale representation of the population from which it is drawn. As such, the sample may produce estimates that differ from the figures that would have been obtained if the whole population had been interviewed. The size of the difference depends on the sample size, the size of the estimate and the design of the survey. Sampling variability is also taken into account in tests of statistical significance. Throughout this report differences are reported which are statistically significant at the five per cent level (i.e. the level at which there is a one in twenty probability of an observed difference being solely due to chance) unless otherwise specified.

Non-response bias. Despite the high response rate (85% for the panel sample; 67% for the fresh), it may be that non-respondents differ in key respects from those who took part. For example, those with particularly chaotic lifestyles or more serious offenders might be difficult to contact and more likely to refuse.

Exclusions from the sample. The results relate to the general household population age from 10 to 25 only. People in institutions (including prisons) or who are homeless are not covered in the OCJS sample. As such there will be relatively few 'serious' offenders included in the sample.

Offence coverage. The survey does not cover all offences. In particular very serious offences including homicide and sexual offences are omitted. The main focus of the OCJS was on the 20 core offences, and the wording of these questions was carefully considered to reflect legal definitions in simple, understandable language which was suitable for a survey including respondents aged as young as ten.

Accuracy of responses. The survey is designed to provide information that is as accurate as possible, e.g. by using self-completion (CASI) for more sensitive questions, and audio-CASI to assist those with literacy problems. However, the accuracy of information obtained through all surveys depends on respondents' ability to understand questions, their ability to recall events accurately, and their willingness to provide complete, honest and accurate responses. These factors may vary across different groups. Respondents were asked at the end of the interview how honest they had been when asked about offending and drug use; 98 per cent said they answered all offending questions honestly.

Source: Roe and Ashe, 2008: 9

can also be argued that this research is narrowly focused. It is **skewed** towards younger people, misses the crimes of the powerful, likely to be perpetrated by those in a position of 'power' and, hence, who are older, and is unlikely to uncover serious crimes of a sexual and/or domestic nature. The issue of attrition – people no longer being involved in the research – is also important. Those who dropped out of the survey between 2003 and 2006 may have done so for a reason. It could be that they had committed offences during this period and did not wish to reveal them to researchers. As a result, the sample becomes more skewed towards non-offenders. Non-disclosure by participants is a particular hazard of offender-based surveys.

Problems with the accuracy of survey data are not limited to participants' failure to disclose information. Failure to account for, and address, **bias** in the research design can also undermine a set of findings. For example, in a classic study into CCTV (surveillance camera) acceptability in Scotland, Ditton (1998) demonstrates how inconsistencies in the structuring of survey questions can lead to wild variations in estimates of public support. Ditton wanted to expose how many studies claiming CCTV cameras were popular were, in fact, methodologically flawed. So, he designed two different surveys, each analysing the same issue but designed to generate different results. Both surveys ended by asking respondents whether or not they were in favour of CCTV. In the first survey, this final question was preceded by a series of questions on the fear of crime. This was designed to elicit a 'pro-CCTV' response to the final question. The second survey, by contrast, first asked respondents about civil liberties issues before asking if they were in favour of CCTV. A sample of 308 pedestrians using a Scottish high street was taken. This sample was then subdivided into three groups. Group one was given the 'pro-CCTV' questionnaire, group two was given the 'civil liberties' questionnaire, and group three were simply asked whether or not they were in favour of CCTV. This led to striking disparities in the levels of support for CCTV between the different groups. The findings ranged from a seemingly overwhelming 91% public support for CCTV among those given the 'pro-CCTV' survey, to a more modest and less conclusive 56% among those whose survey contained questions on civil liberties, while 71% of the 'neutral group' were in favour of CCTV. Ditton's (1998) study demonstrates a 20% 'swing' in public support for CCTV depending on the types of questions the survey contains.

CONDUCTING SURVEYS FOR CRIMINOLOGICAL RESEARCH

Here, we discuss the various elements you need to consider when designing, conducting and analysing your own questionnaires and surveys.

Types of survey

Often, one of the first considerations is to select one of the many types of survey that are available. For university-level projects, three key considerations are:

1. Which is the most appropriate type of survey?
2. Which is achievable?
3. Which most effectively allows access to your research population?

The most commonly used surveys are:

- **Face-to-face surveys**: Advantages include probably reasonably high response rates, for example the amount of people completing the survey, and a high degree of control over sampling. Disadvantages include their potentially more time-consuming nature.
- **Telephone surveys**: Advantages include the ability to access many participants quickly. Disadvantages include the potential cost and the possibility that respondents could find the survey disruptive if participation has not been agreed in advance.
- **Postal surveys**: Allow researchers to question large numbers of participants. However, they are potentially costly and often have lower response rates, for example people do not always return a completed survey.
- *Email surveys*: A cheap and efficient way of accessing large numbers of participants. If unsolicited, emailed surveys may be unwelcome and may have a low response rate. It is also more difficult to compensate for sampling bias (see below) in email surveys.

Types of questions

Another key consideration when planning a questionnaire is the careful choice of types of question to ask. Questionnaire design goes far beyond simply drawing up a list of questions the researcher wants answering. Instead, it is necessary to ensure that the survey is valid, reliable and meets the defined research aims. Many types of question are available. If the research aims dictate a need to discover issues that probe detailed *meanings*, then open questions are often valuable. If a comparison is being sought, ranking questions or attitude scales may be useful. Most well-designed surveys combine the various types of questions to achieve a number of aims. These are the most common types of questions used in questionnaires:

- *Open or closed questions:* Closed questions invite a short answer, normally a 'yes' or 'no'. Although closed questions often limit the range of responses available, the responses are normally quicker to analyse. Open questions invite respondents to answer with greater freedom and offer their own interpretation of the issue. Open questions also require additional effort when coding answers for analysis. Well-designed surveys often combine open and closed questions to great effect. Here, a closed question could be combined with an open question to provide greater detail on a specific point. For example: 'Earlier, you answered that you thought sentences for burglary were too short, could you tell me why you think that?'

- *Classification questions:* Often present in the 'personal', or demographic, part of the questionnaire, they are used to record information such as age, ethnicity, gender and income. Classification questions take many familiar forms, including those that ask respondents to tick a box that best describes their ethnicity. When adopting quota sampling methods (see below), such questions are ideally situated at the start of the survey. This way, important information can be gathered to inform the decision of whether to continue interviewing a particular participant.

- *Fixed-choice questions:* Similar to classification questions, they offer participants a clear set of answers from which to choose. These are perhaps most commonly used in surveys that seek to understand people's voting intentions, such as: 'Which party are you intending on voting for: Labour, Conservative, Liberal Democrat, Green Party, Other?'

- *Factual questions:* Designed to find out certain key facts about a respondent's life, choices or preferences. One example could be a question over which measures are taken to avoid becoming a victim of crime. For surveys, these types of question need to be both clear and specific. The survey could also specifically ask for behaviour within a certain time frame, such as the last six weeks. This would avoid the prospect of comparing descriptions of activity that happened recently and those that rely on the distant memories of respondents.

- *Opinion questions:* Seek to understand how respondents feel about certain things. They may be open or closed in nature, for example: 'Do you think there should be more or less police patrolling the streets?' 'What is your view about the current level of policing on our streets?' Similar to factual questions, opinion questions need to be carefully designed and unambiguous. This type of question is also particularly susceptible to bias and **influence**. For example, slight changes in the way these questions are worded may have a huge influence on their respondent. Additionally, if participants are not alone, they may try to give answers that fit with their peers' perception of them.

- *Scaling and ranking questions:* Often ask for a response that indicates the strength of a participant's view or opinion. Perhaps the most recognizable form are questions that ask respondents to tick whether they 'strongly agree, agree, neither agree nor disagree, disagree, strongly disagree' with a particular statement. Sometimes, questions ask participants to rank their response on a scale of, say, 1–5. This is known as a **Likert scale**.

Phrasing of questions

How questions are phrased may have a significant impact on the answers given. Here, clarity and neutrality are crucial. For general trends and tendencies to be inferred from the survey, it is important that everyone who is asked understands the questionnaire in the same way. A number of techniques can be used to ensure that surveys are **standardized**:

- *Ensure questions are specific:* The more specific a question is, the more likely it will be understood in the same way by different participants. For example, the question: 'What do you think of our prisons?' could be interpreted in many different ways. Some people may answer with reference to whether prison regimes are sufficiently strict in their view. Others may be concerned with the appropriateness of prisons compared to alternative punishments. Another interpretation could relate to the role of rehabilitation in prisons and so on. To avoid such uncertainties, it would be better to have a number of more specific sub-questions. If the questions offer a choice of answers, such as the frequency of a particular action, you must ensure that these are also clear. For example, terms such as 'frequently', 'often' and 'normally' are interpreted in many different ways. Choices such as 'once a month' or 'once a week' are less easily misinterpreted.

- *Ensure questions are easy to understand:* Not everyone holds the same level of understanding of the subject being researched as you do. Indeed, variations of knowledge are the point of many research exercises. It is important that all respondents understand the questionnaire in the same way. To achieve this, questions should be worded in a straightforward manner using simple language. Double negatives, colloquial phrases, overly long questions and, generally, questions containing a statement and then a question, should be avoided.

- *Avoid leading questions:* Questions should be phrased in a neutral manner. Avoid questions that invite a particular answer. For example, 'Should burglars be given longer sentences?' or 'Do you agree that burglars should be given longer sentences?' are both leading questions. These encourage the respondent to answer in a particular way. Instead, the question 'Are current sentences for burglars (a) appropriate, (b) too long, (c) too short?' would be more neutral. In addition to the language used, the way a question is structured may also create a leading question. For example, in multiple-choice questions, care needs to be taken that a reasonable range of potential answers are provided so respondents are not prevented from answering in the way they would wish. As Ditton's (1998) study above demonstrates, careful thought must also be given to the order of questions to prevent this skewing the results in a particular direction.

- *Avoid using emotive language:* This may inspire the respondent to answer in a way they may not have otherwise. Questions asking if prisons are 'tough enough' or if criminals should 'pay' for their crimes are examples of emotive language that you should avoid.
- *Ensure questions are ethical:* In addition to the duty that researchers have towards the wellbeing of their participants, unethical surveys often yield poor-quality data and limited response rates. One form of good practice, for example, is to inform participants that they may withdraw from the survey at any time if they wish. There are a number of approaches that can be used when asking questions that may be of a sensitive nature, yet remain ethical. One option is to give respondents a choice of statements and ask which they are most likely to agree with. This can have the effect of depersonalizing the question to limit the negative impact on the participant.

Piloting research instruments

One simple yet effective way of addressing a number of potential and unanticipated problems, such as those highlighted above, is to conduct a **pilot study**. This involves testing the design of the questionnaire before it is used more widely. Piloting will help you uncover whether respondents find the questions easy to understand, whether sufficient and appropriate options are provided in multiple-choice questions, the need to modify the structure of the questionnaire and so on. One useful approach to piloting is to test the research tools on a population that is as close to the intended sample as possible. If you did some research measuring attitudes among students, then piloting the questionnaire on other students would be the most effective approach.

Sampling

Sampling is a key concept in research methods. An important consideration in any form of research, whether it is in the natural or social sciences, is the notion of generalization. This is also known as **external validity** (and 'ecological validity' in psychology), which refers to the extent to which the findings of a particular piece of research are relevant beyond the immediate context where the research was done. This has implications for the credibility of the conclusions of the research. Sampling is concerned with a number of broad questions:

- Who or what is going to be researched?
- How is the who or what going to be researched?
- What number of people or things are going to be researched?
- How are research participants selected?

Sampling, then, generally refers to decisions surrounding who is selected to participate in the research. Most quantitative research does not engage with every possible participant – the population. In many cases, it would be difficult to imagine, let alone do, any piece of research that would involve an entire population, which is called a census. Instead, a subset of the population is taken, the sample, and the findings are generalized from there. Deciding who should be in this sample, the process of sampling, is of crucial importance to the overall success of the research and whether its findings are meaningful and valid.

If you were to research the attitudes of students towards city-centre violence and only speak to those who rarely travel there, your research will produce skewed and unreliable results. In the context of criminological theory, we saw in Chapter 3 how Lombroso deduced that criminals had small 'cranial capacity'. This could equally be explained by the possibility that he was simply examining the skulls of younger offenders. Unless attempts are made to demonstrate that the specimens are drawn from samples of different age groups, it is difficult to accept the findings as genuinely representative of the wider populations of both criminals and non-criminals. Critics of Lombroso regularly point to the absence of adequate sampling and the failure to use appropriate **control groups** – in this case groups of non-criminals – to compare with, in much of his work. Sampling, then, is a way of ensuring that the findings are representative of the wider population.

There are a number of tried and tested methods that can be used to effectively sample a population. Normally, the key consideration is that the sample resembles the wider population in terms of its main features and characteristics. Although there are many approaches to sampling, they can be categorized into two main groups: probability and non-probability sampling.

Probability sampling

There are several approaches here but they fall under a general category known as **random sampling**, where each unit in a population has a known chance of being chosen. Simple random sampling refers to those instances when each unit is selected by chance, but every unit within a population has an equal likelihood of becoming part of a sample.

How is this done in practice? The starting point is the wider population and a **sampling frame**. A sampling frame is a tool that allows the researcher to identify all the potential participants from the population. A list is the most common form of sampling frame. Once the population and sampling frame have been determined, the researcher must then decide on the size of the sample. For example, a researcher may be interested in the extent of self-harm among 8,000 offenders detained in prison, but they may not have the resources to study this

entire population. So the researcher may decide to use a sample of 400 prisoners. In other words, the probability of being included = 8,000/400 (one in twenty).
This may be expressed in the form of an equation:

Sampling fraction: N/n (N = population, n = sample)

To actually produce a sample, it is first necessary to list all the cases appearing in the sampling frame (that is, 8,000 prisoners), assigning a number to each
of these cases. A table of random numbers (or other approach) is then used to
select the 400.

Although there are others, here we outline just three variations of random
sampling:

- **systematic sampling**: rather than randomly selecting numbers from a sampling frame, cases are selected according to fixed intervals. For instance, the
  researcher would begin by using the first reference taken from a table of random numbers, which shows a number less than 20. The random number may,
  for example, be seven and the researcher would then select every 20th number
  after this (27, 47, 67 and so on) as a participant from the list of 8,000 prisoners.
- **stratified random sampling**: the population is divided into specific categories
  or strata, for example gender or age. For example, if you wanted a sample
  to comprise 49 per cent males and 51 per cent females, the sampling frame
  would be divided so that males and females were listed separately and, then,
  samples would be taken from within these distinct groups. Then, either simple
  random sampling or systematic sampling is used within these two separate
  lists. This approach could be used to stratify a range of variables, including
  class, age and ethnicity.
- **multi-cluster sampling** (such as **area sampling**): often used in nationwide surveys. Because it may not always be practical to speak to participants across a
  large geographical area, researchers adopt methods to sample specific locations. Here, the wider area is broken down into smaller constituent parts, for
  example by postcode, zip or area code. Random sampling is then used a second
  time to select individual participants within these smaller areas. Returning to
  the above example of prisoners and self-harming, it would be possible to select
  a sample of prisons and a sample of prisoners from each prison.

Random sampling is often confused with convenience or opportunity sampling,
where research participants are selected on an ad hoc basis (see below). It is
important to recognize that, in many respects, random sampling is the exact
opposite. As discussed below, convenience/opportunity sampling techniques
involve no prior mathematical calculation and little advance knowledge over who
may be selected to participate in the research.

Overall, random sampling strategies provide an objective approach to selecting participants. The approach is transparent and observers can easily see how the selection processes occurred. Random sampling techniques also have their drawbacks. In many circumstances, sufficient detail of the wider population is not available to researchers at the outset. This may affect the validity of the sampling frame. Another tension occurs when randomly selected individuals are not available or do not wish to be part of the research (see the student examples below). As such, researchers need to incorporate strategies to substitute potential respondents, rather than repeatedly, and potentially unethically, contacting them, should they decline to participate.

Non-probability sampling

Non-probability sampling is the opposite of probability sampling in that the method of selecting units for analysis is not random. Here, it is more likely that some units will be selected from a population than others. For the purposes of this illustration, three broad types of non-probability sampling are commonly used: the convenience sample, the snowball sample (which share much in common), and the quota sample. Repeated users of convenience and snowball sampling approaches are generally less likely to be quantitative researchers committed to positivist values and interested in ensuring their research is representative across wide populations. These kinds of sampling are likely to be justified by appealing to interpretivist principles (see Chapter 2). That said, quantitative and qualitative researchers can and do use non-probability sampling.

1. **Convenience sampling**, sometimes referred to as **opportunity sampling**, is chosen by a researcher on the basis of what is available to them. For example, a serving police officer who is an area commander in charge of several police stations may be interested in the attitudes of rank and file officers towards their capabilities as a police leader and manager. The officer may decide to administer a questionnaire to all the police constables and sergeants in the police station where their office is based. Due to the status of the officer, it is likely that many participants will complete the questionnaire and therefore provide a reasonable response rate. The findings may be of interest but it would not be possible to generalize them because they reflect only the views of officers working in that station and not others and of those who are less likely – or did not have the opportunity – to complete the questionnaire – this is known as non-response bias.

   Convenience sampling therefore lacks scientific rigour. Despite this criticism, it can be used to pilot a questionnaire before it is administered as part of the research project. Convenience sampling is a useful tool for accessing some groups that are hard to research. This may be because it is difficult to identify the population, for example people committing street crimes in your town or city, or the population may prove hard to access, for example homeless persons who have been the victim of a physical assault. In these instances, a researcher may come across a chance to obtain data which may be an opportunity too good to miss. The findings will not be representative but it is arguably better than nothing and accessing hard-to-reach groups often entails compromises in generalizability in exchange for access.

2. **Snowball sampling**, sometimes called **network sampling**, is similar to convenience sampling. It refers to those researchers who, after making contact with just one person or a handful of people, then use these initial connections to make further contacts. These initial contact points are called 'gatekeepers' and are extremely valuable in generating additional participants. The image to bear in mind is a small snowball being pushed from the top of a hill, watching its size increase as it rolls downwards. Again, rather like convenience sampling, the data is not likely to be representative and, for the most part, qualitative researchers prefer this method of sampling where the emphasis is less on broader tendencies and generalizability and more related to meanings and issues in a specific group (see Chapter 2). Snowball sampling techniques are extremely useful when researching groups that are not easily accessible to outsiders. Rawlinson and Fussey's (2010) research into irregular migrants operating in the informal and organized criminal economies relied heavily on this technique. Without being introduced by a well-regarded gatekeeper with access to other criminals, other participants would have simply refused to speak to the researchers. In other contexts, snowball sampling is useful for researching environments that the investigator only partially understands at the beginning of the project, such as policy networks or gang structures.

3. **Quota sampling** is the most frequently used non-probability sampling technique. This technique first requires that the larger target population is divided into segments and variables (see below). For example, if a research project is attempting to understand the differences between male and female attitudes to offending, one important variable is gender. To generate a quota sample, the sample must have the same proportions of each category as the wider population. Remaining with this example, if the wider population comprises 49 per cent males and 51 per cent females, the quotas of males and females in the sample must use the same proportions. Researchers then approach participants from each category until the quotas are filled.

This method has considerable benefits in that it is a relatively uncomplicated way of representing a wider research population. However, quota sampling is more subjective than it initially appears. Researchers decide who

to approach and who to ignore based on more than whether potential participants appear to fit into the requisite categories of, for example, sex, age or
ethnicity. Interviewers may be influenced by additional factors based on prejudices and assumptions, such as whether a potential participant appears
friendly or not. Thus, a sample could comprise people the interviewer likes the
look of, rather than more objective rationales for inclusion.

Overall, when researching a criminological problem, it is not always possible
to consider every case. For each problem, there is a researchable population
and the researcher will normally only be able to access a part of it: a sample. In
quantitative research, it is generally important for the sample to be representative of the characteristics of the whole sample. Nevertheless, for any research
project, sampling is an important feature and may be heavily scrutinized by
observers. Many sampling strategies are available and it is important that you
not only select the most appropriate sampling tool, but also comprehensively
justify your selection.

Variables

Defining, labelling and comparing variables are a key part of quantitative
research projects. In brief, variables are a more formal and scientific way of analysing relationships and refer to something we intend to measure. For example,
age, ethnicity, attitudes on a scale of 1–5 and stated preferences are all variables.
These categories are further divided into independent and dependent variables:

- *Independent variables:* refer to something that changes, for example different
  categories of respondent, such as age, gender, ethnicity, class and so on.
- *Dependent variables:* refer to the measurable *impact* of that change. Something
  that observably changes across these categories, such as particular attitudes
  and so on, is a dependent variable.

As their names suggest, there is normally a relationship between these two
types of variable, with the dependent variable being largely 'dependent' on independent variables. For example, if the relationship between age and the fear of
crime is being measured, age is the independent variable and fear of crime the
dependent variable. This is because the researcher is interested in whether levels of fear *are influenced by*, that is, depend on, whether someone is young or old.
Therefore, different ages (the independent variable) may indicate a difference in
the level of fear (the dependent variable) someone feels.

Another simple example could be seen in a study of whether different
types of prison regime affect whether someone reoffends (recidivism). Here,
the type of prison regime, for example rehabilitative or punitive, would be the

independent variable, and is something that the researcher categorizes, and the level of recidivism would be the dependent variable – something that is affected by the type of prison regime; the independent variable.

In most of the survey projects you are likely to be involved in, much of the analysis centres on the relationship between independent and dependent variables. Therefore, thinking about the types of, and relationships between, variables at the project's planning stages helps provide you with clarity over the likely shape of the research and how the data will be analysed.

Types of data

When attempting to measure the change in variables, consideration needs to be given to the type of data that is being measured. An understanding of the differences between types of data helps to clarify later analysis of variables and their relationships. For example, some types of information are amenable to being compared to each other, while others are not. More commonly, some types of data can be ranked in order of importance, value or preference. In general, there are four mechanisms for scaling statistical data:

- **Ordinal**: the *rank* of the data
- **Nominal**: the *category* of the data
- **Interval**: spaces (intervals) between points on a scale that are consistent wherever they are measured, such as differences in temperature. Unlike other scales, often '0' does not imply the absence of what is being measured in interval data; after all, 0°C does not mean there is 'no' temperature
- **Ratio scales**: differences between measures can be compared and quantified. For example, 2 kg weighs twice as much as 1 kg and '0' implies the absence of what is being measured – 0 kg weighs nothing.

The importance of accounting for these differences is developed in the discussion on data analysis below.

ANALYSING QUANTITATIVE DATA

There are many ways to analyse quantitative data, ranging from simply counting and calculating averages of questionnaire responses to more advanced statistical analyses. To get the most from your data, it is essential to use a computer-based statistical package. With a small amount of training, many of these software programs are, with some patience, quite easy to use and give you a powerful tool to analyse your data.

Microsoft Excel is one commonly used option and does a good job of undertaking basic statistical analysis of the results and presenting the data in a clear and attractive manner. However, the industry standard for quantitative data analysis is a piece of software called Statistical Package for the Social Sciences or SPSS. In many ways, it is as easy to use as Excel but, in addition, is an extremely powerful tool for quantitative data analysis. SPSS is used by professional researchers and has a large number of advanced functions for analysing data. Familiarity with SPSS can also prove to be a distinct advantage if you apply for research-related employment.

We now provide a short introduction to getting started with SPSS, inputting data and undertaking some simple analyses. This brief overview may be supplemented with many of the available excellent guides to SPSS, such as Rodeghier (1996), Pallant (2010) and Griffith (2010), and the large number of internet-based tutorials, including on the official SPSS website (www.spss.com), YouTube and elsewhere (see, for example, UCLA's web-based introduction to SPSS: www.ats.ucla.edu/stat/spss/modules/dataed.htm). The SPSS software package itself also contains extensive help and tutorial sections.

Regardless of whether you adopt SPSS as a data analysis tool, we also provide an overview of how to analyse quantitative data in any form. Issues of coding, frequency and understanding the relationships between variables are particularly important features of any quantitative data analysis and are discussed here too.

Getting started with SPSS: inputting data

When opening SPSS, the opening screen is called the 'Data Editor' (Figure 5.1). This operates in a similar way to other database packages (such as Microsoft Excel) and is where the raw data, the survey responses in this case, is stored. SPSS then allows you to analyse this information. There are two main ways in which to input data into SPSS: manually type it in or, alternatively, import it from other database packages (including Microsoft Excel). This is because most popular data analysis programs have an inbuilt level of compatibility, known as Open Database Connectivity. To import data into SPSS from Microsoft Excel or another source, simply click 'File', 'Open', 'Data' and then search for the file.

The row along the top of the grid is where you input the variables. Normally, these correspond to the questions on a survey. For example, the first column could be 'Age', the second 'Gender', then 'Income', 'Attitudes to prison' and so on. Each row then corresponds with the data collected from each participant.

To input data into SPSS, we first need to give names to these variable fields. To illustrate this process, we will follow a short exercise based on a fictitious survey on attitudes to crime. Following this exercise, we will equip you with the basic skills necessary for undertaking statistical analysis using SPSS.

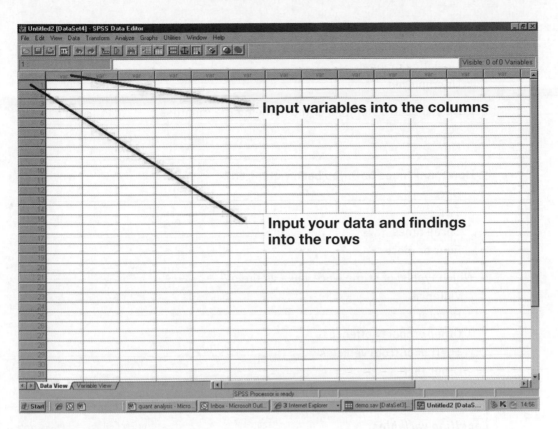

Input variables into the columns

Input your data and findings into the rows

Figure 5.1 *The SPSS Data Editor*
Source: Reproduced with permission of IBM

In this exercise, we will input information from a survey that asked the following questions:

1. Age
   Under 16
   16–24
   25–35
   36–50
   51–75
   Over 75

2. Gender
   Male
   Female

3. Occupational category
   Professional/managerial

Administrative/clerical

Skilled manual

Unskilled manual

Unemployed

4. Have you been a victim of crime in the last 12 months?

Yes

No

5. How many times have you been victimized?

Once

Twice

Three times

Four or more

6. Which type(s) of crime were you a victim of?

Violence

Burglary

Other property offences

Theft of or from vehicles

Other theft

Other (please state)

Labelling variables

The first stage is to give the variables a name. Normally, this is a process of transferring the questions from the survey into the computer. To do so, double-click on
the 'var' label in SPSS's 'Data View' window. This will bring up the 'Variable View'
window (Figure 5.2). We can then submit information about each question.

	Name	Type	Width	Decimals	Label	Values	Missing	Columns	Align	Measure
1	Age	Numeric	8	2	Which Age Category do you fit into?	{1.00, Under 1	999.00	8	Right	Scale
2										
3										

Figure 5.2 *SPSS Variable View*

Source: Reproduced with permission of IBM

Following the above example, 'Age' would be our first variable. This should
be entered under the 'Name' field. The next field, 'Type', allows the choice of the
type of information being entered. Double-clicking on the small grey box brings
up a set of options (Figure 5.3). Here, select 'Numeric'. In other projects, if words
are being entered, we could select 'String' here.

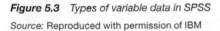

Figure 5.3 *Types of variable data in SPSS*
Source: Reproduced with permission of IBM

The 'Width' field allows us to set how much space is given to each figure. For example, the number '1,000' would have a value of four because it contains four digits. The default setting in SPSS is eight and this is normally sufficient for most student projects. If a project uses larger figures, this value can be increased accordingly. 'Decimals', the next field, refers to the number of digits following a decimal point that we wish to record. Again, SPSS has a default setting (two) that is sufficient for most student projects and this field can often be left alone. 'Label' allows more detail to be provided regarding what the variable means. Here, it is possible to list more information about the question.

Values, the next field, is important and often relates to how data is coded. Coding is when more complex categories are given a simple label to help us interpret and analyse them. For example, we can give the categories of question 1 of our survey (Age) the following labels:

Code/value		Value/label
1	=	Under 16
2	=	16–24
3	=	25–35
4	=	36–50
5	=	51–75
6	=	Over 75

This way, when we enter our survey responses, rather than 'Over 75', we type in '6' each time. Double-clicking on the small grey box brings up a set of options where these codes/values can be entered (see Figure 5.4). Here, the code given for each category, that is, 1, 2, 3, 4 and so on, is inputted to the 'Value' box and the description for each category is submitted to the 'Label' box. Then click 'Add' to progress to the next category. After inputting all categories, click 'OK'.

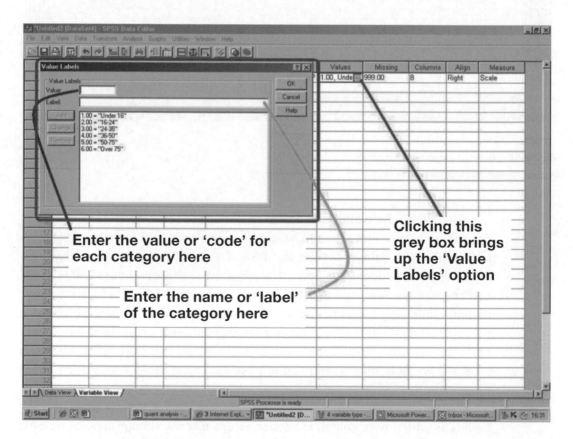

Figure 5.4   *Coding data in SPSS*

Source: Reproduced with permission of IBM

Sometimes, when conducting surveys, interviewers may miss some information. This could happen for a variety of reasons. For example, the respondent may not wish to answer the question or the researcher may not have marked the response down clearly. These omissions can sometimes affect the accuracy of the statistical analysis of the data. The 'Missing' field allows us to overcome this problem by informing SPSS that data in a particular field is missing and should be regarded as such. Here, if '999' is entered, it means that any time '999' is inputted, it is treated as missing data. To input '999', click on the small grey box, then select the 'Discreet missing values' option and input 999 into one of the boxes underneath before selecting 'OK'.

The 'Columns' field allows us to set the width for each variable. This refers to the space each variable will occupy and is different to the earlier 'width' field, which indicates the number of digits to be inputted. The 'Align' field refers to how the data should be presented (left justified, right justified, or centred).

'Measure', the final field, enables us to tell SPSS what type of data is being entered. The dropdown menu provides three choices, 'Scale', 'Nominal' and 'Ordinal', which broadly reflect the discussion on types of data earlier in this chapter. Generally, interval and ratio data are not distinguished in SPSS and are labelled as 'Scale'. You should apply this label when values belong to reasonably clear categories where comparisons between them, and the distance between them, are likely to occur. As a rule of thumb, data relating to income (in numbers) or age are most appropriately labelled as 'Scale'. Nominal variables have values that are not ranked, such as gender, religion, or a place of residence. Ordinal variables have categories that can be ranked in relation to each other. A scale measuring satisfaction with the police, say, from very dissatisfied to very satisfied is an example of an ordinal variable.

To proceed with this exercise, enter the remaining questions into the 'Variable View' of SPSS. To key in the final question, 'Types of crime', we need to adopt a slightly different strategy. One option would be to code the different potential responses; that is, 1 = Violence, 2 = Burglary, 3 = Other property offences and so on, under one variable. However, because the preceding question asks how often our respondents have been victimized, this approach will not allow us to account for people who have been victims of different forms of crime. For example, if someone was a victim of burglary and violence on separate occasions, we would not be able to record this. Instead, because we will probably want to analyse each offence separately, question six can be split into six variables, one for each potential response. Also, for these variables, we do not need to code our responses under the 'Values' heading of the 'Variable View'. Instead, we can just record the number of times someone has been victimized by each form of crime. When it comes to the analysis stage, this will allow a more detailed exploration of the data. The completed version should look something like Figure 5.5.

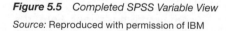

	Name	Type	Width	Decimals	Label	Values	Missing	Columns	Align	Measure
1	Age	Numeric	8	2	Which Age Category do	{1.00, Under 1	999.00	8	Right	Scale
2	Gender	Numeric	8	2		{1.00, Male}...	999.00	8	Right	Nominal
3	Occupation	Numeric	8	2		{1.00, Professi	999.00	8	Right	Nominal
4	Victim	Numeric	8	2	Victim in the last 12 mo	{1.00, Yes}...	999.00	8	Right	Nominal
5	RptVictim	Numeric	8	2	How often victimised?	{1.00, Once}...	999.00	8	Right	Scale
6	Type1Viole	Numeric	8	2	Violence	None	999.00	8	Right	Nominal
7	Type2Burgl	Numeric	8	2	Burglary	None	999.00	8	Right	Nominal
8	Type3Other	Numeric	8	2	Other property offences	None	999.00	8	Right	Nominal
9	Type4VehT	Numeric	8	2	Theft of or from vehicles	None	999.00	8	Right	Nominal
10	Type5Other	Numeric	8	2	Other theft	None	999.00	8	Right	Nominal
11	Type6Other	Numeric	8	2	Other offence	None	999.00	8	Right	Nominal

You can also toggle between 'Data View' and 'Variable View' by clicking on these two tabs

Figure 5.5 *Completed SPSS Variable View*

Source: Reproduced with permission of IBM

Entering responses

Let us say that we gave the survey to 16 participants. Although this is a small sample, it is enough to illustrate how SPSS functions. Having set up our variables, the next stage is the simple, but sometimes time-consuming task of entering the data. In the 'Data View', each of the rows represents one survey respondent. To enter our data, we simply go along each row inputting the information from each participant (referred to as 'cases' by SPSS). The results are illustrated in Table 5.2 and appear in SPSS as shown in Figure 5.6.

Table 5.2 Victimization survey responses

	Age	Gender	Occupation	Victim of crime?	How many times?	No. of violence?	No. of burglary?	No. of other property offences?	No. of theft of/fr vehicles?	No. of other theft?	No. of other offences?
Case1	Under 16	Male	Unemployed	No	None	0	0	0	0	0	0
Case2	Over 75	Female	Unemployed	Yes	Once	0	1	0	0	0	0
Case3	16–24	Female	Unskilled Manual	Yes	Twice	1	0	0	1	0	0
Case4	16–24	Male	Administrative/clerical	No	None	0	0	0	0	0	0
Case5	50–75	Male	Professional/managerial	Yes	Three times	0	3	0	0	0	0
Case6	36–50	Female	Professional/managerial	Yes	Three times	0	1	1	1	0	0
Case7	36–50	Male	Skilled manual	No	None	0	0	0	0	0	0
Case8	24–35	Female	Unskilled manual	Yes	Three times	2	0	0	0	1	0
Case9	Under 16	Female	Unemployed	No	None	0	0	0	0	0	0
Case10	50–75	Female	Administrative/clerical	No	None	0	0	0	0	0	0
Case11	36–50	Male	Skilled manual	No	None	0	0	0	0	0	0
Case12	16–24	Male	Skilled manual	Yes	Once	0	0	0	1	0	0
Case13	24–35	Female	Administrative/clerical	No	None	0	0	0	0	0	0
Case14	50–75	Male	Administrative/clerical	No	None	0	0	0	0	0	0
Case15	16–24	Male	Skilled manual	Yes	Once	0	0	0	1	0	0
Case16	24–35	Female	Unskilled manual	No	None	0	0	0	0	0	0

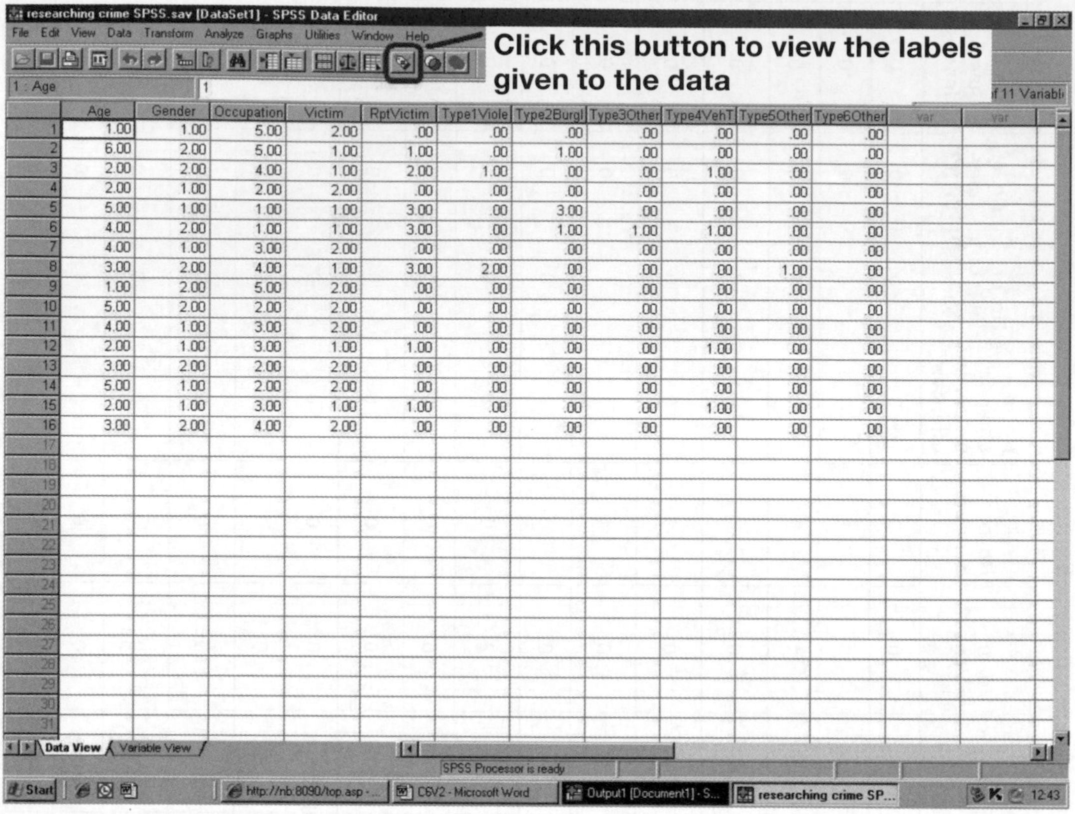

Figure 5.6 *Survey responses in SPSS*

Source: Reproduced with permission of IBM

Data analysis

Quantitative data allows researchers to apply a number of statistical processes to discover a range of information. Mainly, these involve the prevalence or **frequency** of particular occurrences, the relationship between variables, and the significance of the findings. While it is possible to work some of these out in a rudimentary way using pen and paper or a calculator, SPSS allows us to make such calculations instantly and easily enables sophisticated analyses of the data. These main types of analysis are now described with reference to how SPSS can be utilized.

Frequency analysis

Many of the analytical tools you would use for a student project can be found under the 'Analyze' menu on the toolbar (Figure 5.7). To calculate the frequencies of particular variables, click 'Analyze', then 'Descriptive Statistics', then 'Frequencies'.

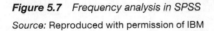

Figure 5.7   *Frequency analysis in SPSS*
Source: Reproduced with permission of IBM

We are then presented with a set of options (Figure 5.8). Here, select the variables you wish to measure in the left-hand box, press the arrow icon to shift your selection across into the 'Variables' box and then press OK. At this stage, it is also possible to present the data as a chart by pressing 'Charts' and selecting the appropriate option before pressing 'OK'.

We are then presented with a pop-out box detailing the statistical frequencies for the selected variables (Figure 5.9). The 'Frequency' column of the chart lists how many cases/participants fall into each category. The 'Percentage' column calculates the percentage of participants that this figure translates into. 'Significance' is discussed below and the final column, 'Cumulative percentage', simply adds the percentages of each category together. Any charts are also displayed here. Using the toolbar, it is possible to edit the charts, for example by adding labels and titles. This additional sheet can be saved as a separate document for future use and each table and chart can be selected by clicking on it, and then copying and pasting into another document.

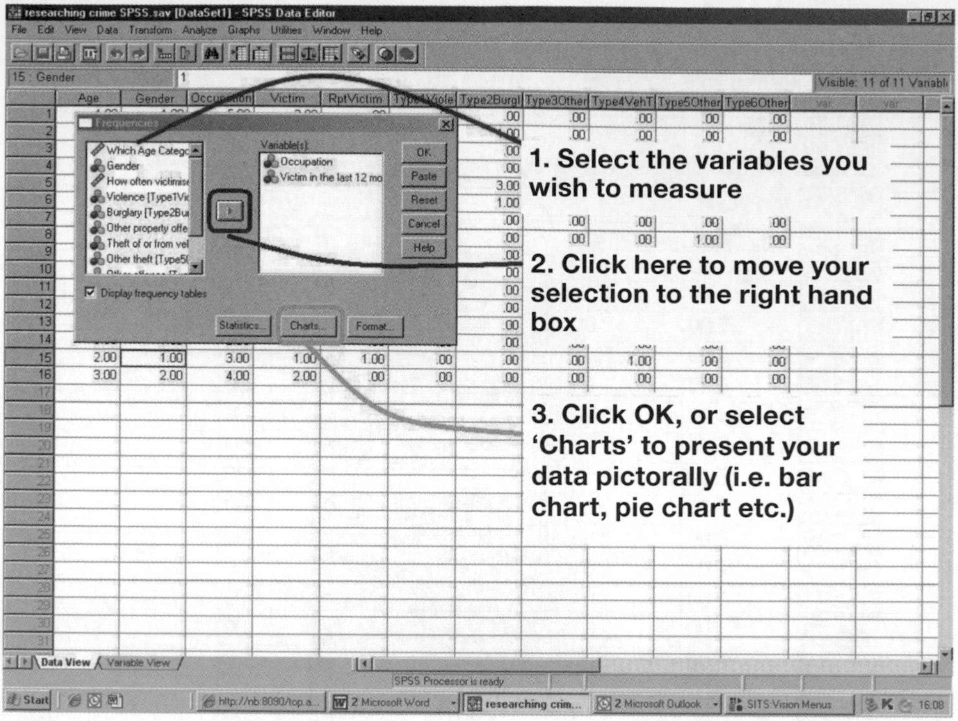

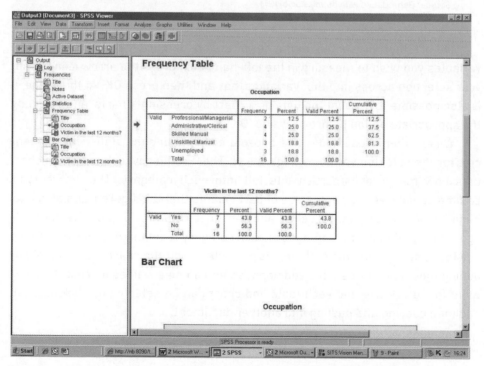

Figure 5.8 *Selecting variables for frequency analysis in SPSS*

Source: Reproduced with permission of IBM

Figure 5.9 *Frequency results for the distribution of victimization by occupation in SPSS*

Source: Reproduced with permission of IBM

Analysing relationships between variables

Most quantitative research projects seek to understand the relationship between variables. In this exercise, we can explore whether there are any relationships between, say, age and victimization; profession and repeat victimization; which groups have been affected by burglary, known as the **distribution** of burglary; and so on. In fact, we can easily analyse any combination of variables.

SPSS can analyse the relationships between variables using a function it calls **Crosstabs**, an abbreviation of **cross-tabulation**. A simple illustration of how this works is if we examine the different victimization rates between males and females in our survey. To do this, again click 'Analyze', then 'Descriptive Statistics', and then select 'Crosstabs'. Using a similar procedure as before, select one variable from the box on the left and transfer it to the right (Figure 5.10). Here, SPSS provides an additional option of whether to place the variables as Row(s) or Column(s). As a general rule, the row should contain the dependent variable (the more constant category) and the column, the independent variable (the thing being measured).

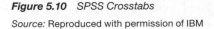

Figure 5.10   *SPSS Crosstabs*

Source: Reproduced with permission of IBM

If 'Gender' is selected in the 'Row' box and 'How often victimized?' in the Column box, SPSS will produce a table that examines their relationship (see Table 5.3).

Table 5.3 Relationship between gender and victimization

Count

		How often victimized?				Total
		None	Once	Twice	Three times	
Gender	Male	5	2	0	1	8
	Female	4	1	1	2	8
Total		9	3	1	3	16

More detailed analysis can be undertaken by examining:

- the percentages these figures represent
- the percentages of each category of victimization as a proportion of overall levels of victimization
- the extent of each category of victimization as a percentage of victimization levels for each gender.

This can be achieved by accessing the 'Crosstabs' menu (see Figure 5.10 above) and clicking on the 'Cells' option. This will bring up another set of options (Figure 5.11). This will then elicit a much more detailed set of results, providing a deeper level of analysis (Table 5.4).

Table 5.4 Gender and prevalence of victimization

			How often victimized?				Total
			None	Once	Twice	Three times	None
Gender	Male	Count	5	2	0	1	8
		% within Gender	62.5%	25.0%	.0%	12.5%	100.0%
		% within How often victimized?	55.6%	66.7%	.0%	33.3%	50.0%
	Female	Count	4	1	1	2	8
		% within Gender	50.0%	12.5%	12.5%	25.0%	100.0%
		% within How often victimized?	44.4%	33.3%	100.0%	66.7%	50.0%
Total		Count	9	3	1	3	16
		% within Gender	56.3%	18.8%	6.3%	18.8%	100.0%
		% within How often victimized?	100.0%	100.0%	100.0%	100.0%	100.0%

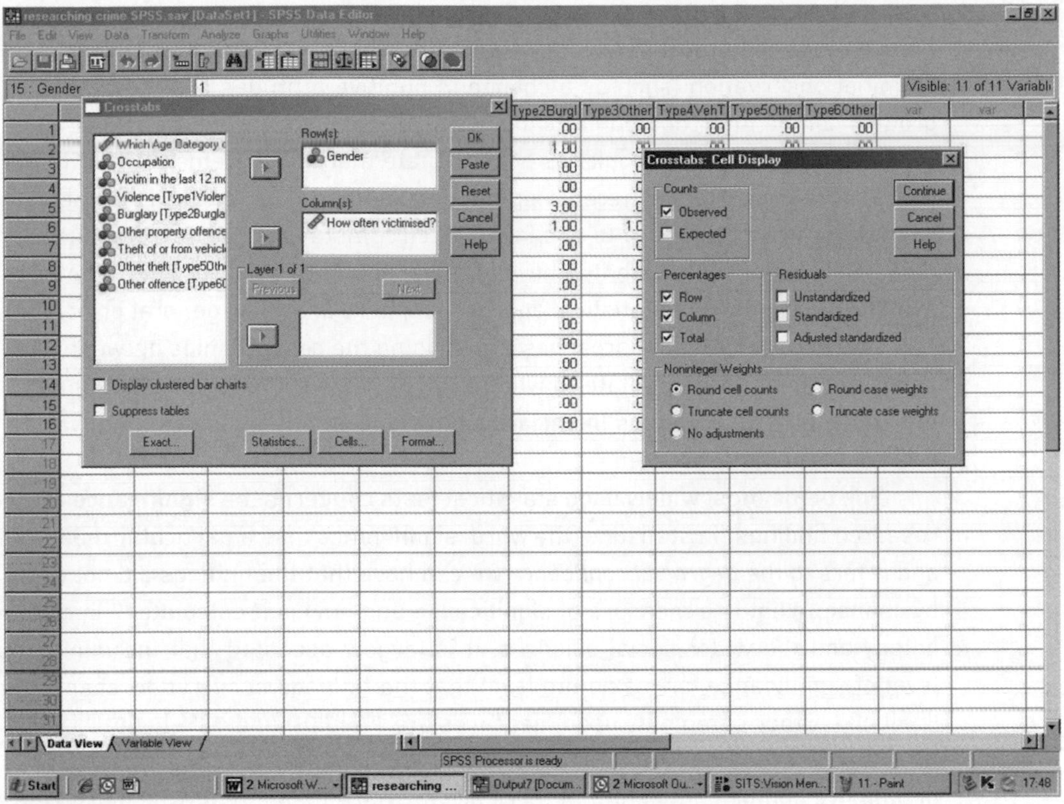

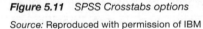

Figure 5.11   *SPSS Crosstabs options*
Source: Reproduced with permission of IBM

This process can be repeated with any combination of variables that feature in the survey and can penetrate the data to provide a detailed and rich set of findings.

Findings can also be presented in the form of bar charts, pie charts and other graphical representations. This can be achieved in a number of ways, although the two most straightforward approaches are bar charts and graphs (creating charts for frequency counts is described above). If a bar chart detailing the association between two variables is needed, simply select the 'Display Clustered Bar Charts' option, while selecting the appropriate variables in the 'Crosstabs' box. Alternatively, selecting the 'Graphs' menu and then the 'Chart Builder' function takes users through a step-by-step process of creating charts and graphs that is similar to the 'Insert/Chart' function in Microsoft Excel.

Going deeper: significance and relationship testing

Once it is apparent that two variables are indeed related, statistical tests can be used to do two things: test the strength of **association** and the significance of that association. In the above examples, we have already begun to test associations through the process of cross-tabulation. What appears to be an association on initial observation (such as a change in punitive attitudes over different age groups) can be interrogated in further detail by using different statistical tests. A constant theme of this book has been to state that, in all elements of criminological research, many different approaches can be taken, and part of the skill is knowing which measure to use in which circumstance. The same applies for statistical testing. Although it is beyond the scope of this text to offer a detailed exploration of different statistical approaches, here are a few general principles.

There are different approaches to analysing the relationships between variables and these largely relate to whether the analysis of one variable (**univariate analysis**), two variables (**bivariate analysis**) or many variables (multivariate analysis) is being conducted.

One of the most widely used statistical tests concerns the **significance** of the research findings. In statistics, the word 'significance' has a particular meaning, and refers to the *degree of confidence* we can have that the findings did not occur by chance. What is a measure of significance and how is it calculated? In criminology and the wider social sciences, it is largely accepted that the minimum level of significance (or maximum level that the findings occurred by chance) is 5% (0.05). Other commonly used measures are 1% (0.01) and 0.1% (0.001). Therefore, a statistical significance value of 5% (or 0.05) means that for each 100 pieces of data, we can be confident that there are no more than 5 that exhibited a relationship that occurred by chance. Or, in other words, no more than 5 exhibited a relationship that may not exist in the wider population. In sum, significance tests indicate the degree to which we can be confident that our findings are not false and, therefore, that the sample is representative of the wider population and avoids **sampling error**.

The most commonly applied test of significance is **Pearson's chi-squared test**, commonly known as the **chi-squared test** or **x² test**. This tests the 'goodness of fit' between a theoretical distribution of frequency and the actual distribution of frequency present in the observed data. However, such statistical tests can only apply to data derived from probability samples. This is because probability samples, such as the random sample, have a concrete and statistically testable relationship to the wider population. Calculations can then be made regarding the generalizability of findings. There is little point conducting a chi-squared test on quota or snowball sampled data as there is insufficient information available about the wider population.

It is also important to note that chi-squared tests only inform us of the likelihood that the findings, say a relationship, did not occur by chance. They do not test the strength of the relationship. To understand this, other statistical tests are needed. Again, the choice of test depends on the circumstances. Here, it relates to whether nominal, ordinal, interval or ratio data is being used. A useful resource in choosing the correct statistical test to use is the online 'Which Test' resource (www.whichtest.info/index.htm). Although aimed at clinical psychologists, its web-based toolkit is equally useful for criminologists.

Two commonly used tests of association (depending on the type of data) are the **phi coefficient** (ϕ) and **Cramer's V**. These attach a numerical value to the association between two variables. In both tests, the values range from 0 to 1. For example, 0.1 would indicate a very weak relationship between two variables, whereas 0.9 would indicate a very strong association. Where relationships do exist, they rarely sit at the extremes (0 or 1) of the scale. The phi coefficient test is normally applied to simple bivariate analyses, where variables are likely to be one of two options, for example people are generally either male or female. Phi coefficient tests are therefore normally applied to '2 x 2' tables of results, where two aspects of a dependent variable are measured against two outcomes of an independent variable. In the above example, a 2 x 2 table consisting of appropriate variables would be an analysis of whether gender (two variables: male or female) is related to whether an individual had been a victim of crime (two variables: yes or no). For larger comparisons involving both greater numbers of variables and, also variables that have a number of possible values, particularly nominal forms, other tests, such as Cramer's V, are often employed by researchers.

To conduct these statistical tests in SPSS, first ensure that you are applying the correct test for the variables that are to be measured, then in the 'Crosstabs' function (Figure 5.10), click the 'Statistics' button and select the tests you wish to run.

Data analysis: final points

For many researchers, the thought of statistically analysing their data is a distant consideration at the start of a project. This chapter has demonstrated there is a lot to do when setting up a quantitative research project. Attention must be given to identifying the research population, structuring the interview questions, ensuring objectivity and eliminating bias wherever possible. Issues of sampling and access also need to be addressed. For many, engaging in fieldwork and speaking to participants in person is an exciting prospect, and something far removed from the statistical and computational analyses that follow. However, an appreciation, at the outset, of how the data will eventually be analysed is critical to ensuring the success of the overall project. Prior consideration to the likely categories of response, the form of data and variables (nominal, ordinal, interval, and ratio) will enable the analyses to progress much more smoothly, and increase the chances that clear and significant findings will be generated. More

than any other research strategy, quantitative research demands an appreciation of the entire likely research process during its planning phases.

Another important consideration relates to the capability of computer analysis tools. While packages such as Excel and SPSS are powerful and impressive,
they cannot perform miracles. Indeed, computer scientists have a saying, 'junk
in, junk out'. If a research project is poorly designed, a software package will not
remedy this, it can only work within the parameters it is given. To further explore
the capabilities of SPSS, it has a useful built-in statistics resource, called 'Statistics Coach' (Figure 5.12). To locate this, click 'Help' and then 'Statistics Coach'.

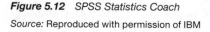

Figure 5.12   *SPSS Statistics Coach*
Source: Reproduced with permission of IBM

The dataset accompanying this chapter is available for you to download from
this textbook's companion website (www.palgrave.com/sociology/researchingcrime).
We recommend that the above exercise is followed to gain an important grounding in
how to set up SPSS and analyse datasets. Indeed, through learning and experi-
mentation, even more detailed statistical analysis could be carried out. Reflecting on the strengths and weaknesses of this survey could allow you to create
more advanced studies. For example, at the design stage, questions could have
been asked over whether victims reported the offence(s) to the police, which
ones, why, what their level of satisfaction was with the police response and so
on. More complex and analytically rich projects could thus be developed from
relatively straightforward planning exercises at the outset.

STUDENT PROJECTS USING QUANTITATIVE RESEARCH

There are a seemingly limitless number of options for students seeking to
develop quantitative research projects. You now have a guide to the key steps
you need to take in order to create a robust survey-based research project. One

of the common mistakes people make is overestimating what can be 'proved' in a dissertation-type project. Indeed, it is unlikely that it would be possible to uncover trends across an entire country, region, or even town in a short-term, dissertation-type project. Also, one of the key elements of successful small-scale research projects is cohesion. By this we mean that the aims, methods, design and analysis fit together as part of the overall research process. To achieve this, two strategies can be deployed: ensuring a common thread, or theme, runs throughout the project, and defining a clear research population. This will prevent the temptation to make grand claims from the project's findings. The following examples of survey-based anonymized student projects address these issues.

Example 1: researching the fear of crime among the students

Alan wanted to research levels of fear of crime among students and decided that a survey was the best way to canvas a large number of respondents. Having discussed the best approach to take with his supervisor, Alan settled on a random sample of 100 students in the Faculty of Social Sciences at his university. Heeding his tutor's advice, Alan set about designing his questionnaire and defining his variables at an early stage.

The first step was to consider the overall aims and objectives of the project. In this case, Alan was keen to understand the levels of anxiety about crime among his fellow students and, in particular, the types of crime they were fearful of. These were to be his dependent variables. He then sought to measure these dependent variables against a set of independent variables, in this case, age, year of study, gender and area of residence.

Next, Alan deliberated over which type of survey to use. In many cases, this decision is closely linked to the type of sampling adopted. Because Alan had settled on a random sampling approach, he faced the potential difficulty of not being able to recognize these participants in person. Feeling that an introductory letter followed by a face-to-face interview may be time-consuming, he elected to use an email-based survey. He then developed a sampling frame based on student enrolment data. To do this, Alan checked the faculty noticeboards and recorded the names of students who had registered for social science modules and whose seminar groups were listed. Out of 300 students, Alan selected 100. He did this by listing the names of each member of his research population and then selecting every third potential participant starting at number three on his list. Correctly assuming that not all students would participate, he then developed a new sampling frame starting at number two on his list of 300 students and then selected each potential participant in intervals of three. The second list would serve as a contingency in case he did not reach 100 participants from the first list. He would use this once he had exhausted the initial sampling frame. Despite this objective approach, ethical issues are raised over the unsolicited inclusion of participants into the research (see below).

Having planned the overall aims of the research, which type of survey to use, established an appropriate sampling framework, and considered the main variables, he then designed his specific survey questions. He used a blend of closed questions, scaling questions (to understand the intensity of participants' fears), and some open questions in order to provide more depth to participants' responses. After assembling his questionnaire, Alan proceeded to 'pilot' his work. He did this by emailing a small group of friends, asking them to complete his survey. Alan then tweaked the order of questions to ensure a more logical progression throughout the survey. He also incorporated an ethical statement at the start of the questionnaire. This detailed respondents' right to withdraw from the survey at any point and promised total anonymity of responses. Having completed this, Alan then began his fieldwork.

It was at this stage that Alan began to encounter some problems. While his friends had been keen to fill out his questionnaire, students who he did not know were less helpful. His original sampling approach yielded a very low response rate, with 18 students returning their completed questionnaires, reflecting a more general pattern of low response rates for email-based surveys. After Alan had exhausted his 'contingency list', he had only received another 20 completed questionnaires. This meant that he had to create another list from his selected population. To do this, he selected the first name on his original list and then every third person after that. This third 'wave' yielded a further 23 responses, meaning that Alan had received 61 responses overall. To reach his stated aim of 100 respondents, he then had to adopt a new sampling strategy. This involved adopting the same approach to students of the Faculty of Arts and Design until he gained an additional 39 completed questionnaires.

This ad hoc approach to sampling meant that his survey was no longer representative of his initial population and therefore threatened to undermine his results. Indeed, had Alan been aware of the issue of low response commonly associated with email questionnaires, he could have adopted a number of different strategies. First, he could have resigned himself to using a smaller sample size. Indeed, if of suitable length, 61 completed questionnaires actually provides a substantial amount of data and his supervisor may have felt it was sufficient for a project of this size. Alternatively, Alan could have used a stratified random sample to conduct a comparative study of levels of fear of crime between students of the Faculty of Social Sciences and the Faculty of Arts and Design.

Nevertheless, having reached 100 responses, Alan then began to code and enter his data into SPSS. While he was doing this, he realized another potential difficulty with his project. This was that the open-ended questions sometimes did not match the responses participants gave to the scaling questions. For example, there appeared to be particular confusion among some respondents over whether they were 'somewhat frightened' by crime or 'a little frightened' by crime. In addition, there were difficulties in coding the open-ended questions, particularly over the differences between people who said they were 'anxious' about crime and those who were 'fearful' of crime. These issues demonstrate the need to be as precise as possible when designing survey questions that deal with the emotional state of the respondent. Careful attention to the existing literature on fear of crime (see, for example, Hale, 1996) at the outset would have alerted Alan to these potential problems. An important lesson here is the necessity of locating research projects within the existing criminological literature on the subject that is to be investigated.

Example 2: public opinions of punishment

Dmitri was interested in issues around punishment, an area of criminology described as 'penology'. He was aware that, over recent years, increasing numbers of people have been imprisoned in his country, and that every new year represented a record in the numbers of those incarcerated. At the same time, from reading tabloid newspapers on his commute to university, he was aware of a high degree of public and media opinion that felt punishment was not 'tough enough'. His classes on penology deepened his interest in the subject and Dimitri was particularly drawn to Pratt's (2007) work on 'penal populism'. Here, Pratt examines the many and sometimes complex relationships between politics, societal attitudes and punishment. Rather than claiming that punitive policies are a 'political football' that politicians evoke whenever in need of a boost in their popularity, a number of complex and often structural processes shape the creation of such policies. For Pratt (2007: 12), a number of processes create a strong 'resonance between populist politicians and extra-establishment forces', such as victim advocacy groups, radio phone-ins and various pressure groups. Politicians have become increasingly reliant on such groups for electoral support and to provide an indicator of public opinion. Discourse around popular punitivism is also argued to tap into (often debatable) beliefs that the criminal justice system favours criminals over victims. For his research project, Dmitri decided to investigate some of these issues further. He elected to survey public opinion to establish whether people felt prisons were sufficiently punitive.

Acting on an instinct that people of different ages and different gender would feel differently about punishment, Dmitri decided to use a quota sample. To set this up, he used the internet to obtain national statistics on the breakdown of different demographic groups in his local area. He then divided the population into different categories of age, gender and ethnicity based on these statistics. Dmitri set up a quota sample to reflect these categories and aimed to interview 100 participants selected by virtue of their membership of these demographic groups. He then developed his questionnaire, paying particular attention to issues of punishment, potential alternatives to prison, and the length of sentences. He also elected to undertake a face-to-face survey in order to accurately ascertain people's demographic grouping.

When conducting his fieldwork, Dmitri realized that quota sampling was not as straightforward as it initially appeared. In particular, he faced problems over the fact that most participants fitted not just one category but three at the same time. For example, each participant has an ethnicity, age and gender. He was therefore unsure whether his sample was representative. This is because although he knew that 16 per cent of the population were over 65, he did not know how this group broke down in terms of ethnicity and gender. Another difficulty he faced related to his inability to speak to participants who were under 16. Indeed, from an ethical point of view, it is often seen as inappropriate to speak to people from this age group for student research projects, because of the more complex nature of issues such as consent and the impact of the researcher on their research participants. He decided that he would shift the focus of his research towards adult perspectives on punishment.

Face-to-face interviewing can be hard work. After several hours on the high street, Dmitri had only gathered 18 completed surveys. He elected to suspend his fieldwork at the end of the day, resolving to return to the high street the following week at the same time of day. This time, Dmitri encountered new difficulties. It was raining heavily and the street was sparsely populated. Those using the street were also not inclined to stop in the rain and answer Dmitri's questions. As his project deadline was looming, Dmitri opted to go to the high street whenever he could to complete his remaining quota of surveys. What initially seemed like a straightforward way of gaining a representative sample of the population generated a number of problems. Nevertheless, Dmitri persevered, collecting the remaining questionnaires, coding and inputting his data and analysing it in SPSS. In the final analysis, Dmitri generated some interesting and theoretically relevant findings, detailing high levels of public support for more punitive prison sentences and regimes. Dmitri then connected his analysis to Pratt's work – by providing new detail on public beliefs over the appropriateness of punishment, and in developing a specific geographical case study of this issue – in an attempt to give his dissertation greater theoretical depth. However, Dmitri's problems with sampling and time management meant he could not accurately generalize his findings across his neighbourhood and, as a result, his conclusions were weaker than he had hoped.

CONCLUSIONS

This chapter has introduced the key considerations and stages related to the design and commission of survey research. There are a number of elements that are important to recognize for survey-based research to succeed. In addition to clarifying the aims and overall method of the project, it is important to consider the entire research process from the outset. This consists of the following broad stages:

- Clarify the type of questionnaire to be used. Is a face-to-face, email, telephone or postal survey most suitable?
- Consider the type of questions used, such as open, closed, scale, categorical, opinion, fixed choice and so on, and how they map against the aims of the research.
- Take care when constructing the questions. Ensure that they are specific, easy to understand, not overly emotive, not 'leading', and do not have the potential to influence the respondent.
- From the outset, consider independent and dependent variables and what specifically needs to be measured.
- Adopt an appropriate and achievable sampling frame that best fits the aims and approaches of your research.
- Consider how the data will be analysed and presented. What strategies will be used? Which software packages may be most helpful?

In addition, an appreciation of the relative strengths and weaknesses of the survey method are key to understanding its correct deployment. Some of these features are listed in Table 5.5.

Table 5.5 Selected strengths and weaknesses of survey-based research

Strengths	Weaknesses
Clear articulation of data	Detailed prior understanding of the research environment is often required
Findings are often generalizable to a wider setting	Meticulous pre-fieldwork planning is needed
The availability of powerful software-based data analysis tools	Limited opportunities to shape the research during the data collection phase
Appeals to those subscribing to objectivist ontology	Potential for sampling bias, particularly in non-face-to-face surveys
Particularly suited to analyses of prevalence and correlation	Difficulties of ensuring consistency of coding
Visible methodologies. Observers can easily see how the data processes occurred	Difficulties of ensuring questions are understood the same way by all participants
The research is potentially replicable in different environments	Sometimes used for excessive and unrealistic claims to an objective 'truth'
	Sometimes used to falsely validate or overstate positivist assumptions
	The impossibility of neutrality

REVIEW QUESTIONS

- List five important considerations when starting to design a survey.

- Define the following words and concepts: dependent variable, independent variable, sampling, piloting, significance and correlation.

- Evaluate the strengths and weaknesses of using random sampling and convenience sampling to consider problem drug use in a local community.

- Critically assess the extent to which surveys can accurately capture the opinions and beliefs of the populations of entire countries.

FURTHER READING

If you were to read one book, our recommendation would be:

Chen, H. (ed.) (2012) *Approaches to Quantitative Research: A Guide for Dissertation Students*. Cork: Oak Tree Press.

In addition to this, we suggest you refer to:

Gorard, S. (2003) *Quantitative Methods in Social Science*. London: Continuum.

Rodeghier, M. (2010) *Surveys with Confidence: A Practical Guide to Survey Research Using SPSS*. Chicago: SPSS Publishing.

A classic criminological study using survey methods is:

Hirschi, T. (1969) *Causes of Delinquency*. Berkeley: University of California Press.

6

TALKING TO PEOPLE ABOUT CRIME: INTERVIEWS AND FOCUS GROUPS

OVERVIEW

The aim of this chapter is to:

- Describe the different types and main features of interviews used by criminologists.
- Demonstrate how interviews can be used to study offenders, victims, criminal justice professionals and members of the public.
- Enable you to design and administer a simple research study using interviews as the research method.
- Evaluate the relative strengths and weaknesses of interviews.

INTRODUCTION

The interview is a popular research method among criminologists and you, like many students, will often think about using interviews to do your own research. This chapter offers a brief summary of the main types of interview: structured, semi-structured, unstructured and focus group interviews. The type of data – quantitative or qualitative – that different types of interview are designed to gather is explained and also linked to the fact that interviews may include open-ended or closed questions. We then look at some examples of how interviewing strategies have been used by criminologists. The rest of the chapter uses examples to show you how these approaches to interviewing can be used in real, concrete research settings, looking at three anonymized student projects. The examples offered here consist of projects at different levels of study. Each research design is examined systematically as a process, beginning with a consideration of the appropriateness of interviews to achieving the aims and objectives of the project. This is followed by the considerations that need to be taken on board when developing an interview schedule, carrying out the interview, working with the data and writing up the research findings. As noted in Chapter 1, practical considerations, in particular resources and ethics, are key influences on the process of interviewing because they determine, to a point, what is actually feasible or doable. Finally, we present some of the pros and cons of using interviews in different types of project, where the issue of resources and the themes of representativeness, validity and reliability are central.

Some of the terminology and a number of the issues that arise in respect to interviews have already been discussed in Chapter 5, notably sampling and framing issues, in addition to considerations regarding the different types of questions that can be used.

RATIONALES AND APPROACHES

To find out why people commit crime, surely it makes sense to ask someone who has committed a crime? For example, only a burglar knows why they broke into their neighbour's home. Similarly, to gain an insight into the policing of organized crime, the most obvious person to ask is a police officer who has, for example, arrested the head of a notorious criminal family. This fits with the view that the only way of discovering anything about the lived realities of crime, deviance and social control is to go out there and talk to the people who *really know* all about it (Cromwell and Olson, 2003; Cromwell, 2010; Caless, 2011). So, on the surface, one of the reasons why you might use interviews is quite straightforward. Another attraction is the similarity between the interview and everyday talk, something that is natural for us as social beings. However, doing an interview involves far more than the equivalent of talking to our friends and family, and there are certain rules that you are obliged to observe. It is not simply a case of going out there to find people with whom we can talk about crime or crime control. A lot of careful planning needs to take place, for example in order to ensure comparability between different interviews.

In short, an **interview** is a face-to-face encounter between the researcher and a research subject or participant, that is, an individual being interviewed, in which the researcher asks questions, which may have been agreed in advance with the person being interviewed or, more typically, are previously unknown to the interviewee. Sometimes, in a large research project, the researchers conducting the interviews will not be the chief researchers, in which case, the interviewers need to be carefully briefed. There are also potentially difficult but not insurmountable issues of access you need to be aware of, especially if it is proposed to interview practitioners or officials.

These are the three main types of interviews – structured, semi-structured or unstructured. A fourth is the focus group, where a group of participants are 'interviewed' at the same time. Deciding which type (or combination of types) of interview you might use in a research project is closely related to the kind of data you are looking for. If you undertake a study in order to record quantitative information about the characteristics of either criminals or practitioners or measure their attitudes – for example 'counting' how many agree with a certain statement – a more structured approach would be advisable. Alternatively, you might want to delve into the deeper thoughts and feelings an individual has about their experiences of committing, controlling, being a victim of, or perceiving crime. Here, a more open-ended, unstructured approach, or the use of focus groups, would be called for, perhaps in combination with a more structured initial round of interviews. There is also some leeway in that 'open-ended' questions may be added to an otherwise 'closed' interview type.

Below, we define the different approaches to interviewing and show you how they relate to one another by using examples to say what they can do and what they can tell us.

Structured interviews

What makes an interview 'structured'? First, the questions are all specified and fixed in advance. Second, like surveys, there is a preference for 'closed' questions, which makes the answers easier to quantify (see Chapter 5). Because all the respondents are asked precisely the same questions, the answers can then be compared in a straightforward manner. These are examples of closed interview questions:

- How many offences have you committed in the last year?
- How many times have you been burgled in the past six months?
- Do you agree with the following statement: 'The death penalty is an effective deterrent'?

The answer to each of these questions will either be a single number or one of two words: 'yes' or 'no'; 'do not know' could possibly be a response. There is not much more you can do other than quantify the number of offences committed or experienced on one, two, three or more occasions. For the death penalty question, the interviewer will be able to count how many respondents said yes or no (see Chapter 5). Because this type of interview is so much like a questionnaire, we do not say much more about it.

Semi-structured interviews

The questions asked in semi-structured interviews will be less closed and more open-ended because here you are seeking more qualitative data. The questions you pose will give more scope for the interviewee to answer in a more discursive way, allowing them to express their own feelings and views. This type of interview may be chosen to gain an insight into the diverse experiences and perceptions individuals have of offending or victimization or, indeed, their role in crime control. Adapting the questions asked above, the line of enquiry could be:

- What made you commit the burglary?
- How did you react when you were a victim of crime for the first time?
- What, in your opinion, are the main arguments for using the death penalty?

Even if the interviewee is reluctant to talk, the responses to questions framed this way are likely to constitute more than one word. Also, with semi-structured interviews, the interviewer can probe and prompt participants by asking supplementary questions. If an interviewee said that when they first became a victim they felt angry, the interviewer could ask them to describe how they showed this anger to the people around them. In doing this, it is possible to flesh out our understanding of the subjective experiences of a crime victim. Although the respondent is given some freedom to talk about the issue, the interviewer still has control over the direction the interview goes. The 'semi-structured' aspect still allows us to compare the responses of different participants discussing the same question. Going beyond the semi-structured format, other researchers aim to allow the interviewee to speak more freely, asking questions that are even more open-ended in their design.

Unstructured interviews

Unstructured interviews would be appropriate for finding out as much as possible about the views someone holds about a criminological issue without overinfluencing the focus of the research and the content of the findings. The illustrative questions asked above would need rephrasing:

- Describe your experiences as a burglar.
- Tell me about your experiences as a victim of crime.
- What are your views about using the death penalty as a deterrent?

These open-ended questions give the person being interviewed the space to express their own often individual and highly personal thoughts. The questions are designed to avoid limiting the control the interviewer has over the outcomes of the interview. During the interview process, there are likely to be silences and some interviewees are more likely to talk at length than others. During the interview, themes will emerge, which can be followed up. Apart from the researcher asking the first question, the interviewee can significantly influence the agenda.

Focus groups

The focus group draws on elements of the above but, instead of interviewing an individual, a group of people are interviewed at the same time. In most cases, focus groups utilize a semi-structured interview schedule, making it possible to obtain the views of those participating in the discussion. Rather than prioritizing the views of an individual, the focus group asks relatively open-ended questions so each member has an opportunity to express their views. The qualitative data generated as part of the discussion is likely to show some common, unifying themes, as well as drawing attention to differences of opinion. The three themes explored by the above questions would be rephrased depending on who was included in the focus group:

- The question, 'What made you commit the burglary?' could be addressed to a group of 10 prisoners in a prison classroom.
- A group of 12 elderly residents living in a high crime area could be asked: 'How did you react when you were a victim of crime for the first time?'
- A group of 6 university students are brought together in the researcher's office and asked: 'What, in your opinion, are the main arguments for using the death penalty as an effective deterrent?'

USING INTERVIEWS IN ACADEMIC RESEARCH

You will now be aware that interviews can focus on questions relating to offenders and those who attempt to control crime and its effects. Winlow and Hall (2006) interviewed offenders to understand the motivations behind their behaviour. This research is consistent with a grounded theory approach, allowing the respondents to speak freely and without undue direction from the interviewers, and emphasizes the salience of cultural and social influences on behaviour. If you look at Farrington et al.'s (2006) work, a longitudinal study established in 1961 by the Cambridge Institute of Criminology, you will see a different account. It includes interviews with a group of young males born in a socially deprived urban area between 1951 and 1954. Unlike the previous example, this study lends support to theoretical work that attributes offending behaviour to psychological factors such as individual temperament and individual social learning. Thus, individual character and immediate environmental circumstances are favoured as explanations instead of external forces. Offenders are perhaps the most obvious group you might want to talk to but what about people who are employed to deal with offending behaviour?

In Reiner's (1991) work, we find a classic study of police chief constables, which demonstrates the strength and usefulness of interview techniques in researching criminal justice professionals. Reiner was interested in the politics of policing, in particular chief constables at the top of police organizations who are of central importance as they constitute a small but powerful elite group who play a major role in determining the directions taken by police policy and practice. To research this target population, Reiner wrote to the 43 chief constables in England and Wales asking for their approval to be interviewed about their background, careers and philosophies and succeeded in interviewing 40 participants, thus ensuring a representative sample (see Chapter 5). In seeking to generate an 'appreciative account' relating a 'faithful flavour of how chief constables do see the world, and the variations which exist among them' (Reiner, 1991: 45, 51), a blend of interviewing strategies was pursued. Key here was the importance of allowing participants to express their views via their own frames of reference, but giving the data from each respondent enough structure to allow their responses to be compared to other participants. Thus, semi-structured interviews were used extensively to generate a set of responses that are easier to interpret than the outputs of an unstructured interview, yet at the same time, while the interviewee is not given absolute freedom, they are free to express their own perceptions. The interview schedule was therefore standardized so that all officers would be asked exactly the same questions in the same order.

The interview schedule comprised eight thematic sections and a total of 67 questions covering themes such as the police function, crime control, public order policing, management of the police, the external environment and the social perspectives held by officers. Some of the early questions were designed to gather quantitative data, for example length of service, previous employment. The remaining questions were qualitative, encouraging respondents to express themselves freely, although some participants were suspicious about Reiner's motives, as a potential critic of the police. From time to time, if an officer did not say much, the interviewer used some probes, an effective strategy in maintaining the momentum of an interview or encouraging the participant to expand on an area of emerging interest. In some cases, officers were reluctant to say much about politically sensitive and controversial issues, and did not talk freely. On other occasions, they unintentionally revealed worrying attitudes towards race relations. To adhere to ethical principles, Reiner (1991) guaranteed that none of the quotations used in the final study would be attributable to individual officers, thus guarding their anonymity, which proved important because several officers were worried about the potential adverse publicity attached to sensitive issues. By allowing the researcher to gather data that may have been previously denied to them, these guarantees of anonymity serve a practical as well as an ethical purpose.

The interviews lasted between one and a half and two hours, producing a lot of data. The quantitative data, that is, prevalence of opinions, was analysed through the use of SPSS (see Chapter 5). The qualitative data was coded, and when Reiner read the interview transcripts, a number of categories emerged, including some that were not included in the interview schedule. These categories were jotted down on index cards and followed up in the analyses. This generation of new themes during qualitative research is a common event (see Chapter 2) and, by being attentive to and able to capitalize on their emergence, researchers are often rewarded with rich and unanticipated research findings.

Reiner's aim was to gain an insight into the understandings and perceptions held by senior police officers and interpret this material with reference to a number of classic sociological texts, not least the theoretical work of Max Weber (1964). Here, Reiner drew on Weber's research into the behaviour of elite groups and the view that the best way of understanding the 'action frame of reference' of police officers, for example how they think and act, is to talk to or interview them. Because elite groups are in positions of power and authority, they are often quite guarded about what they say in order that their status is maintained and not threatened. Put simply, chief officers are not likely to always say what they really mean, but the interview is the best tool we have to attempt this.

USING INTERVIEWS IN RESEARCH PROJECTS

In order to provide a real sense of what is involved in interviewing, here we offer three examples of the types of research project where interviews could quite feasibly be applied by you. The three examples relate to different aspects of the criminal justice system: policing and discrimination; the experiences of women in prison; and sentencing philosophies. Each example is partly based on actual student research projects where interviews have been employed in practice. The anonymized examples are intended to show you both good practice as well as areas where practice could be improved. You are not encouraged to replicate or repeat these studies because you should be aspiring to do a better and original piece of work. The examples serve to focus attention, in a concrete way, on the sort of issues you need to consider when planning and actually conducting an interview. In line with the other chapters in Part 2, each illustration describes the background context of the research and explains why interviewing was considered to be the most suitable research method.

There are two aims in providing these examples:

1. To sketch out how interviews would fit into the research process as a whole, including research design, sampling, ethical considerations, data collection and analysis (see Chapter 1).
2. To show you some of the issues that need to be thought about before deciding to use each of the main types of interview.

Example 1: using interviews to explore the experiences of minority ethnic police officers

Chandani is a student interested in working on a project that focuses on diversity and discrimination within the police, exploring different theoretical models of racism. The problem of police racism has been well documented by criminologists, especially the differential policing experienced by minority ethnic communities in terms of overpolicing suspects and underpolicing victims (Rowe, 2004; Hall et al., 2009). However, Chandani's interest is in the discrimination possibility experienced by minority ethnic police officers from their colleagues. Her choice of topic has been influenced by two factors, one academic, the other personal. First, she is aware of other research studies showing that black and minority ethnic (BME) communities have negative experiences when it comes to their contact with police (Bowling et al., 2008). She also had a general awareness that some research states that these groups are overpoliced on the streets as suspects but underpoliced as victims. This has been attributed to two theoretical explanations:

1. the racist attitudes of individual police officers
2. institutional racism and the workings of organizations such as the police (Webster, 2007).

Chandani wanted to revisit this debate. Second, during her studies, Chandani gained work experience as a police officer and was struck by the fact that she had not experienced any racist attitudes or behaviour from any of her colleagues, although she was aware that a relative, a serving officer in a large police force, had encountered some racism. So she wanted to put together these two elements: studies of policing discrimination towards the public and her own – and her relative's – different experiences of working for the police.

Her literature review (see Chapters 1 and 8) sought to fill the gap. Chandani identified three prominent themes concerning BME police officers: 'recruitment' (joining the police), 'retention' (staying in the organization) and 'promotion' (getting to the top positions). Quite early on in the research process, she formulated a research topic that was reasonably focused, calling her project: 'A study of the opportunities and barriers facing BME police officers'.

Planning and design

Having decided on the focus of her research project, Chandani met her supervisor to consider the most fitting method for her own research. How did she make this decision? Governments across the world have published much statistical data about the number of BME police officers and their career paths and, although an analysis of this quantitative data could reveal distinctive patterns,

Chandani felt that this did not really provide enough detail on the experiences of officers. She wanted to dig deeper to explore this issue from a more qualitative perspective, in particular by interviewing serving BME police officers about their experiences. Her supervisor suggested that Holdaway's work (2009) provided some guidance on the type of questions that could be asked of BME officers in a qualitative study. In light of these recommendations, Chandani decided that her study would combine structured and semi-structured components in a single interview schedule. For her study, she decided to standardize the interviews so that all respondents were asked identical questions in the same format and sequence, similar to the approach adopted by Reiner (1991) above.

As part of the quantitative data generated by the structured section of the interview, Chandani thought it useful to record some basic information about her interviewees, asking them classification questions about their age, gender, ethnic background, length of service and rank (see Chapter 5). These categorical variables would then be complemented and analysed in relation to the qualitative data gleaned from the semi-structured part of the interview. To meet her research aims, these qualitative questions were designed to gain an insight into interviewees' perceptions about the opportunities and barriers they experienced during the recruitment process; whether they had experienced discrimination within their job; if they had ever considered leaving the job and why; and if they had been given a fair chance to follow a career path that matched their ambitions on joining and after being in the organization for a few years. She also included some questions to explore participants' awareness of key explanations of discrimination, drawing a distinction between 'institutional' and 'attitudinal' discrimination on the grounds of race and ethnicity and to see if they thought either of these had had any impact on their experiences of working in the police service (see Appendix 2 for a copy of the interview schedule).

The interview schedule was piloted (tried out) by asking her supervisor to comment on it and she also asked an ex-police officer she knew, to see if he thought it would make sense to a police officer. He suggested that the wording of some of the questions was ambiguous and that there were a few typos.

While Chandani had been working on her literature review and research design, she started to think about whom she could interview. As a sole researcher, with no more than six months to complete the project, and lacking the status and expertise of the academics whose work she was reading, Chandani felt daunted. Her supervisor explained that, although it was unlikely her research would produce any startlingly new findings, and would in any case be limited in terms of evidence, it would still be possible to undertake an interesting exploratory study. During this conversation, the issue of sampling was raised.

In a small study, it would not be possible to interview a number that was in any way representative of the research population. It might be possible to interview several officers and ensure that the proportion of officers from a particular BME group in the sample mirrored that found in the police service as whole. Chandani's supervisor remarked that she was perhaps 'trying to run before she could walk', because she was assuming that she could gain access to police officers. This can never be taken for granted but Chandani was more optimistic in this regard because of her work experience; and her relative was a serving police officer, albeit in another constabulary.

The approach to sampling taken by Chandani is called 'convenience sampling' (see Chapter 5), where she is using her workplace and a relative to help her enter the field. In the constabulary where Chandani worked, she had got to know as many as 15 officers from various BME groups (8 Asian, 7 black) of varying ranks. All of them said that they were more than happy to be interviewed, subject to having enough time at the end of their shift. It was at this stage that Chandani realized it was not possible to simply go into work one day and interview these officers; she would need advance permission from her participants' line manager. She wrote a letter to this person outlining the aims and objectives of the project, adding that her findings might benefit the organization. Her relative, the police constable employed by another constabulary, also consented to her request for an informal interview. He added that some of his colleagues, up to four other BME police officers, would help out by agreeing to be interviewed in an informal setting, thus avoiding having to seek permission from their superiors. Increasing the number of respondents in this way is called 'snowball sampling' (see Chapter 5).

The ethical considerations encountered by all researchers about to start an empirical study are identical and Chandani's planned research is no exception. Before she could write to her participants' line manager, she needed to gain ethical approval from the university's research ethics committee. She completed all the relevant sections on the ethical approval form (see Chapter 1 for a reminder) and submitted it to the committee in a rush because her supervisor had planned a period of leave. Despite being generally well constructed, her application was initially rejected because she had committed a basic yet damaging error. In identifying her potential respondents by name and rank, and in some cases revealing personal information such as mobile telephone numbers, she had failed to preserve the anonymity of her respondents and the confidentiality of her data. In particular, she said nothing about the storage of her interview data. This oversight was especially serious because the issue of discrimination is politically sensitive and to talk about this, especially when personal opinions are offered, can be harmful for the organization and the individuals involved.

There was also no information about where the interviews would be held, raising a concern about Chandani's personal safety. By addressing these issues, Chandani was able to gain ethical approval for the project.

Conducting the fieldwork and analysing the data

Chandani was fortunate because the 15 officers from her own constabulary not only agreed to be interviewed but were also officially permitted to do so by their line manager. Her relative also arranged a date on which he would be interviewed as well as dates for a further four interviews with his colleagues. Each interview lasted between 20 and 75 minutes, with the average being 40 minutes, culminating in around 17 hours of interview data. Chandani had thought about recording and transcribing the interviews before realizing how long transcription would take. More crucially, she decided against using audio recording equipment because of the sensitive and political nature of the subject matter, thus avoiding compromising any of the interviewees. Police officers must record interviews with suspects and are alert to the potentially incriminatory nature of interview data. Instead, she made handwritten notes, which would later be typed up on her home PC and stored in a secure internet-based data storage facility. Due to the shift patterns of the officers at the station where Chandani worked, the interviews were spread over three weeks. For the other interviews, she had to make a 150-mile round trip by train to the police force where her relative worked, which proved expensive and had be self-financed because there was no way of claiming expenses through the university, and she also stayed overnight with her relative, resulting in her missing two lectures.

Although the interviewing was time-consuming and more expensive than envisaged, the interview process ran smoothly in all bar one case. In part, the interviews were straightforward because Chandani knew all the officers from her workplace as well as her relative. It turned out she had fleetingly met the other four officers at a social event so they were acquaintances and not complete strangers. Because she worked for the police, she was able to present herself to the interviewees in a favourable light and could create a 'rapport' without causing suspicion. The participants accepted the researcher so they let her into their world to show her how they thought and felt about their occupation. If the researcher had not had a police background, the relationship between the researcher and researched would certainly be different.

We hinted that one interview did not go too well. All the interviewees talked openly about their experiences as police officers and all seemed quite knowledgeable about the topic of discrimination, although their respective thoughts and feelings on the subject were mixed. One of the interviewees from her relative's constabulary told a story about a senior officer in his force who made openly derogatory and racist remarks to a colleague. The senior officer (a sergeant) threatened both the recipient of the verbal assault and the witness that they should not report this to a senior officer and if they did, 'their lives would be made very difficult'. The interviewee became quite angry and at one stage started to shake and clench his fists. Chandani was not naive and had been prepared for stories about discrimination but not of this nature, nor was she adequately prepared for such a reaction from an interviewee. She used some of the people management skills she used in her role to calm him down, which proved successful, and the officer also helped to compose himself. The interview was terminated at this stage. This is ethically troubling and the matter would have been much more serious if the interviewee was from the same constabulary. The informal nature of this interview also raises questions because, if a formal request had been made to these officers in the other force, it might have been turned down.

Chandani split the interview data into two parts. The structured data (ordinal, interval, nominal) was presented in a table (see Chapter 5). As well as identifying the BME group to which the respondents belonged, it showed that none of the interviewees had served more than 15 years and most had been police officers for less than 5 years. However, the sample was too small to make any claims about statistical significance or representativeness in relation to the general population of BME police officers. Nonetheless, it provided useful, contextual information and enabled deeper analysis of the qualitative data that followed; for example, making judgements on whether length of service may also explain the issues related to career progression. Chandani was familiar with the philosophical and methodological arguments for not relying exclusively on structured interviews. By adopting a more interpretivist perspective, she argued in the methodology chapter of her report that structured interview data channels the lived experience of the respondents into potentially overly rigid and narrow categories created by researchers.

Compared to the numerical information, the data produced by the semistructured part of the interviews was more difficult to manage, owing to the sheer volume of written notes. When it came to typing them up some time after they had been taken, there were some stumbling blocks. There were pages and pages of notes, some of them illegible, and Chandani had created her own idiosyncratic method of shorthand, which seemed meaningful at the time but a month later sometimes proved unintelligible. After writing up the notes for each interview, Chandani structured her analysis by looking at what each interviewee had said in response to each question. She summarized the main points to identify thematic patterns and the extent to which the accounts either shared common features or diverged noticeably. Perhaps surprisingly, with the exception of the interviewee who became upset in interview, the sample all said that they were aware of discrimination before joining the force, this did not put them off the job, and they had all been exposed to some form of verbal discrimination. None of these experiences had prompted them to seriously consider leaving the police and, on the whole, they did not feel that their ethnicity/race would hinder them in developing their career and seeking promotion. Compared to the existing research, Chandani's sample seemed to be suffering fewer hardships (Foster et al., 2005; Holdaway, 2009). She reflected on her interview schedule and wondered if the questions were leading – possibly because her own experience of working for the police had been positive – and had resulted in a biased response. For example, a common criticism of interviews in general concerns the so-called **interviewer effect** or reactivity. This refers to those occasions when the interviewer influences the research environment. By asking a leading question, an interviewee can be steered in a particular direction to say something they do not actually believe. This is potentially theoretically significant because, on the face of it, the results of these interviews showed that experiencing verbal discrimination does not necessarily lead to officers resigning from the force. Chandani decided to err on the side of caution by pointing out that, while this interpretation of the results was valid, the small size of the study and the nature of the sample (convenience) meant that more robust research would be needed to explore this argument in more depth and detail. Her findings were in no way representative of and generalizable to the general population of BME police officers. As a piece of exploratory research, many of the questions asked in her interview could be adapted and used again in a different context or a larger study.

Example 2: interviewing women in prison

Stella was interested in becoming a prison officer and, during her final year of studies, she decided to apply to join the prison service. To support her application, Stella decided that it would be a good idea if her research project focused on an aspect of imprisonment. The topic she selected was 'women in prison', as she felt this would give her a sound basis to draw on if she succeeded in being called for a job interview. Earlier on in the course, Stella had studied penology, finding out that, although fewer women are given custodial sentences compared to men, a disproportionately higher number of women were incarcerated from the mid-1990s onwards. Doing time (Matthews, 2009) in prison is tough for anyone, but as feminist theorists and researchers have demonstrated (see Chapter 3), women seem to have more negative experiences than their male counterparts, with their physical and psychological health being especially bad (Carlen, 2002; Silvestri and Crowther-Dowey, 2008). Stella set her sights on gaining access to a small number of women currently serving a prison sentence to talk to them about their experiences. What happened?

Planning and design

Initially, Stella's aim was to conduct some qualitative semi-structured interviews with a small number of female prisoners or ex-prisoners. Her preference was to talk to women currently in prison because she wanted to speak to women with an immediate experience of living in this setting rather than talking to women drawing on their memories. Memory is always subject to distortion. She felt that by using relatively open but standardized questions, it would be possible to glean some insight into the lived realities of being locked up instead of relying on academic or journalistic accounts of female prisoners' lives. By meeting women experiencing imprisonment first hand and in the present, Stella wanted to enter the participants' mindset. She wanted to discover what these women thought about prison in their own language. However, she did want her questions to be focused as well as giving some scope for flexibility and attention to detail so the respondent could talk about those issues important to them, while making sure that there was not too much drift away from issues of immediate relevance to the research project. Writers such as Audrey Peckham (1985) have published personal accounts of what prison is like for the female offender and this provided Stella with some thoughts on how to structure her exploratory questions. In short, she aspired to explore a range of issues drawn from the academic literature and also more personal accounts but to update knowledge and public understanding about this group of prisoners. In her draft interview schedule, there were four key themes: health; prison conditions; family life; and education, training and employment.

If Stella is to remain focused on current prisoners, then the relevant population for this research is relatively small. It would be straightforward for Stella to identify all the female-only prisons near where she lived, but getting to speak to members of this population is much more difficult and she imagined that she would have to make a formal application to the prison service/department. However, the research ethics committee at the university rejected the proposal, partly because it was contrary to research ethics guidelines and also not feasible. Most universities would not be willing to sanction students speaking directly to offenders because of the risk of being told something about a criminal act that could put the student in a compromising position. Also, it was deemed that some offenders, while being only a small number, may pose a risk to the personal safety of a researcher. As for feasibility, it also must be noted that many prisons no longer support undergraduate research.

Stella discussed these obstacles with her supervisor, who did not want to dissuade her from doing an interesting and important piece of work. Stella had in fact prepared a plan B: to interview a female family member, Jane, who had served several custodial sentences for acquisitive and violent offences. She first went to prison when she turned 18. Now 22 years old, she had been released from her most recent sentence six months before Stella thought about interviewing her. During her last spell in prison, Jane had given birth to a baby girl and, on release, pledged to stay out of trouble. She was living in a women's refuge, keeping herself and her child away from her violent stepfather. Jane agreed to be interviewed for the purpose of this research and Stella resubmitted her ethical approval form. The research ethics committee decided that plan B was, in principle, acceptable. Stella reviewed her methodology so her research aims and objectives were more feasible or achievable and ethical. Stella also explicitly referred to an alternative theoretical approach.

Due to the nature of the subject matter and what Stella already knew about the psychological and physical ill health experienced by female prisoners, Stella reflected on an important issue, the risk that talking about her experiences might cause Jane, the research participant, psychological harm. She reflected on this in her ethical statement, writing that:

> Little is known about the experiences of prisoners, who are often denied a voice in describing their personal experiences so it is important that academics are able to appreciate the lived reality of prison life. It is possible that participants may become upset and even distressed when talking about their prison experience. However, it will be ensured that the participant is aware that she can stop the interview at any time and does not have to give any justifications/reasons to do so.

Although the research ethics committee recognized that the interview could prove distressing, the familial relationship between interviewer and interviewee and the provision of a consent form with a right to withdraw assuaged its concerns. At the time of the interview, Jane signed a consent form and, despite expressing some initial concerns about how the data was to be used, Stella pacified her fears by explaining that the data would be stored in a secure place, destroyed after it was analysed and that Jane's identity would never be known to anyone except the researcher. The assessors of Stella's submitted work would read the data but all identifying features linking the data to Jane would be anonymized or deleted.

While Stella was reading around the research topic, she came across an approach known as 'grounded theory' (Glaser and Strauss, 1967) (see Chapter 2), which resonated with her aspiration to see the world through the eyes of a female prisoner and made her think that even her small piece of research could be part of a wider project of generating important theoretical insights. The basic assumptions underlying grounded theory are that rather than simply confirming and challenging what we can learn from the existing literature, the data gathered through empirical research can generate theory. Unlike scientific/positivist models of research, there is no attempt to formulate and test a hypothesis; she thought this meant the data would speak for itself. Stella did not adopt grounded theory fully, because the general themes outlined in her original plan were retained, broad enough to encourage the interviewee to have free rein to talk about her own experiences and her perceptions of how her fellow prisoners experienced prison life, yet retaining some guidelines and parameters. The discussion was therefore steered in the direction of health, prison conditions, family life, education, training and employment but these topics were not introduced via a standardized interview schedule. Now that Stella was relying on just one interview and because she wanted to glean as much data as possible, she decided to use an unstructured interview instead of a semi-structured interview.

The unstructured interview is, for many qualitative researchers, an 'ideal' research method as, in a sense, it gives them licence to ask a person anything they wish and there are no immediate constraints or restrictions on what can be said. This style of interviewing is often described as 'naturalistic'. Unlike other methods, especially quantitative ones, the researcher makes no attempt to control the research environment and they ensure, as far as is practicable and ethical, that the interviewee is in their own world and that what they have to say should not be unduly influenced by the researcher. In ideal circumstances, an unstructured interview can be viewed as autobiographical, inasmuch as the respondent can tell their own story at a particular moment, producing a narrative that is as detailed as the interviewee desires it to be.

Stella was also conscious of power relations in the research process and even though Jane has a familial bond with her, Stella found herself in a relatively privileged social position due her educational background. This was another reason why Stella tried her best not to impose herself on the research process by keeping quiet and allowing Jane, her interviewee, to do all the talking.

Conducting the fieldwork and analysing the data

Like Chandani, Stella also built up a rapport with her interviewee, probably made easier due to the blood relationship between them. The interview took place at the sheltered accommodation where Jane lived and another relative looked after her small child so she could concentrate on the interview and not be distracted. Stella borrowed audio recording equipment from the university so the interview could be recorded. Jane opened up during the interview and spoke freely for almost two hours. When Stella played back the recording, she calculated that she herself probably spoke for no more than five minutes in total.

At certain moments during the interview, Jane became upset when she relived some of the things she had done and the terrible things that had happened to her. Although tears were shed in the interview, at the end of the exercise and during the debriefing – when the participant is asked if they need any support or have any questions to ask following the interview – Jane said that the experience had 'hurt' but that it was a 'good thing'.

Stella transcribed the interview, which proved to be a time-consuming process, taking over a day to finish. Earlier on, we said that Stella had taken an interest in grounded theory, although when she read more widely about this approach, she soon lost interest because of the technical issues surrounding the coding of the data. Given the limited time available for this activity, Stella decided to focus the analysis on her four initial themes. So, she spent three days reading the interview transcript, looking for themes that emerged from the page, and making notes summarizing what she considered to be the key points, paying particular attention to the issues of health, prison conditions, family life, education, training and employment. It soon became apparent that what Jane was saying, although expressed in her own words, had been said before and everything she said confirmed the existing research data (Carlen and Worrall, 2004; Corston, 2007). Women in prison tend to:

- be vulnerable
- have poor mental and psychological health
- come from poor and deprived backgrounds
- be dependent on alcohol and illegal drugs
- be in relationships with violent partners/families
- be more prone to self-harm and suicide.

Sadly, Jane was saying nothing new in her graphic and shocking descriptions of her own and other prisoners' experiences of being incarcerated. The research, which focused on an individual case, confirmed earlier findings from academic studies that identified experiences common to the wider population of women prisoners. Stella had gained the invaluable experience of planning her research and hands-on experience of doing the interview and analysing the data.

Example 3: using a focus group to study student perceptions of the death penalty

Jordan has an interest in capital punishment (the death penalty), especially the fact that, despite sharing similar cultural and political values, some states in the USA continue to pass the death sentence, but this does not occur in the UK and Australia (Pratt, 2002; Hood and Hoyle, 2008). A popular theme explored in studies of this topic are the arguments for and against its use as a punishment and Jordan revisited this debate but he was also interested in pedagogic or educational issues surrounding the topic. Jordan was required to produce a research proposal based on the following working title: 'An assessment of student attitudes and beliefs to the death penalty'. When searching the death penalty literature, Jordan was inspired by an article written by Falco and Freiberger (2011), who argue that most survey research into this topic adopts quantitative approaches. Jordan wanted to gather some data of this kind but agreed with Falco and Freiberger that the use of focus groups would allow the collection of qualitative data, which would give an insight into the subjective beliefs held by participants. So, instead of just finding out if someone agrees with a statement about the death penalty, they are also asked to outline their reasons behind their answer.

Planning and design

The interview schedule Jordan designed (see Appendix 3) for his focus group included mainly structured questions requiring a quantifiable response, which was followed with a prompt – for example give reasons for your answer, can you tell me a bit more about this and so on – for most questions, encouraging further discussion and the capture of qualitative data. His main objective changed slightly to find out not only what students knew about the death penalty, but also whether there were significant differences between the type of knowledge held by criminology students on his course and those studying different academic disciplines. He selected engineering students as the comparison group, as he shared a flat with several engineering students. In other words, he was thinking about sampling and instead of involving all students at the university, he choose two subgroups within the student population. This is a form of convenience sampling. Thus, he accepted that his data would not be representative of the student population but would be indicative of the views held by two distinct populations, that is, students on two separate degree programmes in their final year of study. There were 20 students on each programme and Jordan proposed setting up two focus groups, one for the criminologists and another for the engineers. The interview schedule used in the focus groups was designed in such a way that it would take no more than one hour to complete.

There were few ethical dilemmas because before asking any questions, Jordan intended to explain the aims and objectives of the research to the participants, informing them that they would need to sign a consent form and that all the information they gave would be anonymized. Second, even though capital punishment is a sensitive and moral issue arousing strong feelings, none of the students had any first-hand knowledge or immediate experience of it and so they would not be psychologically harmed.

Conducting the fieldwork and analysing the data

Jordan did not anticipate that any problems would arise in conducting the focus group but when his proposal was marked, he was penalized for not considering the following issues:

- Jordan had assumed that all the students would agree to take part in the focus group but there was no reason why they should commit their time to the project. There was no guarantee that anyone would help him out, especially the engineering students. In other words, there were no incentives.
- Related to the previous point, he had no contingency plan to find an alternative sample population, that is, other groups of students, if he could not find any willing participants.
- Jordan had not thought about the resources involved, such as when and where the focus group would take place. He did not specify where the interviews would take place, so there was no way of knowing if everyone would be free at the same time. He did not have the authority to book a room for the focus groups as he had not yet obtained a supporting statement from his lecturer, nor had he considered if there was an available room big enough for the focus groups to meet.
- Jordan had no training or prior experience in leading and managing a focus group.

Unfortunately, Jordan's proposal also made no attempt to explain how the data would be collected, for example would it be audio recorded or written down in the form of notes, nor did he explain how the two sets of data would be analysed. Also, what connections would he make between the qualitative and quantitative data?

If Jordan had completed the research, he could have analysed the data thematically, organizing the process in relation to the questions asked in the focus groups. In doing so, he might have hypothesized that while criminology students were more likely to provide greater *detail* in their arguments for and against the death penalty, there would be little difference in the *types* of issues raised or levels of support for the measure. Engineering students would be just as likely to cite issues of morality, costs and practicalities in their assessment of the death penalty as criminology students and they might articulate similar levels of support and opposition to it.

CONCLUSIONS

This chapter has introduced the interview, a particularly popular method among criminologists with an interest in qualitative data and analysis. We have demonstrated the different designs and strategies and their application in the context of basic criminological research. The interview is a favourite method for many because it presents a chance to speak to people who have knowledge and experience of many criminological issues. Many might opt to use interviews for these reasons and also because it appears to be a straightforward way of accessing data. The examples outlined above show something very different: using interviews involves a lot of planning and confronting many obstacles. We close this chapter by summarizing a number of key points that you should be aware of in principle (that is, the simple task of writing an imaginary proposal) and in practice (that is, if you physically do the research yourself):

1. Designing and conducting interviews is part of a process with a clear beginning, middle and end.
2. You must be confident that one of the four kinds of interview is the most appropriate for answering your research question and that the method used will facilitate the collection of the data wanted to answer this question. Think here about epistemology, ontology and ethics (see Chapter 2). To obtain reliable information about how *many* people are stopped and searched on the streets or the *number* of people in the prison population convicted of burglary, choose an alternative method. Of course, you can mix or triangulate interviews with another method, which is a legitimate research strategy (see Chapter 9).
3. While the idea of interviewing an offender, victim or criminal justice worker is exciting and challenging, steps must be taken to ensure that access and ethical approval are attained, and that the time and money required to complete the research are available. Professional researchers often work as part of a team and they may not actually do any interviews themselves. Their involvement is often restricted to project management, data analysis and writing up. By contrast, you might do all these things, although on a smaller scale.
4. Be reflexive about personal values and politics because they may influence your selection of a research topic, your orientation towards it and the kinds of questions you ask in an interview.
5. The idea of preparing an interview is simple but writing a decent interview schedule takes time and patience. Always work closely with your supervisors and seek their constructive criticism in order to make sure that the wording, phrasing and structure are right and the questions address the aims of the research. It is advisable to look at published work in an area related to the topic for pointers and suggestions on how to improve the schedule.
6. It is unlikely that the interviews you undertake for small and basic projects will produce findings that are going to be representative of a particular organization or group of people. As long as you are aware of the rationale for selecting an approach to sampling and its inherent limitations, you are unlikely to be marked down by an assessor. Likewise, the reliability and validity of the

research findings and analysis may not measure up to the standards set by the large-scale projects published by academics and government departments. It is recommended you refrain from overselling the significance and generalizability of your research findings.

As a researcher, all these points, and others, should be considered. Although additional barriers may be faced compared to those confronting an established criminologist, there are still reasons to be positive and, in the process, you too can develop valuable and rewarding research projects. Table 6.1 provides a brief summary of the strengths and weaknesses of interviews and focus groups.

Table 6.1 Selected strengths and weaknesses of interviews and focus groups

Strengths	Weaknesses/challenges
Semi-structured and unstructured interviews and focus groups provide detailed qualitative data	There is no guarantee that interviewees are telling the truth in their responses
They enable you to gain an insight into how social actors perceive the subject matter being explored	Gaining access to interviewees is not easy due to the nature of the subject matter
New themes that were not anticipated by the researcher may come to light	There is the issue of interviewer effect or reactivity, especially when leading questions are asked
They highlight important themes that may not be apparent before the fieldwork commences	The interviewer may have more power than the interviewee, especially when talking to vulnerable groups, such as some offenders
The interviewee is an active participant who can shape the outcome of the interview	Limited possibilities for replicating findings
Apart from unstructured interviews, initial questions tend to be standardized and can be replicated, meaning there is enhanced reliability and validity	Interviewing is a skill and training is advisable
Interview notes/transcripts can be verified by the interviewee	Asking questions of a personally and politically sensitive nature can harm a participant, although research ethics committees can prevent these problems occurring
	Transcribing the recording of an interview or typing up notes can be time-consuming

REVIEW QUESTIONS

- Discuss the main reasons why you might want to use interviews to study crime and its control.

- Describe the main features of structured interviews, semi-structured interviews, unstructured interviews, and focus groups.

- Evaluate the strengths and weaknesses of using interviews in general to explore offending behaviour and the work of criminal justice professionals.

- Critically assess the claim that the research process is 'iterative' (see Introduction and Chapter 1) with reference to the application of interviews in crime research.

FURTHER READING

If you were to read one book, our recommendation would be:

> King, N. and Horrocks, C. (2010) *Interviews in Qualitative Research*. London: Sage.

In addition to this, we suggest you refer to:

> Brookman, F., Noakes, L. and Wincup, E. (1999) *Qualitative Research in Criminology*. Aldershot: Ashgate.

> Silverman, D. (2006) *Interpreting Qualitative Data*. London: Sage.

A classic criminological study using interviews is:

> Hobbs, D. (1995) *Bad Business*. Oxford: Oxford University Press.

CHAPTER

7

WATCHING CRIME AND CRIME CONTROL: ETHNOGRAPHIC AND OBSERVATIONAL RESEARCH

OVERVIEW

The aim of this chapter is to:

- Outline qualitative and quantitative approaches to observing social actors in their natural environments.

- Consider the strengths and weaknesses of these approaches and how they may be applied to criminological research.

- Describe the main features and practical application of observational research, including ethnographic approaches.

INTRODUCTION

This chapter explores the main features of ethnographic and observational research techniques that you can use in criminological research. We look at the origins, rationale, types and criminological applications of ethnographic and observational research. The two main approaches – quantitative/structured observation and qualitative ethnography – are considered here, along with their applications in academic research. These applications are explored in a little more detail than in other chapters to illustrate the differences between quantitative and qualitative approaches to observational research. We then examine the process of conducting ethnographic and observational research in more detail, using two examples of hypothetical projects using structured observation and qualitative ethnography. We conclude by weighing up the pros and cons of adopting these methodologies.

RATIONALES AND APPROACHES

Originating from anthropological fieldwork, observational and ethnographic research is an important tradition across the social sciences and adds an immense contribution to our knowledge and understanding of many criminological issues. Despite this, you might have already observed that these methods are rarely used in state-funded criminological research where political ideologies and values are influential. Why is this? Perhaps the main reason is that ethnographic research tends to yield data that is less structured than other methods, such as surveys or semi-structured interviews (see Chapters 5 and 6). Also, ethnographic research, while generating a rich and detailed picture, usually takes longer, in many cases even years, and often cannot be generalized to other contexts. When crime and criminal justice policy decisions are increasingly scrutinized on measurable performance and short-term impacts, the lack of easily accessible 'results' that can be translated into immediate practical policy is often seen as unattractive, especially to state-funded researchers.

Given these apparent difficulties, what is it that makes ethnography such an attractive method? In brief, no other method can get you as close to the subject matter – and the people involved. For research into closed societies, such as criminal networks, ethnography offers us rich, detailed insights that often challenge commonsense *and* theoretically informed accounts that are merely based on assumptions about how people think and feel. More distanced, quantitative research has an important role, yet it cannot easily access the worlds and experiences of hard-to-reach groups that much groundbreaking ethnographic/observational qualitative work has entered. Some examples of ethnographic criminological work include studies of Chicago's gangs (Thrasher, 1927), rightwing extremism (Fielding, 1982), organized crime and policing (Hobbs, 1988), male violence (Winlow, 2001), youth cultures (Gunter, 2009) and terrorists (Hassan, 2001). A rich understanding of the 'enacted environment' (Hobbs, 1988: 14) – via the researchers' immersion in it – is the key feature of ethnographic research. If you are to understand, say, graffiti artists, as an ethnographer you should be prepared to spend many nights out on the streets and may even pick up a can of spray paint yourself.

Thus, this approach brings the research subject to life in a way that we can rarely achieve by other methods. It is an extremely useful tool in helping us to gain a detailed understanding of how broader processes – such as new policies on drugs or broader social and economic changes like those occurring in the recent period of economic recession – affect particular groups of people. As Bourgeois (2003: 17) put it in his acclaimed research into crack use in Harlem, New York: 'Ethnographic method allows the "pawns" of larger structural forces to emerge as real human beings who shape their own futures.' Ethnographic research usually connects the research subject with an important issue that affects that particular population, which may lead to wider reflections, if not direct applicability.

In writing up their research, ethnographers seek to portray the people they have studied, or their participants, in their own terms, via their own language, settings and perspectives, and often provide sympathetic accounts. One reason for this is to ensure that the presentation of the data is as accurate as possible. Necessarily with this kind of research, 'accuracy' entails far more than, say, recording quotations or actions precisely. The whole point of this research is to understand the frames of meaning in play in order that we can provide appropriate interpretations.

In sum, ethnographic research is based on sustained engagement with the research population. In its purely qualitative form, it is often largely unstructured and inductive, meaning that the key research themes develop as the project progresses. In doing so, ethnographic and **observational methods** yield extremely rich data that normally provides unique insights into the populations of study. Although normally focused on a specific area or group, studies adopting these methods have also managed to tell us a great deal about broader issues, such as the impact of social and economic change or the likelihood that a particular law or policing strategy will be successful. Such methods have a long history and, as Chapter 3 details, were adopted in many of the landmark studies of urban poverty and social change in the nineteenth and early twentieth centuries. Most notably, for criminologists, the Chicago School of sociology spearheaded the wider use of observational and ethnographic methodologies during the 1920s and 30s. This can be seen in works such as *The Hobo* (Anderson, 1923), *The Gang* (Thrasher, 1927) and *The Professional Thief* (Sutherland, 1937). Together, along with important later ethnographic critiques of their work (Wacquant, 2002), they built on years of engagement with their research populations. These initial experiments formed the bedrock from which some of the most important and engaging criminological research ever conducted was developed. Ethnographic research provides crucial insights into the workings of criminal and deviant groups. It provides a richness of detail that is missed by many other methods of understanding crime, such as the quantitatively oriented 'rational choice' and 'crime science' approaches discussed in Chapters 2 and 3. While those methods may have their merits in terms of presenting trends and general tendencies, they often reveal little about how criminals make sense of their tasks; the presumption of rational choice, in particular, imposes a brand of universal rationality that often leaves actual criminal conduct entirely unpredictable. Rawlinson and Fussey's (2010) ongoing ethnographic research into Eastern European organized crime in East London, for example, demonstrates how criminal actors may act in entirely unforeseen and seemingly contradictory ways. Other studies also show that offenders take risks that may not be in their (rationally conceived) best interests, possibly because of the context of particularly chaotic lifestyles or perhaps motivated by a wish to cultivate status. However, observational methods are not only used to study 'deviant' groups. On the contrary, as examples in this chapter show, they have equally been used to explore crime control settings.

Structured observation

Quantitative observational research, also called **structured observation**, concentrates on eliciting something *measurable* from the research environment. Rather than using other quantitative techniques, such as a survey, where you would be distanced and have to rely on the interpretations of the participant, quantitative observational research allows you to be closer to the subject of enquiry and, crucially, provides you with your own interpretations at first hand. To some extent, this helps to eliminate any potential, and inevitable, gaps between what participants say and how they act. For example, interaction with research subjects over a long period of time is likely to provide opportunities for cross-referencing what was said in an interview environment with what an individual does within a range of settings. For these reasons, quantitative observational research has been particularly useful for researchers trying to understand the practices of policing and wider social control.

Qualitative ethnography

Steeped in the traditions of the Chicago School (see Chapter 3), qualitative observation, or ethnography, also sometimes described as participant observation – although some debate exists over the exact definitions of these approaches (see Bryman, 2008) – has generated some of the most important and evocative criminological research studies. You will find that this approach is the most qualitative of the commonly used criminological research strategies, for example, when compared to qualitative interviewing.

Once access to the research population has been negotiated, the strategy for data collection largely relies on the researcher's immersion within the field. In turn, data, themes and issues emerge in an inductive process. Due to its engaged and unstructured nature, ethnographic research is very demanding and anyone attempting it would normally require strong interpersonal skills to navigate an unfamiliar, sometimes unpleasant and often challenging environment, as well as sharp analytical and perceptive skills to identify and capitalize on important themes emerging in the course of the research.

If you were to do a project similar to one conducted by an ethnographer, you might be rewarded with some of the richest and most compelling criminological data that can be produced. Consider these two accounts from ethnographers studying crack dealing in New York and violent masculinities in northeast England respectively:

> ❝ I grabbed him by the back of the neck, and put my 007 [knife] in his back ... right here. And I was jigging him hard ... And I had a big 007. I wasn't playing either.
>
> *Bourgeois, 2003: 79*

> ❝ We pull up outside the pub. About ten men are standing around outside the pub, one of whom is bleeding from the mouth, clasping a toilet roll to the wound. They purposely look away as we skid to a halt and spill out of the car. Right away I get the sense that my companions are going to start hitting people.
>
> *Winlow, 2001: 157*

Ethnography allows us to gain detail and insight into participants' lives in a way that is normally unavailable from other research strategies. In the first quote, trust and rapport with the participant, built over an extended period, had invited him to be open and candid in what he said. It is difficult to conceive that such frankness about engaging in criminal and violent activities could be achieved by a survey.

For many ethnographers, the initial stage of research involves evaluating a broad field of information before embarking on a gradual process of narrowing down and refining to a point where they are collecting material that is relevant to the study. This initial process is normally assisted by the well-used strategy of 'hanging around' (see, for example, Whyte, 1955). At first, it is difficult to judge what may be significant and it is important to build in time to engage with this initial process. The rich and important ethnographic accounts described in this chapter did not arise by chance. Rather, researchers often deploy considerable skill and intuition to position themselves in the right place at the right time and cultivate well-placed gatekeepers who facilitate access to the field. Much is learned during this initial phase. Patience and awareness are therefore key attributes if you want to conduct a successful ethnographic study.

USING ETHNOGRAPHIC AND OBSERVATIONAL TECHNIQUES IN ACADEMIC RESEARCH

Here we focus on some examples of classic criminological research that have drawn on observational and ethnographic techniques.

Structured observation in academic research

Quantitative observation methods need to pay particular attention to how key criteria are objectively defined, captured and measured. In a classic study of the way closed circuit television (CCTV) is used, Norris and Armstrong (1999) conducted a quantitative observational study of camera operators' targeting of individuals they deemed suspicious. Given the sheer volume of data that CCTV camera operators are expected to observe, Norris and Armstrong sought to work out the implicit rules operators used in deciding which individuals or groups to focus on as most likely to be engaged in criminal behaviour. This would allow them to draw conclusions about what the camera operators viewed as suspicious and whether this was based on objective categorization or rationale for suspicion, or commonsense understandings that might, in turn, be based on existing prejudices or other factors.

After negotiating access to three CCTV suites, Norris and Armstrong identified what the operators identified as suspicious. To do this, a quantifiable measure was introduced, identified as 'targeted surveillance', which had two criteria:

1. the operator focused on an individual or group for more than one minute
2. the surveillance was initiated by someone outside the CCTV control room, for example, a shopping centre security guard.

Having found a way to quantify when a camera operator was selecting activity as suspicious, the researchers assessed the characteristics and behaviour of those deemed suspicious on the basis of race/ethnicity, age, gender (and other such categories) and use of space. The researchers then developed a strategy to record four types of data: shift data, targeted suspicion data, person data (of the suspect) and deployment data.

An additional concern, again in common with all quantitative research, was to ensure that the findings based on the study of three CCTV suites were representative of broader practice. This was achieved in two ways:

1. The three different CCTV sites were selected (sampled) to represent different urban areas. These were a major city (population over 500,000), a small to medium-sized town (population over 200,000) and an inner-city district (population over 250,000).
2. The researchers had to ensure enough data was gathered. After all, it is extremely problematic to draw wider conclusions from, say, 10 hours of data. At best, this would only have given an insight into what a particular operator was doing on that day and at that place and little about other operators in different times or places. To address this, Norris and Armstrong observed 592 hours of CCTV operator time across the three sites, the equivalent of 74 eight-hour shifts.

After the fieldwork was completed, the data was analysed in relation to the categories identified in the first stage concerning how CCTV operators constructed suspicion and why they chose to target particular groups and individuals. Norris and Armstrong found that CCTV operators generally did not have much pre-existing information to inform their decisions about whom they should monitor. Instead, operators devised a range of strategies that they believed helped them to identify persons worthy of greater attention. The 'use of space' calculations included appearing out of place in a particular environment; for instance, people running when everyone else was walking or someone begging in a shopping area. However, their most notable finding was that nearly all the people were targeted by CCTV operators for 'no obvious reason' other than the categories to which they belonged. As such, 90 per cent of targeted surveillance was of men and most were based on an individual's membership of a 'particular social or subcultural group' (Norris and Armstrong, 1999: 197). These included economically disadvantaged groups, such as homeless populations, those wearing subcultural attire and, most commonly, people who were young and black. By establishing this process through careful data collection, the researchers had a sound basis for putting forward the conceptual argument that CCTV camera operators reproduce forms of prejudice and suspicion that are present throughout other elements of the criminal justice system, not to mention the general public.

Ethnography and academic research

Observation/ethnography focuses on meaning and the point of view of those being studied. It seeks to convey a 'world'. For this reason, one of the key tasks of ethnographers is to engage with the *context* in which actions and speech take place. Spending time with, for example, groups of offenders or crime control practitioners provides rich insights unavailable through many other research methods. Ethnographies may be the only way to understand a specific issue accurately. Much criminological research attempts to understand offending without speaking to offenders. In the edited collection on crime science (Smith and Tilley, 2005b), for example, there is not one single instance where the researchers convey having spoken to a research participant. Groundbreaking qualitative work is significant because it has succeeded in connecting with hard-to-reach groups, which may be crucial when controversial issues are in the spotlight.

The study of terrorism is a good example. Since 9/11 there has been unprecedented interest in the issue. Yet many – in fact nearly all – researchers writing about the subject have never met or spoken to anyone who has engaged in, or considered engaging in, terrorist activity. Although this does not necessarily undermine all the prior research, studies that have engaged directly with terrorists have given us new and fascinating insights. One such study is Hassan's (2001) ethnographic and qualitative interview-based research with 250 militant Palestinians, and their families, involved in political violence in the Israel–Palestine context. This generated valuable and often unique insights into the recruitment, preparation and motivation of suicide bombers. One particularly important contribution was the way it challenged many mainstream academic accounts of what determined whether someone was likely to become a suicide bomber:

> None of the suicide bombers – they ranged in age from eighteen to thirty-eight – conformed to the typical profile of the suicidal personality. None of them were uneducated, desperately poor, simple-minded, or depressed. Many were middle class and, unless they were fugitives, held paying jobs. More than half of them were refugees from what is now Israel. Two were the sons of millionaires. They all seemed to be entirely normal members of their families.

> *Hassan, 2001: 4*

At this point, though, she confronted another issue. Many explanations had looked at the characteristics of those who had committed attacks – such as their age, socioeconomic background and level of education – and extrapolated, or generalized, their conclusions. Hassan, by contrast, identified an inverse relationship, claiming that, because huge numbers volunteered for suicide missions and only a few were selected, the predominant characteristics were, in fact, those prioritized by the leaders, normally for political reasons. Therefore, it is not the case that, say, wealthy doctors were killing themselves out of political despair; it was because groups such as Hamas would select a wealthy doctor for a mission because this would have greater political and propaganda impact.

This study, like other ethnographies, also questioned the assumed barriers between members of what are perceived to be deviant groups and members of mainstream society, asserting that there is no specific 'type' of person who becomes a terrorist. This is important because ethnography is sometimes, and often wrongly, characterized as entering a special, separate 'world' of the deviant. Another key finding, common to much ethnography and other forms of long-term research, is the way the phenomenon being studied is dynamic and continually shifts. Another notable feature of ethnographic work is that the research itself is **context specific**. It relates to the particular time, place and subject of the research. Other researchers studying a different group of people or event – or even different members of the same group – may generate different data.

For this reason, ethnographic research has been criticized as being highly **subjective** and not representative of wider trends. These complaints often miss the point that such studies are usually not intended to illustrate wider tendencies. Instead, they are intended to provide a rich and detailed account of a particular subject. Other criticisms of ethnographic researchers point to their opaque methods when compared to more quantitative approaches. It is often difficult to see exactly what a researcher did and how they drew their conclusions. This occurs for a number of reasons:

- The length of time and extent of immersion makes it impossible to record everything that occurs during the fieldwork. The researcher therefore uses their judgement to articulate the relevant themes.
- The research subjects may not be amenable to outsiders' questioning, meaning that many of the findings cannot be independently verified.
- Researchers typically have a duty to protect their participants and may even be at risk of repercussions should they provide too much information. As Levi (1994, cited in Hobbs, 1995: 2) memorably noted: 'I would rather receive a bad academic review, however unmerited, than have my face smashed in.'

Again, this points to the role of appropriate choices when designing research strategies. There are no perfect approaches and the researcher needs to select and justify methods that are most advantageous to gaining the necessary data.

USING ETHNOGRAPHIC AND OBSERVATIONAL TECHNIQUES IN RESEARCH PROJECTS

Below are two examples, one of observational research and one of ethnographic research. As in other chapters in Part 2, these examples are partly based on actual student projects and will convey some of the important issues you need to be take into account when carrying out a research project. Rather than providing a detailed template, these anonymized examples are intended to map out the key stages of any project, the major considerations and some of the potential difficulties they may entail. Attending to these issues at the outset will make your project much more manageable and produce a more robust and higher quality piece of work. The projects examined here are a structured observation of a magistrates' court and ethnography of a shopping mall.

Example 1: structured observation of magistrates' courts

Tia was interested in the workings of the criminal justice system and, ever since her 18-year-old brother had appeared in a magistrates' court and received a substantial fine following a driving offence, her interests had turned particularly to the court system. Steering away from what had specifically happened with her brother (she was afraid her feelings that his sentence was disproportionate might bias her approach), for her final year project, Tia decided to look at jury trials.

Tia was aware from her reading of criminological literature that one benefit of quantitative (or 'structured') observation is that it brings the researcher particularly close to their subjects, the individuals or groups whose actions are being studied. Although such fieldwork is often more time-consuming than other quantitative methods and access to the research environment is often more difficult to secure, if done correctly, the researcher can be rewarded with extremely rich data.

Planning and design

One of the first tasks was to establish clear and achievable aims for the project. Her course had discussed the expense, symbolism and bureaucracy of the courts. But, having watched a number of Hollywood court dramas and having spoken to a friend who had recently completed jury service, Tia became particularly interested in the dynamics of jury decision-making processes. While courtroom procedure was highly formal, it occurred to her that, in this less structured environment of the jury room, the outcome of trials could rest on the way some strong personalities in the jury were exerted during their deliberations.

Tia's first step was to examine some of the background literature to ascertain what research had already been done in this area and how previous researchers went about it. Tia began by reviewing the work on jury decision making and quickly found that a wealth of empirical research already existed, with many academics asking similar questions to hers. Many of these studies were conducted by social psychologists, which was good from her point of view as she had done a course in social psychology. From reading them, Tia quickly discovered that jury-based decisions could be influenced by a wide range of prejudices, including the political views of jury members – with those supporting the death penalty being more likely to agree with the prosecution case (Fitzgerald and Ellsworth, 1984) – and whether there was an eyewitness or expert witness giving evidence (even if discredited) at the trial (Loftus, 1974). Tia also discovered that group dynamics played a part. Here, the jury's initial vote was an important influence on their final decision (Kalven and Zeisel, 1967). Many people are susceptible to peer pressure in these unfamiliar settings; indeed, Tia was quite shocked by Asch's (1956) social psychology experiment showing that 75 per cent of people would knowingly give a wrong answer to a question in order to conform to a group.

Following good student research practice (see Chapter 1), she wrote a 500-word draft proposal for her supervisor, summarizing the existing studies she was drawing on, and identifying why direct observation of jury room deliberations was the appropriate method, especially as this would bring her social psychology background into play. She also noted that, realistically, she had to narrow her focus and laid out the options: peer pressure, powerful individual jury members, potential racism, political views. Moreover, jury trials often take days, sometimes weeks. How could she ensure that she had enough time to collect a suitable amount of data? These issues relate to the focus of the project and constitute one of the major challenges that most students face when embarking on their dissertations.

Tia's meeting with her supervisor was a bit of a shock. Her supervisor raised the problem of access. Had Tia paid enough attention to *how* previous researchers had done their research? Tia's supervisor informed her that jury deliberations are held in private with the minimum of outside interference and that many jury studies were, in fact, achieved by using 'mock juries', normally consisting of students. Although in Kalven and Zeisel's (1967) well-known study, jurors were interviewed after the trials were over, it was unlikely that a student would be given permission to do this. Without being able to observe the jury's decision-making processes or interview them, it would be difficult for Tia to undertake her research, even though she had produced a well-designed proposal informed by previous theoretical and empirical work.

Tia had to radically rethink her project. Retaining her interest in bias, she shifted her focus to sentencing. In consultation with her supervisor, she began to reformulate her plan. Because there was relatively little research on magistrates' courts – compared to the police, for example – she decided they would provide a better focus for the research. Tia's supervisor advised her that her research aims could be achieved by using a more quantitative observational approach, informed by analysis of the literature surrounding race, gender and age sentencing. Drawing on existing research in the area, structured observations of the punishments dispensed by magistrates for similar offences could be compared with the demographic characteristics of defendants and provide an overall picture of any discrepancies or potential prejudice. Tia's supervisor also said she must look at the magistrates' court sentencing guidelines to see what factors were supposed to be taken into account.

Now sensitized to the issue of access, Tia checked official online guidance on conducting research in the courts. She was faced with an intimidating looking set of requirements about access, which confirmed what her supervisor had said: to conduct interviews or access court documents, she would need to apply well in advance and would be required to send a detailed methodology. Persevering, she scrolled down further and was pleased to discover that simple court observation would not pose such problems as members of the public are freely allowed to observe most court proceedings, so long as they do not make any audio or visual recordings (prohibited in many countries). Another requirement is sensitivity to the needs and wishes of the parties involved in the proceedings, thus reinforcing, although for different reasons, the methodological notion that researchers should be unobtrusive; indeed, she noted that parties could ask the judge for researchers to be asked to leave. Tia resolved to take written notes, inform court officials of her presence and anonymize her findings, including the names of all defendants, witnesses and even the magistrates. She then consulted her supervisor and applied to her university's research ethics committee, which gave its approval

The next step was to consider how to sample her research population. To accommodate the impact of ethnicity on sentencing, she chose a magistrates' court in one particularly ethnically diverse area to ensure that there were enough relevant cases. In identifying this area, she relied on her local knowl-edge but noted in her methodology section her awareness that using census data would be the ideal. There did not seem to be any geographical way of focus-ing on age- and gender-relevant cases. Her focus on identifying possible bias meant another important decision about the coding and measurement of vari-ables, which she would record in her court observation. Tia identified a number of categories that could be measured against each other. She grouped together type of offence, gravity of offence, past convictions and whether the defendant had pleaded guilty as variables that officially determined sentencing decisions, which she would map first against severity of sentence and then run through again with reference to defendant ethnicity, defendant age and defendant gender. Including guilty pleas was a late decision. Until she read the sentencing guide-lines, she had not realized that they had the almost automatic effect of a one-third sentence 'discount' for guilty pleas.

Tia decided to attend the magistrates' court for three whole days a week over a month. This, she calculated, would provide data from 24 different court sessions (counting morning and afternoon as separate sessions), which, she thought, would involve an average of four cases per session – giving a presumed total of around 96 cases.

Conducting the fieldwork and analysing the data

Tia set off for her first day of court observation, confident that her research project was soundly designed. However, it is difficult to foresee everything in an unfamiliar environment. She had not realized that magistrates' courts run different hearings simultaneously. In her chosen court, a 'main charges court' that dealt with diverse cases, a court focusing on breaches of community sen-tences and a third court for longer running trials were all running at the same time. Tia elected to observe the proceedings of the main charges court but, after a few days, she began to realize that the criminal justice system moved slowly even in magistrates' courts: many of the cases were adjourned to a time that was beyond her research period or remitted to a higher court for sentencing. Should she extend her fieldwork period by an extra week, reducing the overall time to analyse and write up the findings? Should she exclude from her findings any cases that could not be concluded in time? This would lead to a methodological bias in her research towards more simple and clear-cut cases. She also wondered why exactly she had thought she needed to observe entire trials if sentencing was her focus.

Luckily, her decision to inform court staff about her research had an unexpected benefit. One of them told her that there were also sentencing hearings that deal with guilty pleas and she checked this out online. This allowed her to cover many sentencing decisions in one day, although only on guilty pleas. At the same time, she reread some of the background research and noted that defendants' 'demeanour in the courtroom' has been identified as influencing sentencing, which would possibly justify continuing to look at not-guilty pleas, that is, full court hearings as well.

Tia decided just to look at guilty pleas/sentencing hearings because this would allow her to observe the sentencing decisions of a wider sample of BME defendants than if she elected only to observe full trials, as well as giving her a compact set of hearings to attend. She recorded details of pre-sentence reports, bearing in mind Mary Eaton's (1986) research, which emphasized that women and men are judged in terms of how well they fit familial role stereotypes.

After the fieldwork was completed, she began to analyse the results. 'Age' was problematic because she had recorded everyone's exact age. It is difficult to argue that a difference in the sentences between an 18- and a 19-year-old is due to age discrimination. Instead, ages were grouped into categories that, while being less precise, provided more concrete information about discrepancies in the treatment of different age groups. Another problem concerned identifying ethnicity, an issue that has afflicted many research projects of this type. In her study, Tia formulated a distinction between white (British, European and non-European) and non-white (South Asian, East Asian and African Caribbean), based on appearance. Although the ethnicity of some individuals was reasonably clear, this was not always the case; for example, 'mixed parentage' currently comprises the largest self-defined ethnic minority in London. Tia's failure to address this point early on compromised her data. Tia could have used the categories already employed in available statistics on this issue. While this would have generated additional comparability with existing research, it would still leave some 'judgement calls' on her part in assigning people to categories.

After the data had been coded, it was analysed using some of the simple statistical tests available in SPSS (see Chapter 5). Tia was able to ascertain that, in this particular instance, there was some apparent bias against all young people aged 18, which, she argued, was because they were the youngest age judged by adult criteria. She also had evidence that young BME males (as a group) aged 18–20 were more heavily sentenced than white males of the same age. Her findings on women were inconclusive, given the small number of trials involving females observed by Tia. Although the data was compromised and lacked the detail of more intensive academic studies on the subject, Tia was able to present her findings and discuss them in relation to other research. Additionally, she drew on her research diary in the concluding sections of her research report to highlight some of the limitations of the research. This demonstrated to her examiners that she was aware of many of the important broader issues connected with her data and method, and this reduced the negative impact of the project's shortcomings.

One effective way to avoid many of Tia's problems – and this would apply to structured observation more generally – would be to undertake a pilot study. In this case, a few early visits to the magistrates' courts armed with a draft methodology would have allowed Tia to anticipate a number of these issues, the court scheduling being an obvious example. An additional technique used by many researchers is to commence a portion of the data analysis very early on. This allows any necessary refinements to the research design to be made before the bulk of the data is collected.

Example 2: an ethnography of a shopping mall

Jim worked as a part-time security guard in a shopping mall to earn money while he completed his studies. Jim's organization was a large private security company that produced impressive-looking marketing materials highlighting the professionalism, efficiency and quality of the organization. From first-hand experience, Jim knew that this was not always the case in practice. In particular, he was interested in how different people doing similar jobs in the same organization could behave in such diverse ways, which had the ultimate effect of providing uneven forms of security.

Planning and design

Jim discussed his interests with one of his lecturers who suggested that qualitative ethnography could be a useful research tool based on two features of the proposed project:

1. His access to the research field because of his professional background.
2. Jim's proposed project placed substantial emphasis on the importance of environment and the setting in which action occurs, a feature that lends itself to ethnographic study.

Jim's access to the research population would not only provide him with data, it could also be gathered in a way that was sensitive to the environment his participants operated in. This would also capitalize on Jim's existing familiarity with the professional context of his research population and avoid some of the assumptions external researchers may carry with them.

The first issues to address were in the connected areas of focus, timing and approach to fieldwork. Qualitative ethnography is time-consuming. Many of the examples of academic ethnographies discussed earlier in this chapter were carried out over years and involve a scale that is not feasible for most undergraduate research projects, which take place over a few terms or semesters. To overcome this problem, two strategies were considered by Jim.

First, given his existing familiarity with the practices of private security, Jim decided he could focus his research a little more from the outset. Many long-term ethnographies start with only a skeleton framework of aims and broad research questions, with the idea that the substantive research themes will emerge inductively as the fieldwork progresses. Given the limitations of time and scope on undergraduate projects, this is perhaps an overoptimistic way to proceed. Jim decided that, although his work turned on operational detail and hence the observation of actions that would be missed by other research methods such as questionnaires or interviews, he could focus on a number of key areas. To do this, Jim planned a number of core areas of enquiry. These included how colleagues approached their work and what their relationships were with other security operators, such as surveillance camera operators, the police and other private security guards. Jim then defined a number of subthemes. Concerning colleagues' approach to work, this included whether they acted 'pre-emptively', such as targeting areas known to be vulnerable to shoplifters at particular times of day, and whether they acted on 'intelligence', such as reports of known shoplifters in the mall, which overlapped with the issue of relations with other security operators. He was also interested in the question of whether motivation had more of an influence on whether someone was an effective security guard than qualifications or rank. With regard to participants' relationships with other security agents, subthemes included the rapidity and extent to which information was conveyed by the guards to other agents and the degree to which reports from other agencies and companies were acted on by the guards. These general frameworks were not intended to be exhaustive. Jim still allowed significant room for other themes to emerge once the fieldwork was underway.

The second strategy related to timing. For this kind of research, it is essential to begin the fieldwork early on. For Jim, this was less of a problem as he was already employed in the field he wished to research, although timing can prove to be a considerable obstacle for research that requires access to more hard-to-reach groups. Jim therefore consulted his academic project supervisor to find out ways of starting the fieldwork as quickly as possible. He was advised that, before starting, he needed to define his research population and sampling framework and address the potential ethical issues that could arise. Jim defined his research population as all private security guards operating in the shopping mall. Because he had limited access to this environment outside his working hours, he had to sample this population on the basis of the individuals and events that were available to him. This is known as an 'opportunity' or 'convenience' sample (see Chapter 5). Despite their problems, opportunity samples are generally more acceptable when qualitative methodologies are used. For quantitative research, such approaches are less common or acceptable because of the strong preference that findings be 'transferable', that is, representative of broader trends and tendencies. Thus, if the samples are not carefully identified with the aim of being representative of a wider population, which, in the case of opportunity samples, they normally are not, it is difficult to apply the research findings more broadly to other contexts. These issues often apply less to qualitative research, although this is by no means always the case. So Jim needed to consider whether there was any reason to think that guards working the same shifts as him were likely to be unrepresentative of all the private security guards operating in the mall. In the event that follow-up interviews with security personnel were needed, Jim elected to employ snowball sampling to identify and access them.

Jim was essentially adopting participant observation as his method of research, although he does not face the usual problem of gaining access to the group, since he is already an insider. He faced the question of whether to tell his colleagues what he was doing. Covert observation obviously eliminates reactivity issues: by informing people that they are being studied, they may change their behaviour. Nowadays, it is generally felt, particularly by university research ethics committees, that individuals have a right to know they are being studied. In such circumstances, where there is a tension between reactivity and ethics, ethics is almost always the most important consideration. A further ethical consideration is the question of informing Jim's employer about the research.

To address these issues, under his academic supervisor's guidance, Jim submitted an application to his university's research ethics committee and approval was granted on the basis that he must inform his participants about the research, notifying them that they could withdraw from the study any time they wished, and that their anonymity would be ensured. He was advised that he must gain approval from his manager. He also had to advertise the main aims of his research and provide contact details for anyone to gain further details about his study. In addition to speaking to his colleagues and manager, Jim posted a flier on his noticeboard at work detailing these points.

Conducting the fieldwork and analysing the data

Working through the research design process, particularly the ethical approval, took longer than anticipated and it became apparent that this would leave Jim less time to conduct the fieldwork. On the other hand, he had defined a number of open-ended analytical themes, which provided some flexibility. Also, and crucial to the success of this small-scale, time-limited ethnographic study, Jim's prior knowledge of the job puts him in a different position from many researchers using this method. For many ethnographers, the initial stage of research involves evaluating a broad field of information before embarking on a gradual process of narrowing down and refining to a point where the researcher is collecting what is deemed significant for the study. Like all researchers conducting ethnographic fieldwork, Jim needed to devise a strategy of 'data capture'. This involves two main elements: what to record and how to record it. The main challenges here relate to the researcher's ability to take sufficient and accurate notes and to do this in a way that has a minimal influence on the research environment. Similar to the approach used in many ethnographic studies, Jim decided he would write down his findings as close in time as possible to the events he was observing, while avoiding doing so in front of his participants. He allocated his duty breaks to note down what he felt was significant and spent at least an hour after every shift reviewing his notes and adding more detail and, more importantly, his reflections. While many observational researchers merely keep their notes in handwriting, adding additional thoughts in the margin, Jim was thinking of using a computer-assisted qualitative data analysis software (CAQDAS) package and so he typed his field notes into his computer, using different fonts to distinguish his immediate impressions and later reinterpretations. To supplement this data, using a technique common to many ethnographies, Jim later recorded a number of follow-up interviews with colleagues who featured heavily in the research. This data was then used to cross-reference and add further detail to the ethnographic findings.

Well planned though the project is, the pressure of time led him to decide to conduct his observations over 12 shifts covering the busy Christmas period at the mall. He reasoned this would also allow him to concentrate fully on the research. As stated above, although issues of transferability and generalization are normally less relevant to qualitative ethnographic research, Jim still needed to assess the extent to which conducting fieldwork during this exceptionally busy time significantly influenced the behaviour and attitudes of the security guards he was observing. Jim found that the high volume of shoppers in the mall meant that security staff were much busier than normal and often had far less time to act on information supplied by their security colleagues. Given the impact of these exceptional circumstances, particularly in ethnographic research where great importance is afforded to the research environment, researchers are required to account for and explain the form and influence of these exceptional contexts when presenting their data. The danger was that, if based on the Christmas period alone, Jim's results would suggest an atypically low and disconnected security performance.

One significant challenge faced by many ethnographers is knowing what to do with the large volumes of data that have been collected. In recent years, the use of CAQDAS has provided considerable benefits to researchers. Jim's supervisor suggested that he could make sense of his computerized notes using one of the analytical programs available to the university. Perhaps the best known and most widely used is NVivo, a replacement for earlier programs such as NUD*IST, and one that many universities subscribe to. Using NVivo, Jim was able to organize his data into key themes (or 'nodes' in NVivo) and then allow the software to identify and interrogate the relationships between the data. To do this he copied his typed field notes into the software and added codes (such as 'communications' and 'action') to each relevant passage, or item of data. He then applied more sophisticated categories by developing subthemes (such as 'pre-emptive action' and 'responsive action') of these codes. NVivo also allowed him to save considerable time transcribing the follow-up interviews he conducted. Instead of spending many hours painstakingly transcribing his interviews, Jim was able to load MP3 files of his interviews and also attach codes to relevant sections. He was then able to transcribe and present only those elements that were significant to the overall themes as they emerged.

CONCLUSIONS

This chapter has shown you how observational research can take many forms and fulfil many functions. It can also be analysed in a number of ways, largely depending on whether a more quantitative or qualitative approach has been taken. Here, we briefly reflect on the key lessons that can be learned from research projects of this kind. Of these, you should give the following factors particular consideration:

1. It is impossible to conduct effective ethnographic research without some access to the research environment. The time constraints of undergraduate projects mean that you should seriously consider whether you can realistically undertake an adequate amount of fieldwork if you do not have pre-existing access to the research population. Unlike other research methods, because of these time constraints, if you adopted this method, you should consider entering the research field as soon as practicable to give the maximum time for empirical themes to emerge and for them to be written up. Questions to

ask yourself include: Is the population 'available' to the researcher? Can the research population be realistically accessed in the time available? Are there pre-existing relationships that can be drawn on, and what are the special problems this poses?

2. Will the researcher affect the environment they are studying? How might this issue of reactivity be reduced?

3. A recent approach to the above problems of access and reactivity has involved the use of the internet as a site of research. Termed 'netnography' by Kozinets (2009), this approach draws on sales and marketing practices and seeks to distil information from online communities. The main sites of research here include internet blogs, message boards, social networking sites and other online forums. While these sites provide a rich and potentially underused resource in social science research, particularly given the proliferation of social networking, and the fact that the latest version of NVivo has a facility to analyse Twitter feeds, their use has generated debate. Principal among these are arguments over the extent to which rich contextual detail (the currency of ethnography) is lost when identifying opinions and statements in cyberspace. Related to this is the idea that people may hold multiple and mutable identities (Bauman, 2004), that is, selective (or aspirant) projections of specific elements of our identities. While this is true for many social expressions and interactions, traditional ethnographic research – the analysis of behaviour in situ – allows the researcher to gain a more three-dimensional picture.

4. For quantitative observations, can specific variables be quantified and measured? Do they inform the overall focus of the research? For qualitative ethnographies, can key themes in the data, once identified, be organized and catalogued effectively?

5. Who or what is the focus of the research? For quantitative observations, is the sample intended to be representative of a wider population? For qualitative ethnographies, which strategies, for example snowball sampling, can be used to maximize access?

6. The key to validity, accuracy and bias is an awareness of the 'politics' of research (see Chapter 2). Once research findings are in the public domain, they may be taken up by others in a number of ways. As the opening discussion to this chapter highlights, since ethnographies often give details of some unsavoury activities, selecting extracts from ethnographic research may be used to reinforce existing stereotypes. As Nader (1972, cited in Bourgeois, 2003: 18) puts it: 'Don't study the poor and powerless because everything you say about them will be used against them.' Many ethnographic researchers have expressed such concerns. Questions to ask yourself include: What steps can be taken to ensure that the data is articulated fairly and participants are

not represented oversympathetically or dismissively? How can the researcher be certain that participants are telling the truth? How can the findings be presented in as objective manner as possible? What efforts can be made to cross-reference particular findings?

7. Is there sufficient time to conduct the fieldwork and write up the findings? Is there a 'plan B', in case insufficient inductive data can be gathered?

8. Of all the criminological research methods, perhaps ethical concerns arise most strikingly with ethnographic research. Many criminological ethnographers have found themselves in positions of questionable legality. Extended engagement with criminal participants almost inevitably develops relationships that may lead the researcher to overlook or even assist in a participant's criminality. Polsky (1971, cited in Gilbert, 2008) hid a gun in his house on behalf of a participant who was expecting a visit from the police. Hobbs (1995) states that maintaining access to the world of organized criminals meant that one had to turn a blind eye to blatant criminality. In an interview with an individual actively involved in protection rackets in London, Rawlinson and Fussey (2010: 7) were told by one participant that he intended to commit a serious criminal act to settle a debt, stating: 'The Russians are crazy, I believe in God so I use the Albanians.' Such incidents place researchers in difficult situations and should be given due consideration before commencing ethnographic research. Another ethical issue concerns participants' consent. Problems often arise over involving unwitting participants in social research. This is an important point in ethnographic research where detailed and intimate portraits of participants are painted. Many classic ethnographies involved 'covert' participant observation. If consent was granted at the outset, as fieldwork progresses, researchers need to be aware that it may not remain constant. To anticipate and mitigate these ethical concerns in university projects, students should submit their project ideas to their university's research ethics committee before carrying out any fieldwork. As a general rule, student projects that intend to ask people about their offending behaviour and, particularly, plans for future offences are often deemed unsuitable from an ethical perspective and should normally be avoided. Questions to ask yourself include: Which ethical considerations arise from the research? Is there a chance that participants may be adversely affected by the research? How is participant consent assured throughout the duration of the project? Are researchers likely to be placed in difficult, illegal or possibly dangerous situations? Has the project received approval from the university's ethics committee?

A summary of the strengths and weaknesses of observational and ethnographic research is given in Table 7.1.

Table 7.1   Selected strengths and weaknesses of observational and ethnographic research

Strengths	Weaknesses/challenges
Rich and detailed data	Impact of reactivity
Sometimes the only way of reaching closed or hard-to-reach groups	Access issues
Captures important contextual texture and detail	Potential opacity of method
Highlights important themes that may not be apparent before the fieldwork commences	Limited possibilities for generalizing findings
Allows the researcher to shift focus to capitalize on important emerging themes	Limited possibilities for replicating findings
Provides a voice to groups often excluded from other methods of social research	Requires strong interpersonal skills
	Often multiple ethical challenges
	May be time-consuming

REVIEW QUESTIONS

- Describe the main features of ethnographic and observational research.

- Assess three ethical considerations that may affect ethnographic research.

- Critically evaluate the extent to which the lack of transferability of ethnographic research findings limits their scope.

FURTHER READING

If you were to read one book, our recommendation would be:

Hobbs, D. and May, T. (eds) (1993) *Interpreting the Field: Accounts of Ethnography*. Oxford: Oxford University Press.

In addition to this, we suggest you refer to:

Atkinson, P.A., Delamont, S., Coffey, A.J. and Lofland, J. (2007) *Handbook of Ethnography*. London: Sage.

O'Reilly, K. (2009) *Key Concepts in Ethnography*. London: Sage.

Silverman, D. (2006) *Interpreting Qualitative Data*. London: Sage.

A classic criminological study using structured observation is:

Norris, C. and Armstrong, G. (1999) *The Maximum Surveillance Society*. Oxford: Berg.

A classic criminological study using ethnography is:

Bourgeois, P. (2003) *In Search of Respect: Dealing Crack in El Barrio* (2nd edn). Cambridge: Cambridge University Press.

8

USING DOCUMENTS: CONTENT, CONVERSATION AND DISCOURSE ANALYSIS

OVERVIEW

The aim of this chapter is to:

- Consider how documents are used to study crime and social control.
- Demonstrate how you should prepare and write a literature review.
- Introduce a range of research methods that use existing 'text', instead of more traditional research methods.
- Identify how you might use content analysis, conversation analysis and discourse analysis in your own research projects.
- Evaluate the contribution that existing textual sources can make to criminological research.

INTRODUCTION

In this chapter we focus on two issues: the use of documents in the context of library/desk-based studies, and the analysis of text and talk in the field of criminology and criminal justice studies. First, we build on the section in Chapter 1 that outlined the main features of a literature review by showing you how to do a piece of library-based research through a discussion of the things to consider in using the full range of available documentary sources. The systematic preparation and writing up of a literature review is an essential part of the research process, because you will need to write one whenever you plan or do a research project. It is not always possible or necessarily a requirement to do empirical social research like interviews with police officers or surveying victims of crime. Many researchers actually consider the literature review as the sole method in a research project. After taking on board the incentives for doing this type of research, there is a detailed discussion of the skills you need to successfully gather and analyse this readily accessible material. As always, there are some pitfalls with this style of research.

We then demonstrate various methods you can use to analyse texts, including policy documents, newspaper articles, emails, interviews and audiovisual materials. Qualitative researchers exploiting these materials aim to expose the many ways in which language shapes social reality, for instance, through the use of discourse and conversation analysis. Some studies use content analysis, which attempts to quantify the content of texts, although qualitative versions of this approach also exist. Although these methods are quite technical, they are often convenient and cost-effective because, apart from the time they take, they do not require the investment of financial resources. They are also good alternatives to empirical methods like the survey and interview, which involve the constraints of having to negotiate access to participants as well as the increasing influence of research ethics committees in many universities and colleges.

DOING A LITERATURE REVIEW

In Chapter 1 you were introduced to the main features of the literature review. Here, we provide some examples of how you would actually do one, including the use of keywords, the types of publications and their relative merits, and an appraisal of their limitations.

Saeed was asked by one of his tutors to do some exploratory work or a *preliminary review* to find out if anything had been published on the use of 'status dogs' such as pit bull terriers by street corner drug dealers to intimidate those buying drugs off them and to deter rival gangs attacking them. To date, there is not much published academic research on this, and most of the material Saeed found as a result of a quick search via the internet consisted of tabloid newspaper articles and blog sites – the latter included some graphic and brutal images of dog-fighting. Saeed thought the dominance of media-led, sensationalist accounts and the absence of an academic literature was perhaps a justification for exploring an underresearched area through empirical research. On the other hand, Anthea, one of Saeed's friends and fellow student, was tasked with looking into the relationship between substance abuse and youth crime. Here, there was so much material – books, articles, government reports, grey literature (that is, work in progress, or unpublished research) – that it was impossible to make any clear judgements about what this literature was saying. In this case, it would be necessary to do a systematic search of this material by creating a more focused question, such as: 'The relationship between addiction to Class A drugs, young people and acquisitive crime'. The examples of Saeed and Anthea are useful because they show what research material is already out there and that some issues are scrutinized more than others. Saeed and Anthea could then decide if they wanted to base their study on existing literature or go out into the real world to gather some primary data, for example a survey or observational research.

Effective organization is a skill required in both education and employment, and this skill comes to the fore here. Having opted to do a literature review, it is tempting to think it can be done quite quickly, unlike research that requires long hours collecting data through interviews or surveys. You might think you simply need to log onto a PC or visit the library. However, you must not assume that the information you want can be accessed quickly or in the desired format. Finding data may be much easier now we have electronic search engines and databases. Yet, actually accessing key information sources can take many hours, sometimes days and weeks. The information must then be analysed, paying close reference to the research question, and the findings and results must be written up.

Keywords

So what needs to be done as part of a literature search? Once a research topic has been settled on and narrowed down to a provisional working title and/or hypothesis, one approach is to highlight keywords.

Let us take as an example the topic of 'media coverage of state responses to terrorism in the UK and the USA'. There is no single approach we can apply to look for published work on this topic. A priority will be to devise a search strategy that successfully tracks down the items or sources required. The important qualities you will need here are flexibility, patience and perseverance because, in the early stages, this exercise will involve some trial and error. Some searches may take a project in directions you had not even thought about, which may open new lines of enquiry or force you to go back and start again. The results will depend on the keywords used, so finding the right vocabulary is vital and the list of keywords compiled should be closely related to the subject being investigated. There should be a range of words that sum up your research topic, including broad, narrow and related terms. Be aware of synonyms or words that mean the same thing. For our topic, this is an example of a basic search:

Keywords   Terrorism, state, media, UK, USA
Related terms   Journalism, television, newspaper, government

Broader terms	Violence, politics
Narrower terms	BBC, ITV, Sky News, CNN, *The Guardian*, *New York Times*, 7/7, London bombing, 9/11, Twin Towers
Synonyms	Terrorist, news, press, Britain/British, England and Wales, United States, America

Discovering what you think are the right keywords may seem like a simple task; however, in reality, it is quite time-consuming. If the words are wrong, the search is unlikely to be productive. After deciding on the words, the next stage is combining them in a way that means the sources needed to complete the study can be identified. Much database searching is based on the principles of Boolean logic, which refers to the logical relationship among search terms. Boolean logic consists of three 'Boolean operators', 'and', 'or' and 'not'. These words can either widen or narrow a search, depending on what you want to find out. For our topic, 'media coverage of state responses to terrorism in the UK and the USA', we could have the following:

- Terrorism AND government AND media AND UK
- Terrorism AND government or state AND media or television or newspaper AND USA.

A closer look at this list of words shows that 'and' appears frequently in order to limit the search so that the only sources identified will include all the relevant keywords. The other word used is 'or', which widens a search because it uses synonyms. Striking a compromise between a narrow and wide search is not always easy and if you find too many sources, adding to the list of keywords can change the search strategy. The opposite situation may occur and in this case choosing different words could broaden the search.

Another trick worth knowing is how to truncate words. This means a word is shortened by using a wild card symbol (for example *). This symbol will vary from database to database and assistance from a librarian may be needed. The purpose of * is to widen your search without writing a long list of similar words. If we typed in Terror*, the results would include 'terrorist' and 'terrorism'. However, sometimes this method is less useful and searches may generate a list of irrelevant words.

Publications

Because vast quantities of criminological research exist, it is often necessary to find other means of limiting the amount of information revealed by a search. Techniques for refining literature search results include:

- *Type of publication:* a search may be limited to journal articles, websites, newspapers or books. Bear in mind that there is an expectation that as you become more skilled as a researcher, it is essential that you are familiar with the most cutting-edge and up-to-date research, which is found in journals (see the section in Chapter 1 on this issue).

• *Publication date:* it may be necessary to search for material published in the last three years or since 1997. It depends on how historical a research study is. The focus of the study and the research question will help you to make this decision.

• *Language:* most material is published in English but increasingly you will find non-English language sources and unless you are bilingual or multilingual, you can specify the language.

It is now time for you to have a go by doing some experimenting, either by doing a search for the example identified above or by selecting a different topic. What have you discovered by doing your search? The answer to this question will rely in part on the topic selected, with popular topics (at least with many students) such as sexual and violent offences in all likelihood resulting in more hits than plea bargaining in the courts. We noted earlier that it is unlikely that there is a topic out there that has not been researched at all. Even if there is little available information, there will still be something, and a nil finding may be a reflection of the type or quality of question asked. Whatever information is accessed, the next step is to evaluate it by referring to the appropriateness of the data for answering the research question. Below is a checklist of just some of the points that should be taken into account. The relative significance differs according to the type of publication:

1. *Is the author or organization that authored the source a recognized expert in the field?* Most publications by established publishers ensure this partly because they want to sell their journals and books. It also maintains and enhances their reputation. They will check the reputation of the author(s) through the system of peer review where other experts confirm the authority of the author(s).

2. *Does the publisher have a track record of publishing criminological research?* This is important because those publishers with a history of publishing work in the subject area can demonstrate that other authors have confidence in their capacity for commissioning and selling the work of other researchers.

3. *Who is the intended audience of the publication?* Does it target the professional academic researcher, policy maker/practitioner or the novice criminologist or even a reader with a general interest in the field?

4. *Is the publication up to date or out of date?* Some work is timeless, especially theoretical contributions, and if your study is historical, this is not going to be a problem. Other work may be more about the here and now, especially evaluation and policy-relevant research funded by government departments and while theory and history will be evident, the current agenda is far more important.

5. *Is the publication referenced properly and does it cite the most relevant sources?* This may seem like a trivial point, but the use of referencing conventions, such as the Harvard system, is vital because it ensures that you avoid being accused of plagiarism. As well as attributing your sources, this will make it possible for other researchers to replicate or repeat the research project.

Writing up the review

A final thing to think about is how the literature is organized and structured at the stage of writing up the review. There are two main approaches: *thematic* or *chronological*.

Creating a thematic review makes lots of sense because it entails breaking down the research question into different elements and can make the account more coherent. Emily is interested in exploring the factors that motivate girls and women to engage in different types of violent crime. Her review was mainly theoretical and her interest was in looking at the different theoretical explanations used to explain violent crime. The focus of her study was refined, narrowing it down to consider the significance of gender in accounting for the differential involvement of male and female offenders in violence. Because Emily was concerned with different types of violent crime, a decision was taken to concentrate on violent crimes of a sexual nature and violent offences that are non-sexual. She decided to divide her review into four discrete, albeit inter-related, themes:

- theoretical explanations of violent crime
- the relationship between gender and violent crime
- the involvement of and causal influences on females committing acts of sexual violence
- the involvement of and causal influences on females committing acts of non-sexual violence.

Emily could have structured her review chronologically but a thematic approach suited her better because she was exploring theoretical issues of a topic where the general pattern of offending has not changed dramatically across time. Women do commit violent crimes, of all types, but less often than men and the offences are less serious in terms of the harm done to the victim.

Matthew, by contrast, was asked to write a review for the purpose of evaluating the impact of a piece of legislation introduced 10 years ago. Adopting a historical approach, he tackled this subject chronologically by looking at the situation before the legislation and its effects over the following decade. In this way, he could identify changes over time and tease out any evidence to show the extent to which the legislation had proved effective.

Limitations of literature reviews

If you had the time, skills and resources to hand, a literature review would ideally assess all the relevant literature on a given topic, including both published and unpublished work. Journals, books and 'grey literature' should be gathered using electronic and manual techniques. At the beginning, there would be a detailed and transparent explanation of the procedures or how the review was carried out so any reader could see how the material was gathered and interpreted. This is necessary to show the reader that the conclusions you arrive at are balanced and consistent with the material reviewed.

Sometimes, partial reviews of the literature are required, known as **rapid evidence assessments**. These should not be confused with a more substantial literature-based project and, as the phrase implies, time is important and this type of review is intended to be done quickly. When completing an assessment or undertaking an evaluation for an agency, it is possible that information must be accessed, interpreted, and summarized at some speed. Usually, an assessment like this would be done using electronic searches instead of more exhaustive and manual searches of journals, monographs and the grey literature. Such a search is therefore less comprehensive than a full review and for this reason you will need to acknowledge that the conclusions are tentative and subject to revision and updating if a more detailed search was undertaken.

Finally, as discussed in Chapter 2, some sources, in particular journals, are biased in terms of what they publish and favour certain styles of and approaches to research above others. There may be a theoretical bias or the preference for quantitative above qualitative research. Often there are political factors influencing who publishes and what is published in a particular journal. The result will be a selective account that is biased in terms of the type of literature consulted. The main thing is to be honest about the ways in which you searched for and accessed this material. Another limitation is that you may only look at literature that is in line with your research interest. For instance, some people are intimidated by statistics and so quantitative research material of this kind may be ignored, resulting in concentrating more on studies using qualitative approaches. Once again the outcome will be biased, because insufficient attention was given to making comparisons between different bodies of work and important epistemological and ontological debates are ignored.

USING CONTENT ANALYSIS IN CRIMINOLOGICAL RESEARCH

Content analysis is the systematic and objective analysis of existing texts or documents. For the most part, this method does not involve you generating new data. Although you will find there are many approaches to content analysis, it tends to be practised by quantitative researchers. Qualitative researchers do sometimes apply it to look for meanings in the context of text that are not obvious by a superficial reading. Content analysts draw on documentary sources that include newspaper and magazine articles and possibly diaries, as well as audio-visual sources, for example television and radio broadcasts and films. It is less likely, although not impossible, that a content analyst would look at academic books and journal articles. There is nothing to stop a content analysis being based on interview transcripts, but mass media texts are the most commonly accessed sources of data.

A notable application of this technique is studies of the impact of media images of violence on society. In the late 1960s and early 1970s, George Gerbner and his colleagues at the Annenberg School for Communication, University of Pennsylvania, examined the cumulative effects of being regularly exposed to images of violence through mainstream media sources. Gerbner et al. (1976: 1) applied sophisticated quantitative techniques in order to identify the 'context, structure and functions of violence, and what lessons ... children and adults derive from their exposure to [it]'. Put simply, these techniques involved watching US television shows and counting and quantifying the extent and types of violence in addition to the associated value judgements being broadcast. In what has since become a hugely influential and debated body of work (see Carrabine, 2008), Gerbner used the data to develop an idea known as 'cultivation theory'. This theory argues that while people are not necessarily immediately influenced by the violence they see on the screen, prolonged exposure to such images is likely to 'cultivate' certain attitudes and perceptions, notably that the world is more dangerous and hostile than it probably is. He called this the 'mean world syndrome'.

Content analysis is mainly used for the purpose of pure academic research (see Chapter 2), although there is no reason why it cannot be applied in other arenas, for example as an element of the research design for a policy evaluation. For quantitative approaches to content analysis, the main skill required is the ability to create a coding system or predetermined categories, followed by the quantification and tabulation of the contents of the documents studied (see Chapter 5 for a detailed explanation of coding). It is relatively inexpensive and can be used on its own or combined with other research techniques, for example triangulation (see Chapter 9). It is particularly useful for looking at the past where documents are often the only source of information available to researchers.

If you were to choose content analysis as an approach, after formulating a research question, which could focus on an issue like media representations of a certain crime or the diverse representations of a criminological topic found in broadsheet ('quality') and tabloid ('popular') newspapers, there are several stages you would need to follow when using this method.

A first consideration is choosing the material. Is the project going to look at newspapers and if so, what type? If the focus is on media representations more generally, including television and radio programmes, is the focus on headlines or randomly chosen paragraphs or sentences? Another important factor is the time period your research is going to span, for example days, months, years, decades and centuries, and making sure the required resources – time, tools and money – are to hand (Chapter 1).

Second, there is the design of the research instrument. Sampling and the selection of material to be used in the research is key, especially the criteria used to choose texts. Make sure that the sample is manageable and that you keep an eye on its representativeness, validity and reliability. At this stage, the coding scheme and categories must be developed and the analyst should determine what material belongs to each of the categories. The reader of such research needs to be clear how the data you use for analysis is allocated to each of these categories.

Your project supervisor – and possibly the research ethics committee – will then play an important role. They will need to scrutinize your coding scheme and categories to detect any biases that are built into your research design. It is expected that, because the categories have been coded openly and in an objective manner, anyone should be able to undertake the analysis, and not just the person who designed the instrument. They will also examine the material chosen for the analysis.

Example: newspaper representations of youth crime

Paul was asked to experiment with a form of content analysis in a small research study exploring newspaper accounts of antisocial behaviour among young people. The title of his study was: 'A content analysis of popular and quality newspaper accounts of the causes of youth crime with reference to family structure'.

Since the death of an old man at the hands of some youths a month ago, the national newspapers, especially the tabloids, had been blaming young people as a group for this isolated, albeit tragic, incident. Reports had also apportioned blame to family structure, in particular the high number of single-parent families headed by women, echoing right realist criminological theories of the 'underclass' (see Murray, 1990, 2000). The rationale behind the research was Paul's concern about the negative images of young people and the tendency for media commentators to blame single mothers for the crimes of their children, thus ignoring other possible causal influences such as those identified by left realist criminologists (see Chapter 3).

Planning and designing the research

As well as completing an academic exercise, Paul wanted to write a letter to the local newspaper, framed in terms of the notion of a 'moral panic', suggesting that the media sometimes criticize young people by lumping together their boisterousness with crime and disorder. Because content analysis is associated with quantitative research, it is sometimes described as being 'atheoretical', but this is not necessarily the case, hence the reference to the notion of a 'moral panic'. As noted in Chapter 2, this concept refers to 'a person or group of persons [who] emerges to become defined as a threat to societal values and interests' (Cohen, 2002: 1).

In line with the notion of 'moral panic', Paul speculated that despite the reality of youth crime, its actual extent and prevalence, as well as seriousness, would be blown out of proportion, resulting in the stigmatization and stereotyping of young people, especially the poor, and the families to which they belong. All social problems, such as youth crime, are real, but the meanings attached to them are socially constructed and vary depending on the interests of those involved. Newspapers are printed to make money but may also help to shape public opinion, which, in turn, reflects wider political values. At the time Paul did his research, many media and government sources were talking about the link between crime and family structure, specifically the lack of discipline and social control single-parent families have over their young children. In talking about youth in this way, it is possible to 'define a group or act as deviant and focus on it to the exclusion of almost anything else' (Jewkes, 2004: 64).

Paul also wanted to use the evidence to back up his argument that rather than criminalizing and dehumanizing young people, local government and the voluntary and community sector should provide more youth clubs and safe places for young people to socialize. He felt that because he was approaching the subject objectively and systematically, his evidence would 'prove' that some sections of the media tend to distort social reality.

Conducting the fieldwork and analysing the data

Choosing two national tabloid newspapers, Paul decided to analyse stories about young people, their perceived problematic behaviour and how this relates to the theme of family structure. Because he was interested in assessing the extent to which tabloid newspapers printed negative representations, he also looked at two quality newspapers. His sample included all relevant articles taken from the four newspapers, including those published a week before the murder of the elderly gentleman and those published in the month following the incident.

Drawing on the guidance given in Chapter 5, Paul then set about developing a coding system to measure the frequency of references to young people and family structure and to quantify them by splitting the responses into three main categories:

Young people
1. positive accounts
2. neutral accounts
3. negative accounts.

Family structure
1. positive accounts
2. neutral accounts
3. negative accounts.

This is a simple coding system and Bryman (2008) offers general but detailed guidance on how this can be done. All we have done here is outline the basic principles. For some content analysis, there is considerable leeway here for interpretation on the part of the researcher, which may compromise the objectivity of the research. In defence of Paul, the codes are not totally subjective because there is broad agreement about whether or not a word is *positive*, *negative* or *neutral*. Despite this limitation, these categories enabled Paul to discern thematic patterns and the extent to which there was consistency in terms of the coverage of these stories.

His hypothesis was that there would be more 'negative accounts' referring to the poor behaviour of young people in general, and, because of the often sensational tone of tabloid reportage, the language used would present youth as a 'criminal "other"'. For example, rather than referring to young people as simply young people, terms such as 'yobs', 'kids running wild', 'feral children', and references to 'crime', 'violence' and 'antisocial behaviour', including the fear these groups create in the wider population, would be used. He applied the same principle when analysing the language used to discuss how the family unit related to crime and disorder. Was the family simply described as the family or were words such as 'irresponsible' and 'dysfunctional' used alongside this word? 'Neutral accounts' referred to stories and articles about young people that are descriptive, and 'positive accounts' described stories where journalists 'sang the praises', or expressed approval, of a young person. Paul spent a lot of time identifying variables that fitted into each of these categories, as well as thinking about words and terms that are thematically consistent.

Paul found that most stories in the tabloid press during the five weeks of his study were 'negative' and there were very few stories highlighting anything to the contrary. The broadsheets tended to be more 'neutral' and there were no obviously 'positive' representations of young people during this period. Paul's research concerns a concrete social problem and, in part, he did the research to apply the knowledge he acquired at the end of the project. Referring to the concept of 'moral panic' meant that the study could have contained a theoretical dimension, although, common to many applications of this concept, Paul only partially engaged with the theory. Often, the concept of 'moral panic' is used to describe a media story that exaggerates the risk of something, such as a 'scare story' about child abduction. Yet such stories do not necessarily assert moral values nor do they induce panic among readers. Instead, a more careful reading of Cohen's (2002) work reveals that 'moral panics' are said to exist when a specific set of processes and events take place, such as the political condemnation of certain actions, the presentation of ordinary events as extraordinary and the reinforcement of certain moral boundaries.

Content analysis and policy-relevant research

Other researchers may have no obvious interest in theory and utilize content analysis to study a policy-relevant issue, such as the effectiveness of a procedure introduced by an organization. The same principles apply if you take this route and you would look at the content or information in several documents and compare them using a coding system. Researchers in a policy environment are likely to look at the policy process, including the inception, design and implementation of a programme of reform such as a strategy to disrupt drugs markets in a city. The content analyst would identify a sample and may choose to look at a range of documents, comparing what was said at different stages of the process. Ideally, the implementation of the programme will reflect the inception and design stage but this is not always the case. Put another way, a policy may change at discrete stages of the policy process. In this instance, content analysis would reveal if there were any changes in emphasis or direction across the lifetime of the programme being studied. The use of this method in isolation from others may not expose much and it would make sense to triangulate it with other methods such as semi-structured interviews.

In short, content analysis is a relatively cheap method of analysing readily available and accessible data. In principle, through coding, content analysis allows an objective approach to the quantification of data, and the procedures for gathering and analysing the data are both transparent and replicable by other researchers. The individual researcher therefore has minimal impact on the technique itself and the outcomes of the analysis. In practice, things are a little more complicated because coding necessarily involves some subjectivity and interpretation. As we are dealing with language, there are inevitably variations of meaning across cultures.

USING CONVERSATION ANALYSIS IN CRIMINOLOGICAL RESEARCH

In **conversation analysis** (CA), a phrase that is very evident is 'naturally occurring data', which in this instance refers to talk and text. Texts include not only the written word and conventionally recognized documents, but also the spoken word as well as audio and video recordings. A pioneer of CA was Sacks (1984), who attempted to develop a scientific way of collecting and analysing data through using tape-recorded conversations.

Carter (2011) applies CA to interpret transcripts of police recorded interviews with suspects. As well as looking at the language used by both parties to communicate with each other, she also acknowledged sounds, such as laughter, which are an integral aspect of the police interview. Laughter can be employed informally to challenge the story a suspect is telling officers. Strictly speaking, laughter does not comply with recognized interviewing procedures, but the likelihood of an officer being reprimanded for using this tactic is negligible. According to Carter (2011: 2), CA makes it possible to access 'hidden layers of communication' that are at play in the interaction and 'co-construction and negotiation' occurring between police and suspects.

Planning and designing the research

If, like Carter (2011), you are contemplating using CA, an essential reference point is inevitably Sacks (1984). He adheres to the view that a tape recording is a permanent record and amenable to **replication** by researchers in the future. Originally, CA concentrated on everyday talk, but as Carter shows, its focus has broadened to look at conversation in institutional settings such as the criminal justice system. What sets CA apart from other methods used to gather these sources of data is that conversation analysts look at the use of words by people in everyday settings.

There are also theoretical and epistemological considerations. The CA approach has strong links with the micro-level sociology of ethnomethodologists (Travers, 2001). The insight this research tradition imparts is that language is a big part of the 'methods' we use to make sense of the world around us. Language is crucial because it enables us to communicate with other people and it helps us explain to them the meaning of our actions. Echoing ethnomethodology, CA looks at the procedures and rules of interaction taking place between people as they converse or communicate with one another. It shows that our interactions and what we say to each other, and how we say it, are central to shaping and structuring social order. In other words, there are regular patterns in conversation otherwise known as 'structures of interaction' (Atkinson and Heritage, 1984).

An important concept is 'turn-taking analysis' or the detailed interpretation of a dialogue between two or more people. When we listen to any conversation or dialogue, for most of the time it appears to be an orderly act and the participants in the conversation, as well as the listener, are aware of certain assumptions about when to talk. For example:

- a question is followed by an answer
- people know when to stop talking if more than one person talks at the same time
- if someone says hello to you, there is the expectation that you will return the greeting.

These examples of taken for granted expectations about conversation are called 'adjacency pairs'. If a person involved in a conversation fails to do what is expected, we might think they are rude or haven't yet learned the art of conversation. If you think about watching a news programme on television where a journalist interviews two or three politicians about crime policy, sometimes turn-taking and adjacency pairs are both jettisoned. How many times have you seen a journalist ask a question and the other speakers go off track, failing to answer the question and talking past each other?

The potential application of CA in the context of applied criminological studies is arguably not as straightforward as 'naturally occurring' talk in everyday conversation between friends and family, because the turn-taking can operate in environments where there are more rigid rules, such as in the courts, or the dialogue between a police officer and a suspect on the streets or at the police station.

Conducting the fieldwork and analysing the data

Everything going on in a conversation is treated as important and in need of being registered. So, although the words used in conversations are important, the timing of pauses and interruptions alongside expressions such as 'er' and 'erm' are significant too. Conversation analysts use an elaborate method of transcribing recorded interviews and every word and pause, including the length of it, is accounted for. Bryman (2008: 356) gives some examples of the symbols used:

- We:ll   a colon indicates that the sound that occurs directly before the colon is prolonged. More than one colon means further prolongation, for example ::::

- .hh   indicates an intake of breath
- hh   indicates breathing out
- (0.8)   a figure in parentheses indicates the length of a period of silence, usu-
          ally measured in tenths of one second. Thus, (0.8) signals eight-tenths
          of a second of silence
- <u>You</u>   indicates an emphasis in the speaker's talk
- (.)   indicates a slight pause.

These sometimes obvious yet subtle details can tell a conversation analyst quite a bit about the meaning attached to the words and phrases used by the speaker. In a similar way, we can tell quite a bit about people if we observe their body language when we are talking to them, such as whether they are friendly, open, aggressive, shy or distracted.

USING DISCOURSE ANALYSIS IN CRIMINOLOGICAL RESEARCH

We can analyse documents using a number of techniques, although they share in common an interest in the role of language in shaping the social world. One such approach is **discourse analysis**. There are many variants of discourse analysis, produced in the disciplines of sociology, cultural studies and psychology. You can use discourse analysis – where language is the main focus – to scrutinize textual representations and the reporting of crime issues. It can demonstrate that discourse is used to serve the interests of different groups and the analyst uses the method to expose the hidden values and agendas of organizations and agencies. To give an example, when politicians and policy makers deliver speeches about law and order, they use rhetorical devices to persuade the audience that their policies are the right and, sometimes, the only ones. The discourse analyst investigates how the rhetoric in a speech is a form 'spin', which can end up with the audience believing what they have been told even though they have actually been misled.

What follows is an introduction to two influential versions that have been used by some established academics who have applied these tools to explore crime, deviance and other social problems. First, we discuss Michel Foucault's (1967, 1977) archaeological and genealogical approach, also known as the Foucauldian approach, and then the free association narrative interview method (Hollway and Jefferson, 2000).

Foucauldian approach to discourse analysis

If you refer back to Chapter 3, you'll see that many postmodern and poststructuralist thinkers reject the view that there is an external reality, and claim instead that social relations are expressed through language. This claim was a challenge to the thought of Jean-Paul Sartre, the existentialist thinker who talked about the individual person attempting to present a coherent sense of self to the external world. Foucault (1967) rejected the view that the individual human subject – that is, you and those around you – can be conscious in this way. More than this, human consciousness is just an idea and can only be expressed and produced through language (Gutting, 2011). Discourse refers to everyday talk and speech, but Foucault, in his early work, uses it in a different sense, as a way of talking about the rules and protocols influencing how language is used and how it influences our day-to-day lives. Language is not something we use to communicate with each other on our own terms, but is a linguistic structure that exists independently of people. To take this to an extreme, Jacques Derrida, a contemporary of Foucault, is often cited as arguing that: 'There is nothing outside the text' (Gutting, 2011).

Discourse is about the relationship between power and knowledge and the social construction of meaning. All social relations are a product of discourse and power/knowledge relations. Thus, a discourse is a product of a particular context – or time and place – and its meaning is localized and contextually specific. The basic point is that society is not a product of external social structures or individual psychology, but of language. This is a rather abstract theory, but some of Foucault's ideas have been used by criminologists. Foucault's account of power/knowledge asserts that power is not held in the hands of a single, dominant group such as the ruling class or state elite. Power is actually all-pervasive and penetrates every area of social life, across institutions, such as the criminal justice system. For example, you could build on Foucault's insights to explore penal policy in your home country. To do this, you might analyse the notion that the prison service is a powerful organization but the prisoner also has power. Because power is dispersed everywhere rather than being in the hands of one group or individual, it is not possible for it to be challenged at a societal level and all that remains are localized struggles, such as prisoners campaigning for better prison conditions. This becomes a little clearer if we look at Foucault's (1967) method.

Planning and designing the research

The methods used by Foucault do not resemble any we have examined thus far and in some ways his many works are essentially extended critical syntheses of documents, including academic research, historical records and a disparate collection of other archival materials. He named the approach 'interpretative analytics', which includes two key ideas: 'archaeology' and 'genealogy'. The former attempts to identify the most influential forms of knowledge or philosophical and cultural ideas at a particular moment in history. The reason Foucault did this was to show that all ideas – for instance justice, truth and fairness – are not absolute and universal but belong to a specific historical context or time and place. To apply this to a criminological issue, you could consider the expansion of the prison population in the USA and the UK and how this is related to political discourses of punishment in the two countries.

The 'genealogical' approach is all about the way knowledge and ideas have an effect on what we do, hence Foucault's interest in power. In a book that has proved to be important in contemporary penological debates, *Discipline and Punish* (1977), Foucault shows how the prison emerged at a particular time and place as a method of dealing with deviant populations. The origins of the prison coincided with a growing reluctance to use the death penalty and extreme forms of torture, and was presented as a more civilized and progressive method of containing problem populations. In reality, the prison is symbolic of wider threats to human freedom spreading across society because of the permanent presence of power in all social environments.

Conducting the fieldwork and analysing the data

If you compare content and conversation analysis with Foucault's contribution, he gave few explicit guidelines to take you through the research process. This lack of transparency is a common criticism. Add to this the fact that his method does not lead to the creation of any empirical data and a powerful critique begins to emerge. Some commentators on postmodern thought have said this misses the point, because it is more apt if we see his work as a philosophical critique, not only of power and its effects across societies but also a critical commentary on the potentially negative and oppressive use of research methods. In the words of Travers (2001: 154), Foucault

> suggest[s] that social scientific methods, including the social survey but also the various techniques used by qualitative researchers, can be viewed as tools used by the state, and professional occupations, to regulate and control human populations. The methods courses you are taking at college are, if you like, part of the problem rather than the solution from a Foucauldian perspective, because they teach an instrumental way of thinking about human beings, and are intended to give you technical skills which serve the needs of government.

Free association narrative interview method

Criminologist Gadd (2000, 2006) has created the so-called **free association narrative interview (FANI) method**. This consists of certain strands of psychology and psychoanalysis that make up what they call a 'psychosocial' perspective. Research of this type typically uses interviews but because of the epistemological underpinnings, it is more appropriate to assess it in this chapter, specifically because it stresses the importance of discourse and language and how it is used by offenders to describe their actions. Gadd (2003: 338) suggests that the main feature distinguishing the FANI from the typical semi-structured/unstructured interview is that the researcher aims to get the research participant to free associate – or speak freely – when talking about their experiences. It is expected that the interviewer will have minimal input into the interview and will avoid asking questions such as 'Why?' After an initial interview, the researcher analyses the data and identifies 'absences, avoidances, contradictions and changes of emotional tone' (Gadd, 2003: 338). These are followed up in another interview when the participant is asked other questions based on the original narrative, drawing attention to the emotions of the interviewee and asking them to say more about their lived experience.

Simon was asked by his tutor to critically evaluate the potential application of FANI for a study exploring the relationship between masculinities and violent offending behaviour. So, he examined how this style of research is planned and designed, how fieldwork is conducted and the ways data is analysed. He found that to come to terms with masculinities and crime, it is necessary to foreground the psyche, which has its own irreducible determinants and its own rules (Jefferson, 1997; Jefferson and Gadd, 2008). By looking at the psyche, Simon noted that there is an acceptance of both conscious and unconscious processes, including hidden desires. These processes are linked to contradictory emotions in the mind of an individual person and create anxiety and a threat to the self, which need to be handled by their psyche regardless of factors such as the class or ethnicity of the individual man. As human beings, our psyche is the place where we split and project different parts of our personality. A key issue is how, in reality, men deal with their own life histories and psychic formations with regard to masculinities. This is done intersubjectively because of the centrality of 'biographically mediated difference between men' (Gadd, 2003: 333). Each man has his own highly personalized and diverse experiences and trajectories that are made meaningful by taking on board particular discursive positions to deal with or defend against a sense of anxiety and powerlessness.

Simon found that the above points are illustrated in one of Jefferson's (1996, 1998) case studies, which focuses on Mike Tyson, the former world heavyweight boxing champion. Tyson was imprisoned for the rape of Desiree Washington, followed by the decline of his status as a champion and his psychological disintegration. Some commentators explained Tyson's life in terms of his class (working) and race (black), but Jefferson's analysis considers the ambivalence and contradictions that Tyson's psyche had to deal with. On the surface he was a huge and powerful man, although this concealed a more troubled personality. This is apparent in Jefferson's (1996) account of Tyson's transformation from 'a little fairy boy' to a 'complete destroyer', which shows how the biography of this sportsman was full of contradictions. What Jefferson (1996) does is show Tyson as a young man who had a lisp and who lacked the physique he later acquired as a result of years of pumping iron in the gym. Tyson became 'Iron Mike' by splitting off, or rejecting, his own perceived deficiencies and projecting the resulting violent feelings towards his opponents in the ring. The victim is then blamed for the perceived weaknesses of the perpetrator. In other words, Tyson's life cannot be explained in terms of structural factors alone and intersubjective factors are important too, especially the irreducibility of the psyche, which has its own determining rules.

Simon also discovered that Gadd and Farrall (2004) applied a psychosocial approach to draw attention to men's subjectivities and the workings of unconscious processes. Their research concentrates on the criminal careers and desistance literature, digging deeper to look at the 'latent or unconscious meanings embedded in offenders' narratives' (Gadd and Farrall, 2004: 148). More than this, they call for researchers to ascertain the meanings offenders invest in factors such as unemployment, social exclusion and drug misuse. In order to understand the criminal behaviour of men, we must be aware of the unique biographies of individual men. An appreciation of men and their subjectivities shows the complex processes whereby they 'identify' and 'dis-identify' themselves with particular reference points, including real figures in their lives, for example their father, a sibling, and 'cultural stereotypes' (Gadd and Farrall, 2004: 149), such as alcoholics and drug addicts. It is necessary, as Gadd (2000: 431) puts it, to

> expose the disparity between what violent men feel, say and do, the interface of men's psychic investment in social discourses and practices. This is where changes could occur.

Simon noted that elsewhere Gadd (2002) questions a view held by some criminologists that domestic violence is an example of 'accomplishing masculinity' (Messerschmidt, 1993). Rather than wife beating being seen as a situational response by men to reassert their damaged sense of masculinity, violence is more likely to culminate in a sense of shame and guilt. Like Jefferson (1997), Gadd scrutinizes emotional and psychic complexity and attends to the dilemmas involved with 'uniting social and psychic processes, which pull in different directions'. Drawing on the account of an individual offender, Gadd (2002) suggests that those men who are violent towards the significant women in their lives do not necessarily find their behaviour acceptable when they describe what they have done. While men can consciously and unconsciously invest in discourse that condones their violence, there is also the issue of public condemnation. Men who were violent attempted to distance themselves from identifying with 'violent, dangerous men', thus seeing themselves as different. Violent men also feel persecuted, even if this feeling cannot be expressed orally, a problem that makes it even more difficult to handle emotions. Defences in the psyche allow the splitting of unwanted parts of the self, which are projected onto the victim. Basically, men recognize that their behaviour is problematic and talk about changing their ways but persist with their violent behaviour. Gadd (2002) argues persuasively that the nature of the relationship many heterosexual men have with women is based on ambivalence and contradiction, where women are 'idealized' and 'denigrated'. This can be explained, in part, with reference to 'gender relations' but also the multifaceted emotions making up men's subjectivities and their tendency to 'split off' and 'reject' what they dislike or do not understand. Indeed, male offenders end up blaming their female victims for their own weaknesses. Perhaps the most important insight offered by the psychosocial approach is that it rests on an understanding of change, so despite the presence of 'stubborn psychic investments', men can be pushed into changing by representing violence against women in terms of 'emasculating weakness' (Gadd, 2000: 445).

CONCLUSIONS

We have learned that every research study entails the use of literature and documents to some extent. The following themes are important:

1. A literature review is a core component of any academic study and at the very least is a springboard for empirical research.
2. If you must complete a mini-research project or dissertation on your course, do not listen to those who say that a library-based study – one that can be turned into a critical literature review – will result in you being given a lower mark than you would receive for an empirical study. This is wrong. A well-planned and organized literature review can offer an original synthesis of what has been written about a given topic.
3. Because all research refers to literature, which is a form of text, there are other methods or approaches to research involving the use of texts that are more than a literature review. Texts include a range of documents, such as academic research, policy statements and legislation, as well as newspaper reports, movies and PC games.
4. Some methods use texts as the main source of data; for example, content analysis and conversation analysis use elaborate and sophisticated methods to gather and analyse documents and other textual material.
5. Other methods, such as some variants of discourse analysis, have drawn on elements of the above as well as more traditional research methods, that is,

interviews, but thinkers such as Foucault use texts as a method of critiquing social systems and the practice of social research.

6. Texts and existing literature can be used in methodologically robust studies but some approaches, most notably Foucault, hold radical views about the nature of language and discourse, suggesting that there is no empirical reality nor any conscious human subjects existing beyond language. This is a form of solipsism (where a thinker lives in their own head, seeing nothing beyond their inner thoughts) and linguistic determinism (where existence is determined or shaped by linguistic structures), which, epistemologically speaking, is an example of relativism, where there are no absolute values, just contextually specific and highly provisional 'truths' – for example, the meaning of 'criminal justice' varies from place to place and over time. In extreme cases like this, there is a strong case for going out into the world and doing some fieldwork to investigate what people and organizations are doing.

Table 8.1 provides a summary of the strengths and weaknesses of content, conversation and discourse analysis.

Table 8.1   Selected strengths and weaknesses of content, conversation and discourse analysis

Strengths	Weaknesses/challenges
Data is readily accessible	A researcher can be accused of selective reading or the argument that the texts chosen are not representative of the literature in a given area
The cost is low	Ontologically, these approaches are anti-realist and relativist. This means there is nothing to judge their validity/reliability outside discourse
Ethical considerations are likely to be negligible or nonexistent	It may be difficult to generalize from any findings
There are clear rules and protocols guiding content analysis and conversation analysis	Some versions of discourse analysis lack clear rules and protocols
Replication of a research project is possible because each researcher will revisit the same text	

REVIEW QUESTIONS

- Explain how to plan and conduct a literature review on a criminological topic of your choice.

- Critically assess the potential contribution of Foucault's archaeological and genealogical methods to criminological research.

- Evaluate the utility of the 'free association narrative interview' method and the psychosocial approach to explain different forms of offending behaviour.

FURTHER READING

If you were to read one book, our recommendation would be:

> Travers, M. (2001) *Qualitative Research through Case Studies*, London: Sage. Chapters 5, 6 and 8.

In addition to this, we suggest you refer to:

> Jefferson, T. and Gadd, D. (2008) *Psychosocial Criminology*. London: Sage.

> Taylor, S. (2001) 'Locating and conducting discourse analytic research', in M. Wetherell, S. Taylor and S. Yates (eds) *Discourse as Data: A Guide for Analysis*. London: Sage.

> Wooffitt, R. (2001) 'Researching psychic practitioners: Conversation analysis', in M. Wetherell, S. Taylor and S. Yates (eds) *Discourse as Data: A Guide for Analysis*. London: Sage.

A classic criminological study using content analysis is:

> Williams, P. and Dickinson, J. (1993) 'Fear of crime: Read all about it? The relationship between newspaper crime reporting and fear of crime', *British Journal of Criminology*, 33(1): 33–56.

A classic criminological study using conversation analysis is:

> Carter, E. (2011) *Laughter, Confessions and the Tape: Analysing Police Interviews*. London: Continuum.

A classic criminological study using discourse analysis is:

> Foucault, M. (1977) *Discipline and Punish: The Birth of the Prison*. Harmondsworth: Penguin.

CHAPTER

9

MIXED METHODS AND TRIANGULATION

OVERVIEW

The aim of this chapter is to:

- Describe the main features of triangulation.
- Explain why you would consider using triangulation.
- Evaluate the practicalities and philosophical issues relating to triangulating methods, data, investigators and theory when you think about and do some basic research projects.

INTRODUCTION

The term 'triangulation' describes using mixed methods or a combination of methods in a single research project. We begin by outlining the basic ideas associated with triangulation, and then trace the conceptual history of triangulation, showing that the idea belongs to surveying and navigation where it refers to the ways in which a fixed entity or item is measured in different ways. You will see that the aim is to gather a variety of evidence in different ways about various aspects of the subject being researched. There are four main types of triangulation:

1. methodological triangulation, including within method triangulation and between method triangulation
2. data triangulation
3. investigator triangulation
4. theoretical triangulation.

Due to the type and scale of research you are likely to undertake, we pay more attention to the first two types. Most student and small-scale research projects do not have the resources needed to do the third type and few are required to attempt the fourth type.

We go on to outline an example of how to do some basic research informed by the principles of triangulation. Finally, we reflect on the uses of triangulation and advise you to be aware of an important point: although research methods and data can be combined and mixed, important epistemological and ontological issues must be noted (see Chapter 2). This is especially so when attempts are made to triangulate theory.

THE PRINCIPLES BEHIND TRIANGULATION

In Chapters 4–8, we dealt with each research method on its own, including questionnaires and surveys, interviews and observational research. However, this may raise a number of questions. For example:

- *Why can't I use more than one method?:* Alan, the student in Chapter 5, who used a survey to explore the fear of crime and levels of anxiety, adopted a blended approach and his survey included closed, scaled as well as open questions. When he came to analysing the survey data, he found that his respondents were sometimes confused about the differences between 'fear' and 'anxiety' about crime and the data he gathered was not as analytically useful as he had originally hoped. If Alan had had more time, and the 'know-how', he could have also explored the ambiguities surrounding 'fear' and 'anxiety' through semi-structured or unstructured interviews. This qualitative data would have given his research participants an opportunity to say more about the source and nature of their confusion and the more nuanced meanings they attached to the words 'anxiety' and 'fear'. The lesson Alan learned is that some methods are good at finding out some things but not all things.

- *Why can't I use more types of data?:* In Chapter 8 we discussed discourse analysis. We saw how this method might be appropriate for researching violent crime. In another example of a student project, Maria investigated this issue and attempted to apply discourse analysis based on Foucault's (1977) genealogical method. She found that tabloid newspapers gave the impression that most violent criminals were predatory strangers who did not know their victims before the attack. After completing her project, Maria's supervisor pointed that by paying such close attention to media representations of this social problem, other sources of data had been neglected, such as official statistics and some large-scale, funded academic and government projects. This other research material showed that most violent offenders either know their victim as an intimate or at the very least are acquainted with them. This body of work does not deny the reality of predatory strangers; instead, it shows their involvement in this crime is relatively rare. The simple message is that different data can be used to research the same issue and generate greater analytical depth.

• *Why can't I look at data in different ways?:* Gareth decided to use semi-structured interviews with football supporters to investigate their perceptions of soccer violence. When his work was assessed, his tutor commented that he could have interpreted his data through competing theoretical perspectives, in particular rational choice theory and cultural criminology. The former approach would argue that the violence committed by hooligans is an outcome of each actor thinking rationally about their actions and calculating the type of violence needed to achieve a particular preconceived or planned goal, for example to deter rival fans from walking onto their territory. The cultural criminologist would be more interested in gathering information about the emotions invested in the violence and the pleasures derived from it, which transcend any conscious and rational calculations. Gareth learned from this observation that there are many ways of seeing an apparently straightforward issue.

It is quite right to raise these questions and you probably have others. The rest of the chapter explains that all these things are achievable but they need to be done in a systematic way. It is necessary for us to think carefully about and plan how each of these things are carried out. Often criminologists will draw on more than one approach and perspective, even in a single project. Their approach may be *eclectic*, that is, choose material from lots of sources, or an attempt to *synthesize*, that is, bring material together from several places. This is what the word 'triangulation' is used to describe. It may seem that by taking each method in its own right, we have perhaps only told part of the story of what criminological researchers actually do. Our view is that it is advisable to grasp each method as fully as possible, in its own right, before attempting to combine or 'triangulate' methods and data. This is because even if, superficially, triangulation looks like an obvious, uncomplicated principle and easy to do in practice, the research is more likely to be robust and successful if each method is carried out correctly. To successfully triangulate, some of the key practical and intellectual skills you have acquired from reading the earlier chapters need further development and refinement. It is important to account for the following factors:

• criminological theory
• the main sources and types of criminological data
• the key principles underscoring each of the main research methods.

Drawing mainly on Denzin's (1970, 1978) characterization of triangulation, we show how combining different methods and approaches to research makes it possible to obtain different types of data, often resulting in a more rounded analysis. This enhances the validity and reliability of research findings, a point well made by Maguire (2000: 137), who commented that triangulation:

> is one of the most valuable of all basic approaches to research in the criminological field. One is almost always dealing with topics on which there is absolutely no reliable information, but if findings from a number of different methods (however weak they may be individually) all point clearly in the same direction, one can have a great deal more confidence in making general statements.

What Maguire (2000) is getting at is that social research, especially the kind done by criminologists, is exploring legally and ethically sensitive and controversial issues. Many offenders may be reluctant to talk to you about how they 'do' crime because they may fear being caught. When offenders do want to talk, you might be worried for ethical reasons, especially if a respondent were to disclose details about an illegal act. Practitioners may cooperate with you but due to the demands placed on criminal justice organizations and the necessity for secrecy about some operational activities, obtaining data can sometimes prove difficult and, in some cases, almost impossible. Even when it comes to less controversial issues, you can think creatively about picking and mixing approaches and methods.

Let us consider a study seeking to understand the relevance of age in relation to offending behaviour. While it is possible to look at official statistics gathered by the police (see Chapter 4), this will only shed light on police activity, that is, who they choose to stop and search, arrest, caution and charge. These statistics will not reveal the full extent of the involvement of people from different age groups in crime. Nor will it reveal anything about the factors causing particular age groups to have a higher involvement in crime compared to other groups. Other sources, such as crime surveys and self-report studies, can complement this data and although there will be variations in terms of the absolute numbers of different age groups and their participation in crime, the likely pattern that will emerge is a higher involvement of young people. This observation also applies to other social divisions, such as gender, ethnicity, disability and sexuality.

Other issues may be less clear-cut and different sources of data about a topic may not confirm each other. In fact, a different data source may reveal something very different altogether. For example, if you wanted to consider the impact, if any, of sexist attitudes on the opportunity women have to gain promotion in the police service, it is possible that contradictory evidence emerges and different evidence gathered by the use of different methods does not, as Maguire's quote (2000) above indicates, 'point clearly in the same direction'. A starting point could be official statistics, which show that there are disproportionately fewer women in senior posts compared to their representation in the junior ranks. It is possible for you to interpret this as evidence of differential treatment, even sexism, yet drawing this conclusion simply by looking at numbers would be unwise. Thus, it would be apt for you to look at documentary sources such as the policy statements issued by the government and police, which state quite clearly that the police service is an equal opportunities employer and that men and women are treated exactly the same. Relying on this data presents a very different picture yet it should not be taken at face value because there is often a gap between policy in writing and policy in action. It may then be decided that a survey of, or interview with, police officers is appropriate, facilitating an insight into less visible processes and systems that influence who gets promoted. It is likely that divergent views will be voiced and they could point in either direction – there is sexist discrimination or both sexes receive equal treatment. The results will depend on the research design, the questions asked and the samples used and could be presented either as evidence pointing towards discrimination or equal treatment. Either way, in such a study, it would be difficult to arrive at any firm conclusions.

Having considered some initial key points about triangulation, the approach is now explored more systematically and in more depth.

TRIANGULATION AND ITS USES

Social scientists, including criminologists, often use terms and methods belonging to other disciplines. The introduction and Chapter 2 showed the influence of the natural sciences on the creation and ongoing evolution of some criminological theories. The concept of triangulation is another example of the criminologist borrowing an idea from a different subject, in this case navigation and land surveying. What has an idea used to guide a ship through a river or across the seas, or to measure and map a geographical area, got do with the study of crime? What Porter (1994: 68) has to say goes some way towards answering this question:

> [Triangulation] ... is borrowed from surveying and navigation. The navigation analogy is more accurate referring to the process whereby a position is 'fixed' using, preferably, different kinds of measures, for example compass bearings, depth surroundings and radio bearings or at least 'position lines' drawn from different positions. The underlying idea is that the wider variety of evidence you can bring to bear, the smaller the area of doubt in your position.

Like us, you are probably unfamiliar with the navigational terms used in this quotation, although it is an effective metaphor showing the main assumptions underlying the idea and an example of how it may be applied in practice. A good illustration is the way a satellite navigation system works. This has a map, showing the distance and directions based on streets and physical objects such as green spaces and waterways. If you use it to find out how to get from A to B, the beginning and end of the journey are the same but the way there and the guides used along the way are all different. On many mobile phones, one of the applications, through the use of global positioning system, can show you a map of where you are standing. We can either zoom in to see the exact spot or zoom out to see the general area we are in. The details shown are very different although they both pinpoint our location.

Another way of defining triangulation is to say that it enables a criminologist to get a better view of something by looking at it from more than one direction and in different ways. This is still a little abstract, so it may be more helpful if we say that it is the collection of different types of data from different sources in relation to a single research problem or question. To use another metaphor, that of mining or excavation, to triangulate is to dig or drill deeper to reveal different levels of social reality.

Denzin (1970) provides a framework to clarify matters, asking what is meant by triangulation, why it is used, and in what ways. As we said, there are four types of triangulation. These are now discussed in turn along with criminologically relevant illustrations.

Methodological triangulation

Denzin (1970: 300) applied the concept of triangulation to refer to the 'combination of methodologies in the study of phenomena' or the combining of multiple/different research methods. In order to triangulate methodologically, you should have chosen to do this because you wanted to use different methods to gather different types of data about the same research topic. It is a good way of responding to unexpected results that may be highlighted by a piece of research, enabling you to check if your expectations were justified. There are two main types of methodological triangulation.

Within method triangulation

Within method triangulation refers to the use of different strategies within the same method, for example, the use of different types of interviews in the same project. Fran, for instance, was asked to design a survey. The set research topic was to explore the relevance of gender, age and educational achievement for attitudes towards drug addicts. She decided to use forced choice items to measure the influence of gender, age and education. Fran considered using similar questions to elicit her respondents' views about this group of people but thought the use of Likert scales and other attitudinal scales (see Chapter 5) would best capture the myriad and complex views of her sample. After piloting her survey, some of the participants expressed the view that Fran could learn more about their attitudes if they were asked some slightly more open-ended questions. She listened to her critics and took their advice, incorporating some questions of this type into her survey. By triangulating in this way, a particular research method is being used in as many ways as possible to maximize the potential data that can be produced.

Between method triangulation

Between method triangulation is also known as 'cross method triangulation'. The main premise is that it is possible to use different data collection methods to look at the same issue. You may decide to use an ethnographic approach to observe the power relations existing between a probation officer and their clients, combining this with one or a mix of the following:

- an analysis of texts such as discourse analysis, for example the reports probation officers write about their clients, designed to understand how social relations are arranged and structured via power through language and talk (see Chapter 8)
- a qualitative, semi-structured interview with the probation officer and a sample of their clients, either speaking to the clients individually or possibly through the use of a focus group
- by administering a quantitative survey exploring client attitudes towards their probation officer and their experiences of how they are treated.

The logic behind mixing methods is that all research methods have strengths and weaknesses, and that combining them can in some way provide compensation for any shortcomings. Taking the example of the probation officer, the analysis of texts will be based more on the methodological rules used to inform the interpretation and analysis of the discourse analyst. By focusing on text, there is a tendency to see social reality as something that can be reduced to the effects of language, with the outcome that other layers or levels of social reality beyond language are neglected. It would not be possible, through discourse analysis, to grasp the meanings negotiated through the social interaction or conversation between the two parties involved. There are other issues that may arise that are more amenable to quantitative measurement such as attitude scales.

Between method triangulation is best used when it is adopted in a systematic way or as part of a process. For some research projects, it may be judged that the best approach is to start by looking at relevant documentary sources. For example, Samuel is interested in the experiences of providers (police officers) and recipients (members of the public) of crime prevention advice in the form of a leaflet given to householders in the aftermath of a burglary. He first analyses the leaflet to identify points of interest and specific forms of advice. To understand how this advice has been received, Samuel established a second stage of fieldwork: a small self-completed questionnaire to representative samples of both populations, that is, crime prevention officers and victims of burglary. The quantitative study would also enable Samuel to produce hypotheses, define terminology, and look at key concepts. Because some of the issues raised by the survey attend to emotions, such as fear of burglary, and subjective beliefs, such as individuals' steps to reduce their perceived risks of burglary, Samuel developed a third approach: qualitative interviews with a small number of crime prevention officers and the victims of burglary.

Samuel found that the policy statements were very clear and in principle provided the advice and support required by service users. The interviews with the providers of crime prevention advice showed that they were committed to the scheme and clearly understood their respective roles and responsibilities. In their view, the people receiving advice seemed happy with the work they were doing. The small numbers of service users interviewed were also positive. However, the self-completed questionnaire distributed to a wider group of burglary victims revealed the opposite findings, there was less willingness to rely on police advice and more likelihood of relying on their own assumptions of what crime prevention should involve. Samuel was more confident in the validity of the self-completed questionnaire because the sample population was more representative of all service users rather than a self-selected, less representative population. If Samuel had based his report on the interviews, he may well have based his findings on incorrect conclusions.

There are clear benefits to conducting research using methodological triangulation, not least because it compels you to reflect on the appropriateness of a particular method by seeking confirmation and verification of research findings. There is a significant pitfall, though, because it potentially exposes major philosophical differences. The choice of a method, especially when a choice is made between quantitative or qualitative methods, and when there are competing epistemological and ontological frameworks, can be based on diametrically opposed values and assumptions about the criminological world (see Chapter 2). For example, if you are a quantitative criminologist, you may view the topic of study as amenable to techniques of counting and quantifying. Some qualitative criminologists might argue that such approaches are not capable of capturing deeper thoughts, feelings and motivations attached to things. This is a problem that we revisit in the concluding section of the chapter.

Data triangulation

The main point of **data triangulation** is that you can combine data from more than one source. At a basic level, it means that in a particular research project, a range of different types of data may be collected, which could include either various sources of quantitative or qualitative data or elements of both. Thus, the different pieces of data that are collected, albeit from different sources, will attempt to address a single research question. In one sense, many pieces of empirical research could be said to draw on more than one type of data because all research projects necessarily begin with a literature review (see Chapter 8 for a fuller account) to identify hypotheses requiring further testing or to identify gaps in our knowledge of specific criminological issues. In other words, we all engage in dialogue or a conversation with previous research through contextual reading and cross-referencing. This is true enough but it is more usual to talk about this type of triangulation when using fieldwork data or data obtained through interviews, surveys or observational research.

When triangulating data, criminologists often refer to three reference points: time, space and person. To give an example, imagine you have been asked to produce a research design to explore perceptions of personal safety in a city centre at night at weekends. This is the time of week when many people go out to watch a film or play, go out for a meal or go out to drink and party. The reasons why people go out are diverse, although there is also a greater likelihood of witnessing antisocial behaviour, disorder and the threat of violent crime during these times. Even if these are not visible, people will be aware of the factual existence of these problems and may adjust their behaviour accordingly. To explore these issues using our example, the following need to be considered:

1. *Time:* Data could be gathered from various sources at three points in the year – every four months – including Christmas/New Year, spring and the end of summer. It is quite likely that drunkenness and disorder is high at Christmas/New Year and possibly, if the weather is warm, in the summer. Alternatively, a researcher may choose to gather data at four, four hourly intervals: 8 pm, 11 pm, 2 am and 5 am. There is likely to be a correlation between these intervals and the level of alcohol consumption and drunkenness, with drinking and disorder increasing into the late/early hours.

2. *Space:* There are key places and settings in the city centre, for example the areas where the theatres and cinemas are concentrated, and those areas with a high density of bars and clubs and restaurants respectively. As you will know from first-hand experience, often the boundaries between these areas will be blurred and overlapping, but the experience of antisocial behaviour and perceived and actual threats to personal safety are likely to be highest in close proximity to the bars and clubs. Data gathered by survey, interview and observational methods is likely to confirm this finding.

3. *Person/groups:* Although some overlap is likely, there is a chance that an older crowd will be using the space differently, for example going out for a meal

and to see a show, than a younger crowd going out to drink and socialize. If so, their feelings of safety are likely to be noticeably different. Also, it is possible to think about other people who have direct experience of the same environment, such as police officers, security staff and staff employed in the different venues.

For some researchers, triangulating different types of data may be quite controversial and earlier chapters have shown how some quantitative researchers of a positivist orientation will favour handling statistical data and qualitative researchers who are committed interpretivists will favour looking at social action and the uses of language. Bottoms (2000: 21–2) describes this attitude towards data as a consequence of 'methodological pigeonholing' that all too often is counterproductive and stops a researcher providing a more rounded and balanced evidence base with which to work.

Investigator triangulation

In **investigator triangulation**, more than one researcher is often involved in a research project. While many university projects involve being assessed as an individual, on some modules you may be asked to produce a research design in principle which may require working as a team. In the workplace, working as part of a research team is common. In some of the research you do, you will also be asked to reflect on the research process and identify ways of improving future research. One way may be working in partnership with other researchers.

There is more to investigator triangulation than just doing research with other people, and research projects using this approach tend to be based on several considerations. Criminologists may use multiple investigators in studies using a single research method as well as those where more than one method is used. Opting to use two or more investigators will be based on two main considerations: logistical and analytical.

1. **Logistical factors**: The volume of work being done, say, in a face-to-face survey that is administered to a large sample population may require a team of researchers to ensure that the workloads are manageable and the study is completed within a fixed time limit. To take another example, in a multimethod study, which combines a survey with semi-structured interviews and content analysis, it is unlikely that all researchers are equally competent when it comes to all the available research methods. Some criminologists can do everything and even though many of them will have knowledge and understanding of all research methods, on the whole, individual researchers tend to specialize and be skilled in particular methodological approaches. Some researchers are highly numerate, such as econometricians, but they may have never done

any discourse analysis or ethnographic research. Some qualitative research-ers are anxious about numbers and the thought of using a statistical package, such as SPSS. In some studies where methods are combined, the division of labour may be a result of convenience and the accessibility of researchers.

2. *Analytical factors:* Using more than one investigator creates the scope for a study to incorporate different angles on a particular issue. This could reflect the respective orientations of the different researchers towards qualitative or quantitative methods and data. Even if the investigators share a similar out-look, there is an opportunity to check and challenge individual interpretations. This can be used to eliminate errors or add a unique take on a topic.

Theoretical triangulation

Theoretical triangulation is probably the hardest type of triangulation to grasp both as an idea and to carry out in practice. However, the principle is fairly sim-ple: it is all about looking at data from different theoretical positions. You would use it if you wanted to consider how the different assumptions underpinning a theoretical approach affect how data is interpreted. Imagine the divergent explanations of rape advanced by a rational choice theorist, on the one hand, who may see rape in relation to opportunity and rewards for the offender and, on the other, a radical feminist, who may emphasize structural and cultural fac-tors relating to the disadvantaging of women. It is unlikely that they will agree on much here. There is also a recognition that there needs to be an ongoing interaction between theory and research, specifically a continuous process of refutation (disproving) and confirmation (proving). Sometimes, research data will lend support to a theory and at other times it will show that a theory is out of kilter with empirical reality.

There are no restrictions regarding the type of data that can be looked at, so we could be looking at statistical datasets (see Chapter 5) or interview tran-scripts (see Chapter 6). A researcher can consider testing as many proposi-tions and theories as possible in relation to offending, victimization and criminal justice workers. By using just one theory, other possibilities may be excluded, thus limiting the theoretical lessons that can be learned from a project. You need to be aware that, even though there are many alternative and competing theoretical frameworks which can be drawn on (see Chapter 3), they need to be approached with caution.

Theoretical triangulation gives room to situate criminological research in the context of wider debates in the social sciences, such as the relative signifi-cance of rational choice or cultural factors for explaining crime and disorder or various strategies of social control (see Chapter 3). The selection of theories will be based on the importance attached to social structure at a macro-level and the agency employed in social interaction at a micro-level. Some criminological theories, notably left realism, synthesize a range of criminological approaches, providing a holistic, multidimensional approach. Other criminologists may not be convinced by an attempt to integrate sometimes incompatible perspectives. It could be argued that using criminological theory in this way is problematic because of the radically different value frameworks, and epistemological and ontological assumptions that are at the heart of individual theoretical perspectives. Can the accounts of critical criminologists, who draw attention to the inequalities and injustices experienced by minority ethnic groups and women, really be combined with those of administrative criminologists and crime scientists, who are inclined to discuss these as technical or politically motivated considerations?

DOING TRIANGULATION: AN EXAMPLE

Edward was a mature, part-time student who combined his studies with working for an organization called Crimebusters, based in a medium-sized city called Eastown. His line manager, a key stakeholder in the partnership, suggested he could apply some of his criminological skills and knowledge by doing a small piece of research that was of direct relevance to his job and which may work in his favour for his future personal career development. When Edward was required to do some research as part of his degree, this coincided with an initiative called Operation Crackdown, led by Crimebusters, and his employer was interested in evaluating the impact of this initiative on crime, disorder and antisocial behaviour (see the 'broken windows' thesis in Chapter 3) in two areas of Eastown, Upperton and Lowerton. The operation was given this strapline because it was a term used by Nick Tilley, a leading crime scientist, to describe short, intensive bursts of activity to target particular offences such as drug dealing, street robberies and prostitution. Operation Crackdown was introduced for a month in both places, and was designed as an intensive, focused initiative involving a range of statutory and voluntary sector agencies working together. It included law enforcement, crime prevention and community safety strategies.

Crimebusters was an organization that brought together many agencies from the statutory, commercial/private and voluntary community sectors to work in partnership to tackle crime and disorder. Crimebusters, and similar organizations, are put in place to integrate the work of the police, local government, probation and service providers in the fields of health, housing, education and social services among others. Every organization, even those in the private sector such as businesses and retailers, has to consider crime and disorder and develop joined-up solutions to crime. A good example of this is pubs and nightclubs where the risk of alcohol-related violence is high. The licensing authorities must think about pub opening hours and their attitudes to drunkenness because the criminality and disorderliness associated with this have a knock-on effect on the wider community and people living and working there.

Edward had several ideas for his project, although his employer was keen that the research should be relevant to the needs and working of Crimebusters; this pressure placed on the researcher by the employer demonstrates the influence of politics (see Chapter 2) on the research process. It was made clear to Edward that if he refused to base his research on these priorities, he would not be given permission to go ahead with the project. Edward consented to the requests of his employer because he wanted to get a degree and hopefully, sometime in the future, gain promotion at work. Edward's line manager told him that Crimebusters wanted to explore four themes:

1. The impact of Operation Crackdown in terms of the reduction of crime and disorder in Upperton and Lowerton.
2. Public perceptions of crime and disorder in relation to Operation Crackdown.
3. The success of Operation Crackdown, that is, has it reduced the fear of crime?
4. The nature and effectiveness of partnership working resulting from Operation Crackdown.

Edward had little choice and followed the wishes of his paymaster but he did some theoretical 'smuggling' and he wanted to test out a theoretical observation made by Tilley (2005a) about 'crackdowns'. He argued that crackdowns tend to be controlled and dominated by the police and that partnership working was not always achieved. Another criminologist added that partnership working of this kind is not always carried on after the crackdown itself and that communities who benefit from these initiatives over a short-term period soon forget any positive achievements (Hopkins Burke, 2009).

To comprehend these issues, Edward felt that no single research method or type of data, on its own, would provide a satisfactory response to the four aims and objectives. He remembered one of his lecturers talking about 'triangulation' and concluded this would be a promising option.

Planning and designing the research

Edward decided to use a **case study**, one for Upperton and another for Lowerton. Like many researchers, Edward preferred the case study approach because he wanted to glean a holistic impression of what was occurring in both geographical areas. By concentrating on two well-defined contexts, he was able to piece together a comprehensive picture, encapsulating what was going on in each section. In policy evaluations like Edward's, the triangulation of methods and data means that multiple understandings of a policy like Operation Crackdown could be revealed. He could also see how each agency implemented the operation and the different perspectives held by diverse actors about their own actions and the actions of others. The fact that this information included quantitative and qualitative data resulted in a fine-grained account of the complex processes and actions involving Crimebusters and other organizations and individual players.

In addition, case studies were adopted because Edward thought that it was not feasible to study his chosen research topic satisfactorily in a social context other than in the actual location itself. These two geographical areas of Eastown were selected because although Operation Crackdown was introduced across the whole city over the period of three months, these were the first and last places where the initiative was implemented. Edward thought that given the limited time and resources available for him to finish the study, he could carry out the field-work and data analysis for the first area and then carry out the second one once that was out of the way. To address the objectives of the research, he decided on triangulating both different research methods and sources of data. He used:

- Qualitative semi-structured interviews, selected by convenience sampling, with 32 practitioners representing all the agencies involved in Operation Crackdown, including 15 from Upperton and 17 from Lowerton. At the outset, and because Edward worked for Crimebusters, he set his mind on doing face-to-face interviews.
- A focus group – a variation on an interview – was used to gather the perceptions of 6 senior members of the Crimebusters partnership in Eastown that included his line manager (see Chapter 6). The 32 practitioners were involved in designing the initiative at a strategic level and the 6 focus group members for implementing it at an operational level. Edward judged it was important to gain some understanding of what Operation Crackdown was supposed to achieve in principle and what it actually achieved in practice.
- Because another aim of the research was to look at public perceptions, Edward produced a quantitative, face-to-face survey (see Chapter 5), which would be completed by 50 residents in both the Upperton and Lowerton areas, totalling 100 respondents.
- These methods were supported by desk-based research, including an analysis of available crime statistics obtained by the police and Crimebusters and a review of media coverage of Operation Crackdown, based loosely on the principles of content analysis (see Chapter 8).

Because of Edward's status as an employee, he was confident that he would easily gain access to the employees contributing to Operation Crackdown, especially because his line manager was a senior figure in running Crimebusters.

Identifying all the organizations collaborating in the implementation of the oper-ation in the two areas of the city produced the sample. In the first instance, these individuals were contacted via an email outlining the aims and objectives of the research. The initial response was very disappointing and when Edward fed this back to his line manager, he instructed Edward to emphasize that the project 'had his full backing' and that an introductory statement in the email indicating this would increase the response rate. The university where Edward was study-ing was in the early stages of a process of introducing a research ethics commit-tee and it was not necessary for him to formally consider this factor. If you were a critical reader, you might have thought that the role of his line manager raised an ethical issue about the degree of the consent exercised by the research partic-ipants. For example, it would appear that the participants were compelled to participate because they were put under some pressure by a senior figure who had contributed towards the design and implementation of the operation. There is the potential here that, when interviewed, these individuals would give the answers they thought the researcher wanted to hear. Setting up the focus group proved far more straightforward because the intended participants were the individuals responsible for the planning and design of the initiative and had an interest in getting the research done.

In order to gain community feedback from Upperton and Lowerton, Edward decided he would conduct a survey of residents of both areas to acquire quan-titative data. This would guarantee that feedback would be obtained from the intended beneficiaries of the Operation Crackdown initiative. To this end, Edward attended popular and prominent locations in both Upperton and Lowerton and accessed the views of individuals who lived in the area using a process of random sampling. In total, 100 face-to-face surveys interviews were undertaken (50 in each area).

Conducting the fieldwork and analysing the data

For the semi-structured intewrviews, it took up to seven attempts to contact the individuals. Eventually, a full response was achieved but this took longer than Edward had planned and he decided to adapt his plans. Arranging and doing face-to-face interviews could prove both expensive and time-consuming so he did telephone interviews instead and where this was not practicable, the partici-pants were asked to complete the interview schedule electronically, via email.

None of these interviews were tape recorded but notes were taken and used to elicit key themes relating to the evaluation. The respondents spoke most freely in relation to the evaluation criteria. It was recognized that some of the issues and debates addressed were potentially of a politically sensitive nature and for this reason the interview data was anonymized as far as possible. Rather than potentially identifying individuals through the use of extensive quotations, Edward extracted key themes and, where appropriate, the identity of particular agencies, for example police, fire and rescue service, local authority, providers of health services, was occasionally noted.

The focus group, face-to-face surveys and content analysis ran smoothly and according to plan.

The interpretation of the data by Edward was completed in four stages, based on the four aims and objectives of the evaluation. The desk-based research, where Edward reviewed the statistical data to find out if there had been any increases and decreases in the number of crimes committed, was an element of research aim 1.

In the few years before Operation Crackdown was implemented, statistical data showed that crime and disorder had been going down across Eastown. The data gathered for the specific purpose of his evaluation did show a fall in crime and disorder in both areas:

- In Upperton, following Operation Crackdown there were fewer burglaries (−75%), incidents of criminal damage (−38%) and robberies (−55%).
- In Lowerton, car crime, burglary, robbery and violence against the person and incidents of antisocial behaviour and criminal damage all fell.

Edward was aware of the limitations of this statistical data (see Chapters 4 and 5), in particular that it is not possible to conclude with any certainty that crime rates are influenced by a particular operation, especially one running over such a short time period. Criminologists need to be aware that other factors, such as the time of year and the complex mix of initiatives, could all impact in complex ways.

Turning to aim 2 of the research – public perceptions of Operation Crackdown – it was apparent that the media supported the initiative and there were positive articles in local newspapers and features on regional television and radio broadcasts, all reporting a number of success stories. We know that the media has an influence on public perceptions of crime and justice issues and that for many people what they see, read and hear is the only knowledge they have of the 'reality' of crime (see Chapter 2). As noted above, this was why Edward designed a survey to ask residents if they had any first-hand knowledge and experience of Operation Crackdown. The small sample used for the survey made it difficult to draw any generalizations, although many of those who had direct contact with the initiative expressed positive views – there were a few more negative respondents and a significant number who lacked any awareness of what had happened.

Aim 3 of the research was to see if Operation Crackdown impacted on the fear of crime. When Edward did this research in the late 2000s, fear of crime was a priority in crime policy across the world. Thus, many crime reduction strategies were underpinned by the assumption that the fear of crime is as important as the reality, something confirmed by community consultation where the residents in Uppertown and Lowertown were asked for their views about fear of crime. A key finding relating to aim 2 was that some members of the public said they did not know much about Operation Crackdown, yet the survey showed that other respondents felt it addressed their fear of crime either in practice or in principle. The survey showed that some respondents felt more confident, secure and safe as a result of an increased police presence during the two crackdowns. There was a deliberate decision by Crimebusters in Eastown to increase the visibility of police officers on patrol – both on foot and in vehicles – and by crime prevention officers making door to door visits advising people on how to protect their property from burglars. They also saw increased activity by other agencies from the statutory and voluntary and community sectors that all got involved in addressing criminal and antisocial behaviour.

Aim 4 of the research addressed the nature and effectiveness of partnership working. The data provided evidence of effective partnership working. The interview and focus group data demonstrated that the different agencies, from all the sectors, were working together to tackle the social problems identified as targets of Operation Crackdown. The respondents also noted that, during the specific weeks when the operation ran in the two areas of Eastown, new networks and opportunities were created for effective joined-up responses to criminality and disorderliness.

CONCLUSIONS

The aim of this chapter was to show that the main purpose of triangulation is to verify or broaden and deepen our understanding of criminological issues:

1. The most popular types of triangulation are *methodological* and *data* and although *investigator* and *theoretical* forms are both important, they are less frequently used.
2. An emergent theme here is that if you choose to triangulate, you need to come to terms with the practical, philosophical and political considerations arising in relation to each method and type of data; an exercise further complicated by combining different types. Perhaps the main objective underlying triangulation is the idea that in order to have an insight into the 'truth' about any phenomenon, we need as many different types of evidence as possible to verify and confirm what is known. To use the crime scene as a metaphor, we have the location and the criminal act, but without other forms of material evidence we are very much in the dark. For this reason, those investigating the crime

scene will use various *methods* to gather forensic evidence or *data* – such as DNA traces, items used to commit the crime – and evidence from people who have witnessed the crime or have some knowledge of the place or persons involved in the crime. There will be various *investigators* including, among others, law enforcement personnel, scientists and IT specialists. All those involved and other commentators such as journalists and academics may refer to a range of *theories*, depending on the crime, to explain why it was committed and how to solve it. Although it is unlikely we will ever know and verify exactly what happened at a particular crime scene, we would be able to build up a picture and offer a plausible account. So we can aspire to formulate a rounded overview.

3. Perhaps the most important benefit to be gained from all forms of triangulation is that they are useful for revealing questions that remain unanswered, inconsistencies and areas in need of elaboration.

4. The downside is that we can never find the right answers to anything, only the most plausible and persuasive one based on the tools we have to hand.

Table 9.1 provides a summary of the strengths and weaknesses of triangulation.

Table 9.1   Selected strengths and weaknesses of triangulation

Strengths	Weaknesses/challenges
All the strengths of the methods described in Chapters 4–8 apply here too	All the weaknesses of the methods described in Chapters 4–8 apply here too
By mixing methods and data, it is possible to appreciate the multidimensionality of the particular issue being studied	Some critics argue that combining qualitative and quantitative methods and data presents insurmountable epistemological problems
Reliability and validity can be enhanced	The particular combination of data and/or methods may not be appropriate for the issue being studied
Using multiple observers can limit the problem of bias	Investigator triangulation requires additional steps to ensure the consistency of data collection

REVIEW QUESTIONS

- Outline the advantages and drawbacks of the following: methodological triangulation, including 'within' and 'between' method triangulation; data triangulation; investigator triangulation; and theoretical triangulation.

- Evaluate the logistical and analytical benefits of data triangulation.

- Critically examine the ontological and epistemological tensions when triangulating with quantitative and qualitative methods.

FURTHER READING

If you were to read one book, our recommendation would be:

> Denzin, N.K. (1978) *Sociological Methods: A Sourcebook* (2nd edn). New York: McGraw-Hill.

In addition to this, we suggest you refer to:

> Creswell, J.W. (2003) *Research Design: Qualitative, Quantitative and Mixed Methods Approaches* (2nd edn). London: Sage. Chapter 11.

> Denscombe, M. (2010) *The Good Research Guide for Small-scale Research Projects* (4th edn). Milton Keynes: Open University Press. Chapter 8.

A classic criminological study that triangulates methods is:

> Shaw, C. and McKay, H. (1942) *Juvenile Delinquency and Urban Areas*. Chicago: University of Chicago Press.

CONCLUSION

This brief final chapter summarizes and reflects on the three themes contained in the subtitle of this book: approaches, methods and application. We hope this is a useful framework to help you with the practicalities of doing research and suggest you refer to this whenever you are asked to evaluate the research of others, but principally when you are planning and doing your own research.

APPROACHES, METHODS AND APPLICATION

How you *approach* any research exercise will be based on you giving thought to a range of issues, although key considerations include criminological theories, epistemological and ontological assumptions, different styles of research, as well as political and ethical considerations. These are the issues we looked at in Part 1. There is a diverse, rich body of work that has been published by criminologists from many disciplines and traditions, spanning at least three centuries. We suggest that an essential prerequisite for doing your own research is some familiarity with the main currents in criminological thought and research and an appreciation of how they are related. What contribution has been made by quantitative and qualitative research? Is theoretical research superior to empirical research funded by the state, with its vested interests in proving a point? Another key lesson to learn is that every piece of criminological research you look at will have dealt with wider theoretical and methodological questions and probably drawn on specific research methods in particular. When you look at any study, it is important to appraise and evaluate the methods used by the researchers responsible for producing the study. To what extent were the selected methods the appropriate tools to answer their research questions? Did they choose the right methods? If yes, why, if no, why not? Questions like this will help you to plan your own research. The contextual details belonging to Part 1 are an important backdrop, but it is in Part 2 that we moved beyond these framing issues to discuss the *methods* you can use and the key issues arising in their *application*. Throughout the book, we have demonstrated that:

- the issue of *methods* is all about identifying the most appropriate tools for addressing and/or answering your research questions
- the *application* of research is all about actually doing research, using specified methods and thinking about the wider theoretical and practical relevance of what you are doing.

A CHECKLIST FOR DOING RESEARCH

1.   What is the overall focus of the research?
To answer this question, it is necessary to be clear in your own mind about the issue or topic the research is looking at. For some research projects an assignment will be set for you, which is likely to include guidance on the various tasks to be carried out. On other occasions, it will be your responsibility to think about the focus of your research and formulate your own research question. It is essential that the question posed is both meaningful and one that can be answered. Typically, the achievement of these goals is based on the focus of the study being sufficiently narrow and specific.

2.   How does your work relate to existing work in this area?
Awareness of existing published research is an important foundation of all research, and you should demonstrate with some confidence that you know what is already out there. Are you adding to the large volume of work by repeating an aspect of the work done by other researchers, or are you carving out a niche with the aim of producing an original piece of work?

3.   What are the key aims of the research?
Being ambitious is not a bad thing but your aims need to be realistic and appreciate that most research studies do not change the world or redefine criminology. Like the focus of a research project, the aims need to be manageable, especially in light of the constraints confronting all researchers. Is the research curiosity driven or is it applied? Above all, if the aims are to be achievable, they need to be realistic.

4.   What are the main ethical dilemmas posed by the research?
Ethical considerations are often central to any empirical research project. Notwithstanding the increasingly litigious world where people are inclined to sue organizations for any harm they come to as a result of organizational activities, it is imperative that the health and safety of the researcher(s) and research participant(s) are taken into account. What are the implications of your research on those you are researching?

5.   Are you trying to prove, identify, explain, understand relationships, assess the prevalence of something and so on?

Finding out about something that happens is an integral feature of criminological enquiry and all natural and social scientific researchers are oriented towards this goal. Yet, in contrast with the natural sciences, it is highly unlikely that any research you undertake will prove or identify any causal links between two factors – for example whether the introduction of surveillance cameras in a car park reduces the theft of motor vehicles – but it may reveal a correlation, association or relationship that is crying out for further research. If your aspiration is to understand and explain why something happens, it is important to make sure you choose the appropriate method(s), which are likely to produce the most reliable and valid explanation of what is occurring.

6.   Which general approaches to research are appropriate? Is your research inductive or deductive?

This is yet another important consideration and you will need to decide if you are gathering research data to explore existing theories by testing out hypotheses, or if you are going to allow the data to speak for itself.

7.   What is your likely level of access to the research population?

This question is germane to all research, but especially empirical studies. A library-based study relying exclusively on documents and texts, if it is to be successful, relies on the relevant literature being accessed, which should not always be taken for granted, especially if a study is time limited. For projects involving fieldwork, access is of vital importance. However focused and coherent the focus of a study is, it does not automatically follow that you will survey, interview or observe your intended participants. Gaining access is far from straightforward, especially if you have no personal contacts and have to contact individuals and/or organizations cold. Even when a researcher knows their intended participants, either in a professional or personal capacity, there are no guarantees that they are going to accede to your requests for assistance in completing your research project.

8.   How much do you know about the research environment before undertaking fieldwork?

A factor motivating a researcher to study a topic is often personal interest, which could be academic or professional. This interest may mean that you are familiar with the organizational setting or groups of people involved in the research process. Even if you feel that you have the requisite level of familiarity, it is advisable that you do as much background, contextual research as possible.

9. What are the strengths and weaknesses of your chosen method?

A simple rule that is applicable to any piece of research is that there are always areas for improvement or refinement, however appropriate your choice of method(s) appear to be on paper. A common dispute arises between researchers who are committed to different epistemological, ontological and methodological standpoints. Some qualitative studies are criticized by quantitative criminologists because the data gathered is deemed not valid and representative of the wider population. The material is too subjective and cannot easily be verified. A quantitative study drawing exclusively on statistical data may not be well received by a qualitative analyst who may consider that numerical data glosses over the meanings human agents attach to their actions. Even when this dispute is not evident, all researchers need to be reflexive and think critically about any piece of research they complete. More data, a more representative sample, more time, the triangulation of data and methods are just a few of the things that could lead to the enhancement of a study.

10. Which alternative research methods could be employed? Why were they not chosen?

This connects with the previous point and although most researchers will refer to this theme in their evaluation and review of their own work, it is not always desirable and practicable to use other methods. Most crucially, some methods are not appropriate for answering particular research questions. The trick is to have a clear idea of and make explicit the rationale for using a specific method/combination of methods. Many readers of research will be committed to certain approaches and styles to research but if a study outlines in a transparent way why their methods were chosen, they will, in most cases, agree to differ, recognizing the richness and diversity of the endeavours of criminological researchers.

11. Can you justify your choice of data categories to a critical audience?

For most of you, the critic is going to be the person assessing your work and ensuring you write a persuasive statement outlining the case for this choice is essential.

12. Does your sample need to be representative? If so, how will this be achieved?

Some researchers, principally if they are doing ethnographic and some other forms of qualitative analysis, are not troubled by this question, not least because this is not one of their main aims. Their research could be exploratory or explicitly about a single context where the population studied, whether an organization, person or documentary source, is never intended to display characteristics belonging to the general population. A driver underlying much quantitative research, especially surveys, is the quest for identifying patterns and potential causal links or at least a correlation between variables that are based on a sample that is representative of the general population. Large-scale surveys are consciously designed to be representative and even a small study, say an undergraduate dissertation, could be designed to be representative. It is unlikely, however, that, in practice, the latter will satisfy these requirements but it is likely to be considered as a benchmark to show what the researcher would liked to have done if circumstances allowed it.

13. If you are undertaking quantitative research, how many participants are needed in order to generalize the findings to a wider population?

In a sense, this is a 'how long is a piece of string?' question but if you look more closely at it, it poses a quandary for most small-scale studies, especially quantitative ones. For example, a survey of 30 students in your university is probably not representative of the population in the university or further afield than that. As there is little chance that you are going to be able to design and administer a large-scale, national survey, it is unlikely that you will be penalized for not producing a representative study. The situation to avoid is overselling or overstating the significance of your findings. So, ensure that you are honest about the scope and wider applicability of your research.

14. How much time do you have to undertake the fieldwork?

Time is not the only resource you have at your disposal, but in contrast to professional researchers who will be managing funded projects, money should not be a major consideration. Time is limited, though, depending on the assessment you are completing. If your task is to write a proposal, you can be more generous in allocating the right amount of time to the different components of the study. A dissertation or other small-scale study will be time limited and the important rule is to plan every activity. If a project includes fieldwork, make allowances for the design of the research instrument as well as its application. Setting up interviews and administering surveys can take hours, and the transcription of data can eat up hours and days. Even the smallest jobs, like printing off copies of your report, getting it bound and so on, are deceptively time-consuming.

15. How do you plan to analyse your data?

A lot of small-scale studies amass a relatively small volume of research data, but never underestimate the work involved in analysing this material. Most student projects that use quantitative methods result in statistical data that can be counted manually and basic graphs can be used to present this descriptive data. Some more advanced studies are better served by using packages such as SPSS (see Chapter 5); if you need to use one, make sure you have some knowledge of how it works, because you do not want to have to learn how to do this late on in the research process. A similar observation is also germane for qualitative studies, where the researcher can pick out themes from their data by careful repeated reading of their interview transcripts. There are computer packages that assist with qualitative analysis, such as NVivo and MAXQDA, but the previous observation about knowing how to use them is also pertinent.

16.   Have you drawn up a realistic research plan?

This checklist has addressed various activities at different stages of the research process, and an appreciation of the fact that research is a process is at the heart of successful project planning. Any such project, and this is not exclusive to criminological research, needs to be planned with forethought and the assignment needs breaking down into manageable chunks. Some of these activities will be performed at the same time and there will be overlaps between them. Doing research is very much like juggling and multitasking. The latter skill is very much in demand. The list below includes what you would need to do for a typical study:

- Read and write constantly
- Submit a research proposal
- Respond to feedback on the proposal and revise accordingly
- Conduct a literature review
- Think about epistemological, ontological and methodological issues
- Decide on an approach and method(s) that are appropriate for your study
- Consider the resources required and reflect on any ethical issues
- Focus on research design
- If the study is empirical, gather your data
- Analyse the data
- Write up the research

Simple advice such as using a calendar or diary to highlight milestones is all too often forgotten, but it is essential if a project is to be completed successfully. Effective planning and timekeeping are key to delivering good research, on time. The content and findings are clearly more significant but without a sensible, logical plan, this may never come to light.

We wish you luck with any research projects you have to undertake and hope, most of all, that you enjoy the challenges the process throws at you.

APPENDICES

APPENDIX 1
AN INTERNET GUIDE FOR CRIMINOLOGY STUDENTS

The guide is divided into two parts. First, guidance is given on the tools of research: online facilities that can inform and shape university-level research projects in criminology. It is assumed that there is a degree of familiarity with university library facilities, which differ across institutions but normally provide extensive guidance and induction schemes (see Giddens, 1997: 554-7 on 'how to use libraries'), and so emphasis is centred on the role of the internet as a research tool.

Second, key online criminological resources are highlighted. Rather than simply listing a range of 'useful sites', in the way that 'links' pages are often structured, commentary is offered on the content and relative importance of key sites. These links also connect with the discussion of online 'research resources' offered in Chapter 4.

RESEARCH TOOLS

Internal university pages

These are a useful place to start. There are usually at least three areas of a university website of considerable use for criminology students:

1. *The department, school or faculty page:* Often contains information about the course, its wider context and links to other sites (see below).
2. *Virtual learning environments (VLEs):* Online intranet sites such as 'blackboard' or 'moodle' accompany many courses. They are repositories for a wealth of course-related information – lecture slides, additional reading, links, interesting information and opportunities to engage with tutors and other students.

3. *University library websites:* Maintained by professional librarians, they are an extremely valuable resource. They often have connections to course reading lists and key materials and, crucially, provide a gateway to electronic journals.

Most universities hosting a criminology course will subscribe to journals such as *The British Journal of Criminology, The Australian & New Zealand Journal of Criminology, The American Journal of Criminal Justice, Theoretical Criminology, Criminology and Criminal Justice, Punishment and Society* and others. Depending on the system individual universities use, many electronic journals can either be accessed directly through the library website or via a third party provider, such as an 'Athens' (sometimes listed as OpenAthens or My Athens) account. Athens is a portal (or access management system) that allows users access to particular resources on behalf of their university. Students can normally open an Athens account via their library's website when using a university-networked computer. Another form of remote access is an institutional login, sometimes called a 'Shibboleth login'. These allow individuals to access third party sites (such as ingentaconnect, see below) using their university login details. Depending on your university's subscriptions, other third party sites may enable you to download academic articles. In criminology, one commonly used third party portal is SwetsWise: www.swetswise.com.

Online literature searches

Most research projects involve a review of related research and literature (Chapters 1 and 8). These are often conducted via a search of academic libraries such as those housed at universities. Students can, however, search beyond these boundaries. Some of the most comprehensively stocked libraries in the world are the British Library in London, the Library of Congress in the USA and the National Library of Australia:

> www.bl.uk/
> www.loc.gov/index.html
> www.nla.gov.au/libraries/

Internationally, there are many databases that conduct searches of millions of academic publications and provide other services including online access to articles (normally for a fee) and also allow search results to be emailed or downloaded. Perhaps the most prominent of these is ingentaconnect:

> www.ingentaconnect.com

This can be accessed via Athens, Shibboleth or an individual account and is an extremely useful tool to help understand the range of existing work conducted on a particular area of criminology, as well as most other academic disciplines.

Search engine-based resources

Existing internet search engines are often the first port of call for many researchers. Within some search engines are academically focused mini-engines, designed to prioritize academic outputs. Perhaps the best known and most comprehensive of these is Google Scholar:

http://scholar.google.co.uk/

A related resource is Google Books, a utility that enables access to an ever-expanding library of books that may be viewed online:

http://books.google.com/

Dedicated online 'meta-search' tools also exist that are efficient ways of searching through specific discipline-related fields. In the UK (and internationally), Intute originated from a consortium of universities to provide an online research tool that supplied detailed search results on a number of academic subjects. This has now expanded to be a freely available and highly effective research tool:

www.intute.ac.uk/socialsciences/

Other discipline-specific searches also exist, including:

www.abacon.com/internetguides/soc/weblink.html

Other research tools include the mechanisms for accessing raw data from other research studies. The most notable of these are highlighted in the following section.

RESEARCH SOURCES

Important caveats apply to the use of online resources for criminological research. Given the volume of information on the internet, researchers need to be judicious about where they source their materials from. A useful rule of thumb is to focus internet searches on the following areas:

- *Government and state resources:* The internet is an extremely quick and relatively easy way of getting hold of official information on crime, both in terms of raw statistical data and in-depth reports and research. Relevant government agencies with a significant web presence include the Home Office and Office of National Statistics (UK), the Bureau of Justice Statistics and FBI Uniform Crime Reports section (USA) and, for Australia, via the Australian Institute of Criminology. European and wider international agencies include the European Union International Crime Survey (EU ICS), UN Office of Drugs and Crime, UN Interregional Crime and Justice Research Institute and Europol.
- *Quality mainstream media sources:* Numerous media sources provide valuable research tools for criminologists. This can be in terms of providing general

information about a form of crime or, for analyses of crime and the media, as a source of primary data, for example if a project was analysing the way the media report crime. In addition to up-to-date commentaries, many of these sites archive old articles. However, caution needs to be exercised as papers often have a particular agenda and, as most criminologists are aware, articulate a partial view of crime and justice (see Chapter 2). Most major newspapers can be accessed online and can be found by entering their title into an internet search engine. Some newspapers also organize their articles and analysis thematically.

◄ *Academic and charitable organizations:* The websites of academic organizations such as the British Society of Criminology and the American Society of Criminology may be used as portals to access a number of important criminological resources. In addition, respected campaigning organizations such as Liberty or the American Civil Liberties Union provide useful briefings on a number of often contentious issues in the fields of criminal justice and policing.

Government and state resources

The UK

◄ Useful information can be found on the Home Office Research Development and Statistics website at:

www.homeoffice.gov.uk/rds/

There are a number of ways to use this site effectively:

1. Click the 'subjects' heading for access to official research and analysis on a broad range of criminological areas.
2. Home Office publications are grouped by type under a range of headings, such as 'Research Reports', 'Statistical publications' and summarized 'Findings'. To access these, click on 'publications'. The current URL is:

http://rds.homeoffice.gov.uk/rds/pubsintro1.html

3. The website allows users to isolate official statistical studies, including the British Crime Survey, from other reports via the 'Official Statistics' option on the homepage. The current URL is:

http://rds.homeoffice.gov.uk/rds/statsprog1.html

◄ For other useful information and developments, see the general Home Office website at:

www.homeoffice.gov.uk

There is also an area devoted to crime reduction:

www.gov.uk/government/policies/reducing-and-preventing-crime--2

- Other government statistics, covering a range of social and economic issues, can be accessed from the Office for National Statistics:

www.statistics.gov.uk/

This has its own dedicated crime and Justice section:

www.ons.gov.uk/ons/taxonomy/index.html?nscl=Crime+and+Justice

- It is also possible to analyse statistics relating to specific neighbourhoods:

www.neighbourhood.statistics.gov.uk/

This facility largely draws on national census data to provide statistics on crime and a raft of other social and economic issues, including income, measures of wellbeing, education, services, deprivation and migration. It provides a fascinating overview of the areas in which we live. The maps record crime statistics across England, Wales and Northern Ireland.

- This site was launched in February 2011 and enabled other geographical analyses:

http://www.police.uk/

- There are a number of useful online sources relating to the criminal justice system. These include:

The Ministry of Justice: www.justice.gov.uk/

HM Courts & Tribunals Service: www.justice.gov.uk/about/hmcts/

The USA

- The government hosts a website dedicated to crime statistics, the Bureau of Justice Statistics:

http://bjs.gov/index.cfm

This agency produces the National Crime Victimization Survey (discussed in Chapter 4):

http://bjs.ojp.usdoj.gov/index.cfm?ty=dcdetail&iid=245

- Statistics of crimes reported to US law enforcement agencies – the FBI Uniform Crime Reports (see Chapter 4) – are available from the FBI website:

www.fbi.gov/about-us/cjis/ucr/ucr

- Other sources of official data can be accessed from the Department of Justice website:

www.justice.gov/

Australia

- National crime and justice issues are undertaken by and available from the same official information source, the Australian Institute of Criminology:

www.aic.gov.au/

Similar to the UK Home Office site, the website allows users to isolate official statistical studies from other reports via the 'Statistics' tab:

www.aic.gov.au/statistics.html

International crime and victimization studies

- European Union International Crime Survey (EU ICS):

www.europeansafetyobservatory.eu/

- International Crime Victims Survey (ICVS), available from the United Nations Interregional Crime and Justice Research Institute (UNCRI):

www.unicri.it/services/library_documentation/publications/icvs/

- European Sourcebook of Crime and Criminal Justice Statistics:

www.europeansourcebook.org

Transnational and organized crime

A number of international policing and government agencies conduct high-quality research into transnational criminal activities. Some of the most useful sources include:

- *Drug trafficking*: The UN's annual World Drug Report is a touchstone for research into international drug markets. It covers a range of different substances, trafficking networks, geopolitical factors and demand issues. It is free and available from:

www.unodc.org/unodc/data-and-analysis/WDR.html

The report is commissioned by the UN Office on Drugs and Crime (UNODC). Its website is also a useful repository of information on many forms of transnational and organized crime:

www.unodc.org/

- *Trafficking in human beings*: There are a number of national, international and third sector (charity) agencies looking at this issue. The US State Department produces an annual 'Trafficking in Persons Report' that can be accessed at:

www.state.gov/g/tip/rls/tiprpt/index.htm

Other sources for this type of criminality can be found at:
Council of Europe:

www.coe.int/t/dghl/monitoring/trafficking/default_en.asp

International Organization for Migration:

www.iom.int/jahia/Jahia/pid/748

Transnational policing

- Europol:

www.europol.europa.eu/

- Interpol:

www.interpol.int/

- The UN also funds its own research department, the United Nations Interregional Crime and Justice Research Institute (UNICRI), which analyses a range of criminological issues. The large proportion of the website concerns policy statements but nonetheless contains useful information for researchers:

www.unicri.it/

Quality mainstream media sources

Some free to view examples of media sources containing dedicated sections on crime include:

- *The Guardian* (UK):

www.guardian.co.uk/uk/ukcrime

- *The Telegraph* (UK):

www.telegraph.co.uk/news/uknews/crime/

- *The New York Times* (USA):

http://topics.nytimes.com/topics/reference/timestopics/subjects/c/crime_and_criminals/index.html

- *Sydney Morning Herald* (AUS):

www.smh.com.au/opinion/society-and-culture/urban-affairs/crime

Academic and charitable organizations

- UK Data Service, which makes data from previous research projects available to researchers (see Chapter 4):

  http://ukdataservice.ac.uk

- Centre for Crime and Justice Studies:

  www.crimeandjustice.org.uk/crimeinfo.html

- General information on sociology:

  www.sociologyonline.co.uk/

- The British Society of Criminology (BSC):

  www.britsoccrim.org

- BSC links page:

  www.britsoccrim.org/links.htm

- University of Oxford Centre for Criminology links page:

  www.crim.ox.ac.uk/Links/index.htm

- John Jay College of Criminal Justice links page:

  www.jjay.cuny.edu/links.php

- Liberty (UK):

  www.liberty-human-rights.org.uk

- Australian and New Zealand Society of Criminology:

  www.anzsoc.org/

- American Civil Liberties Union:

  www.aclu.org

APPENDIX 2

INTERVIEW SCHEDULE FOR 'A STUDY OF THE OPPORTUNITIES AND BARRIERS FACING BME POLICE OFFICERS'

1. What is your age?

2. How long have you been a police officer?
   a. 1–5 years
   b. 6–10 years
   c. 11–15 years
   d. 16–20 years
   e. 21–25 years
   f. More than 25 years

3. Are you:
   a. female
   b. male?

4. Define your ethnicity:
   a. Black
   b. Asian
   c. White
   d. Other (please specify)

5. What is your rank?

6. Why did you decide to join the police service?

7. Was the decision to join the police the right one for you? Please give your reasons.

8. Before joining, were you aware that some minority ethnic officers experienced discrimination? If yes, did this influence your career choice?

9. During the recruitment process, did you feel that you were discriminated against due to your ethnicity? If yes, please explain.

10. In the time you have served as a police officer, have you experienced any discrimination directed towards yourself on the grounds of your ethnicity? If yes, please elaborate.

11. In the time you have served as a police officer, have you seen any discrimination directed towards your colleagues on the grounds of their ethnicity? If yes, please elaborate.

12. How did these experiences make you feel?

13. What, if anything, did you do in response to such experiences?

14. Did these experiences ever lead you to consider leaving the police? Explain your answer.

15. Have you applied for promotion during your career? If you have done so, did your ethnicity have any influence on your decision to apply and the outcome?

16. Have any of your colleagues applied for promotion during their career? If they have done so, did their ethnicity have any influence on their decision to apply and the outcome?

17. On the whole, are the opportunities and barriers experienced by police officers at the different stages of a police career influenced by their ethnic background? If yes, please explain.

18. What is your understanding of institutional and individual discrimination?

19. If you have seen or personally experienced discrimination, has this discrimination been 'individual' or 'institutional'? Please give reasons for your answer.

APPENDIX 3

INTERVIEW SCHEDULE FOR 'AN ASSESSMENT OF STUDENT ATTITUDES TO THE DEATH PENALTY'

NB The same schedule will be administered to students on criminology and engineering degree programmes.

Prompt

1. Do you support or oppose the use of the death penalty in cases when a person is convicted of murder?

   SUPPORT   OPPOSE   UNSURE

   Give reasons for your answer.

2. If you support the use of the death penalty, what are your justifications?

3. In your view, is the death penalty used too frequently, about the right amount, or not frequently enough?

   TOO FREQUENTLY   ABOUT RIGHT   NOT FREQUENTLY ENOUGH   UNSURE

   Why do you say this?

4. Overall, in the USA, do you think the death penalty is used justly or unjustly?

   JUSTLY   UNJUSTLY   UNSURE

   Why did you say this?

5. Where there is no opportunity for parole or another sentence, what is your preferred punishment for individuals convicted of murder: the death penalty or life in prison?

   DEATH PENALTY   LIFE IN PRISON   UNSURE

   Could you say a bit more about this?

6. If you were to reintroduce the death penalty, what crimes would you use it for?

   What is your thinking behind this answer?

7. In your view, does the execution of individuals convicted of murder deter others from committing this crime or has no noticeable effect?

   DETERS OTHERS   NOT MUCH EFFECT   UNSURE

   Explain.

8. In your view, are innocent people ever convicted of murder or does this never happen?

   SOMETIMES   NEVER   UNSURE

   Expand on your answer.

9. How many countries do you believe currently use the death penalty?

10. How many people lost their life in the past 12 months due to capital punishment?

11. Does it cost more or less for a country or state to employ capital punishment instead of imprisoning them for the rest of their life?

    Tell me a bit more about the evidence on which your answer was based.

12. What method of capital punishment would be the most appropriate if a government took the decision to reintroduce it?

    Why did you say this?

13. How and to what extent do you believe attitudes towards capital punishment have changed since the nineteenth century?

GLOSSARY

Access: The availability of the research population to the researcher.

Applied research: Research that explores concrete social problems and tends to be policy oriented.

Area sampling: Selecting particular locations for inclusion in a piece of research.

Association: A relationship between two or more variables.

Between method triangulation: The use of different methods, for example a survey and focus group, to explore the same issue.

Bias: Some influence has exerted itself on the research findings and reduces their objectivity.

Bivariate analysis: Where variables are likely to be one of two options, for example, people are either male or female.

Blue-skies research: This research is driven by the curiosity and interest a researcher has about a particular topic, rather than being asked to do research for a specific reason such as to meet the needs of the organization funding the research.

British Crime Survey: First conducted in 1982, this annual survey focuses on a representative sample of the population in Britain to explore their experiences of crime. It was introduced to provide an alternative account of crime to the one produced by the police service. Now called the Crime Survey of England and Wales.

Case study: Concentrating on a single entity of analysis and often drawing on multiple sources of evidence.

Causation: One thing, normally a particular variable, brings about a change in something else.

Census: Research that encompasses an entire research population and all potential participants.

Chi-squared test: See Pearson's chi-squared test.

Coding: The process of giving data a particular value so it can be examined in more detail and in relation to other variables.

Constructivism: An ontological position that considers social realities as generated and constructed by those participating in social activity.

Content analysis: Analysis of documents and other media. Usually adopted in quantitative research to capture the occurrences of particular items, issues or other phenomena.

Context specific: Something that only applies to a particular setting.

Control groups: Groups that are neutral and are normally used to discern whether changes in the researched group occur irrespective of the issue being researched. For example, medical trials often measure changes in people who have been given a drug, and compare that to control groups of people who have not been given any drugs.

Convenience sampling: Selecting an immediately available group for participants in research.

Conversation analysis (CA): A way of analysing dialogue that attempts to capture a range of contextual information beyond just the words spoken, including pauses, silences and different emphases used in speech.

Correlations: A coherent relationship between two or more variables.

Cramer's V: A statistical test of association between variables. Normally applied to multiple numbers of variables and also variables that have a number of possible values.

Critical realism: A form of realist epistemology that regards structure and action as distinct yet connected phenomena. Like realism, this approach acknowledges the influence of external, identifiable and measurable structures on the social world, but argues they are not deterministic; instead, they generate opportunities for subjective social action to flourish.

Cross-tabulation/crosstabs: A way of measuring the relationships between variables in SPSS.

Curiosity-driven research: See blue-skies research.

Dark figure of crime: Criminal events not captured by crime statistics.

Data analysis: The process of interrogating the information collected during fieldwork.

Data collection: The process of gathering information by deploying various research tools, such as interviews or surveys.

Data triangulation: The use of different types of data in relation to the same research question, for example police statistics about theft and interviews with thieves.

Deductive/deduction: The act of looking at data in relation to preformed questions or concepts.

Dependent variable: Normally refers to the measurable impact of something that changes, for example particular attitudes and beliefs and so on. In a study of voting intentions in relation to different ages, age is the independent variable and voting intention is the dependent variable.

Discourse analysis: Principally a qualitative technique used to access the deeper meanings, embedded values and intentions contained within text.

Distribution: The clustering of statistics in particular areas.

Epistemology: How we derive our knowledge and understanding of things.

Ethics: A consideration of the moral values guiding the research and incorporation of safeguards to protect the interests of participants, the researcher and research funders.

Ethnography: A qualitative technique where the researcher derives a deep understanding through immersion within and attentive observation of the research environment.

Ethnomethodological: A sociological approach concerned with the everyday methods people use to make sense of the social world around them.

Evaluation research: A piece of research that considers if a policy is effective and efficient, or if it works.

Evidence-based/evidence-led policy: Where various policies or crime control initiatives are developed after consulting empirical research on a particular issue.

External validity: The extent to which the findings of a particular piece of research are relevant beyond the immediate context where the research was done.

Face-to-face survey: A quantitative survey that is conducted in the presence of the participant, as opposed to emailed or telephone surveys.

Focus groups: A qualitative technique that explores research questions in detail with a small group of participants.

Free association narrative interview (FANI) method: A psychological/psychosocial interview-based approach. Allows the participant to speak with minimal constraints and seeks to understand a range of complex conscious and unconscious processes.

Frequency: The prevalence of something, or the amount of times something occurs.

Gatekeepers: Participants who enable further access to the research field. Often associated with snowball sampling.

Generalization/generalizability: The notion that research findings relating to one thing may also apply to a wider setting.

Grey literature: Documents that are not traditional academic forms of publication, such as books or academic journal articles, but which are still deemed important. Government reports, think-tank analyses, statistical bulletins and studies conducted by charities are all examples of grey literature.

Grounded theory: Associated with the work of Glaser and Strauss, an approach to qualitative data analysis involving the organization of information into progressively broader groupings, from codes, concepts, categories to theories.

Hypothesis: An assumption tested by the research process.

Independent review board: A US panel of university employees that scrutinizes research proposals on issues such as research ethics.

Independent variable: Normally refers to something that changes but is not influenced by the subject of research, for example age, gender, ethnicity, class and so on.

Inductive/induction: Developing conceptual and theoretical notions as the research progresses.

Influence: See bias.

Interpretivism: An epistemological position that acknowledges differences between the social and natural worlds. Argues that the social realm is interpreted and made sense of by its participants. Many consider interpretivism the opposite of positivism.

Interval data: Spaces (intervals) between points on a scale that is consistent wherever they are measured – such as differences in temperature.

Interviewer effect: A researcher can influence the responses of the research participants. Ideally, the views of a participant should not be shaped by the person doing the research. See reactivity.

Interviews: A method used to ask questions about an issue, which to varying degrees allows the respondent or participant scope to answer questions on their own terms, in contrast to a survey with fixed, standardized questions.

Investigator triangulation: The use of more than one researcher in a single research project. This can be used to minimize interviewer effect as well as to gain a more balanced view of the research issue.

Likert scale: A quantitative tool used to elicit where a participant's response is ranked on a scale. Commonly, a scale of 1–5, where '1' represents strong agreement and '5' strong disagreement, and participants are asked to rank their opinion.

Literature review: All research studies need to summarize relevant previous research that has been carried out in a particular field.

Logistical factors: Awareness of the time and costs involved in a project is a major consideration, that is, travel and equipment.

Longitudinal analysis: Research conducted over a long period, usually with the aim of understanding how the research subject or topic develops or changes over time.

Meta-analysis: The analysis of different pieces of research in one study.

Methodology: A general plan used to guide a researcher to ensure that their research project achieves the aims and objectives of the study.

Multi-cluster sampling: Selection of multiple separate areas, such as geographic regions, each of which is then further subjected to additional sampling approaches.

Multivariate analysis: Analysis involving more than two variables.

Natural sciences: Traditional sciences such as physics, chemistry and biology, which seek to explore more naturally occurring, as opposed to socially constructed, phenomena.

Network sampling: See snowball sampling.

Nodes: The grouping of data into different themes. Often associated with the NVivo software package.

Nominal data: The category that data fits into, and is not ranked, such as gender.

Non-response bias: When research findings may be biased because important groups of people or sources data were not included in the study.

NVivo: A qualitative data analysis software package.

Objectivism/objectivity: An ontological position that considers social realities to exist separately from and irrespective of social actors.

Observational methods: Research involving the researcher watching a group of actors in their own, natural environment. The observer may simply watch what is happening or, to varying degrees, participate in what they are researching.

Ontology: Debates over how the social world can be observed and understood. These debates largely question whether the social world is something that exists *externally to* (or irrespective of) its actors, or whether it is something that is *constructed by* them.

Opportunity sampling: See convenience sampling.

Ordinal data: The statistical rank of particular data.

Participant observation: The data a researcher collects will be based on their observations or the issue they are researching.

Pearson's chi-squared test: A statistical test to ascertain the significance of research findings.

Phenomenological: A philosophical approach to research, which focuses on human consciousness and is concerned with how we experience things and make events meaningful.

Phi coefficient: A statistical test of association between variables. Normally applied to bivariate analysis.

Piloting: The act of conducting a pilot study.

Pilot study: A small-scale study designed to test the research methodology prior to more substantive fieldwork.

Population: The wider group of participants or units available for research.

Positivism: An epistemological position influenced by the natural sciences that posits a belief that there are clear and objectively observable processes that impact on various social phenomena.

Postal survey: A survey disseminated through the post.

Prevalence: The frequency with which something occurs.

Primary research: Research that cultivates new data.

Qualitative methods: Methods used to explore the meanings people attach to their experiences of social phenomenon.

Qualitative research: An approach that usually draws on methods to access the meanings people attribute to things, their emotions or other often subjective phenomena.

Quantitative methods: Methods designed to generate data amenable to statistical analysis including surveys, quantitative observation and, often, content analysis.

Quantitative observation: A form of research where participants are watched and normally involves the recording of the frequency in which something occurs.

Quantitative research: An approach to research that usually emphasizes statistical measures and often seeks to generate understanding of broad trends and processes.

Quota sampling: The subdivision and sampling of a wider population based on the prevalence of particular groups, components or variables.

Random sampling: A technique where each unit in a population has a known chance of being chosen for inclusion in the research.

Rapid evidence assessment: A quick and often cursory look at existing research and analysis into a particular issue.

Ratio scales: Where differences between two things can be compared and quantified. For example, 2 kg weighs twice as much as 1 kg (2:1).

Raw data: Information gathered in the course of research, which has not yet been analysed.

Reactivity: The influence a researcher has on the environment being studied.

Realism: An epistemological position that lies between positivism and interpretivism. It acknowledges the existence and influence of external, identifiable and measurable structures on the social world.

Reliability: The certainty that data is well founded and collected through valid and robust processes.

Replication: The ability to conduct the same piece of research again.

Representativeness/representative: The data and findings reflect the wider population from which the sample of participants is drawn.

Research aims: A clarification of what the research is intending to discover.

Research design: The process of selecting the appropriate tools to address the aims of the research and establishing how the work can be undertaken in a practical sense.

Research ethics committee: A UK body of individuals who scrutinize the ethical probity of proposed research projects. Most empirical work requires prior ethical approval in this way.

Research population: The group of potential participants in a research project.

Resources: The available materials to conduct the research such as time, money and tools.

Sample: A group drawn from a wider population and selected to take part in the research.

Sampling: The selection of research participants from a wider pool of potential candidates.

Sampling error: The sample has been incorrectly selected and does not reflect the wider population or allow anything significant to be surmised about this wider group.

Sampling frame: A mechanism to facilitate random sampling. Allows the researcher to identify all the potential participants from the population.

Secondary analysis: The use of existing data for subsequent research purposes.

Secondary data: Data that has been collected as part of a previous piece of research.

Secondary research: Research that draws on and reinterprets data collected during a previous research project.

Semi-structured interviews: A qualitative technique that allows scope for the participant to express themselves in their own way but has consistent questions that allow the interview data to be tied to the aims of the research and also compared across participants.

Significance: An agreed threshold that the findings are noteworthy.

Skewed: The research findings reflect a particular bias.

Snowball sampling: The use of research participants to facilitate further access to the research field.

SPSS (Statistical Package for Social Sciences): A software tool to analyse quantitative data.

Standardization: The same methodological approach is used for different settings.

Stratified random sampling: Where the population is divided into various categories or strata and then sampled within each of these groups.

Structured observation: A quantitative technique that involves observing a particular phenomena and capturing data in predefined categories.

Subjectivity: The notion that people see things differently to others and that research findings may only be relevant to a particular participant and therefore may not be generalizable to others.

Survey: A highly structured interview schedule used in quantitative research.

Symbolic interactionist: A theoretical perspective social scientists use to look at how people interact with each other and the meanings they attach to this interaction. A key issue is the symbols social actors use to communicate and interpret the world around them.

Systematic sampling: Units of research are selected from a list or other directory of the population according to fixed intervals.

Telephone survey: A survey conducted over the telephone.

Thematic coding: Organizing data according to themes.

Thick description: An account of context and its influence, rather than solely focusing on the actions, beliefs or statements of participants.

Triangulation: The combination of different kinds of data and methods to analyse the same issue in a single project.

Univariate analysis: Analysis relating to a single variable, for example an analysis of frequency.

Unstructured interviews: A qualitative technique that allows the participant to speak freely about a particular issue.

Valid/validity: The data reaches particular standards of objectivity.

Values: This has two meanings. It may refer to biases and beliefs that influence a research project. Alternatively, in quantitative research, usually refers to figures or other statistical data.

Variables: The characterization of something that is intended to be measured, for example age, ethnicity and attitudes on a scale.

Victimization surveys: Surveys designed to overcome the underreporting and underrecording of crime in official statistics by asking people if they have been victims of crime.

Within method triangulation: The use of different forms of the same research method, for example the combination of attitudinal scales and open questions to research a particular issue.

x^2 test: See Pearson's chi-squared test.

REFERENCES

Anderson, N. (1923) *The Hobo: The Sociology of the Homeless Man*. Chicago: University of Chicago Press.

Asch, S.E. (1956) 'Studies of independence and conformity: A minority of one against a unanimous majority', *Psychological Monographs*, 70(9): 1–70.

Atkinson, J.M. and Heritage, J. (eds) (1984) *Structures of Social Action: Studies in Conversation Analysis*. Cambridge: Cambridge University Press.

Baille, S. (2003) 'Epistemology', in R.L. Miller and J.D. Brewer (eds) *The A–Z of Social Research*. London: Sage.

Barclay, G.C. and Tavares, C. (1999) *Digest 4: Information on the Criminal Justice System in England and Wales*. London: Home Office.

Bauman, Z. (2004) *Identity*. Cambridge: Polity Press.

Becker, H. (1967) 'Whose side are we on?', *Social Problems*, 14(3): 239–47.

Bhaskar, R. (1989) *Reclaiming Reality: A Critical Introduction to Contemporary Philosophy*, London: Verso.

Bhaskar, R. (1998) *The Possibility of Naturalism: A Philosophical Critique of the Contemporary Human Sciences*. London: Routledge.

Bottoms, A. (2000) 'The relationship between theory and research in criminology', in R.D. King and E. Wincup (eds) *Doing Research on Crime and Justice*. Oxford: Oxford University Press.

Bottoms, A. (2007) 'Place, space, crime and disorder', in M. Maguire, R. Morgan and R. Reiner (eds) *The Oxford Handbook of Criminology*. Oxford: Oxford University Press.

Bourgeois, P. (2003) *In Search of Respect: Dealing Crack in El Barrio* (2nd edn). Cambridge: Cambridge University Press.

Bowling, B. (1999) 'The rise and fall of murder: Zero tolerance or crack's decline?', *British Journal of Criminology*, 39(4): 531–54.

Bowling, B. and Phillips, C. (2002) *Racism, Crime and Justice*. Harlow: Pearson.

Brantingham, P.J. and Brantingham, P.L. (1993) 'Environment, routine and situation: Toward a pattern theory of crime', in R.V. Clarke and M. Felson (eds) *Routine Activity and Rational Choice*. Brunswick, NJ: Transaction.

Bryman, A. (2008) *Social Research Methods* (3rd edn). Oxford: Oxford University Press.

Burgess, E. (1925) 'The growth of the city: An introduction to a research project,' in R. Park, E. Burgess and R. McKenzie (eds) *The City*. Chicago: University of Chicago Press.

Burgess, E. (1942) 'Foreword', in C. Shaw and H. McKay, *Juvenile Delinquency and Urban Areas*. Chicago: University of Chicago Press.

Burt, C. (1925) *The Young Delinquent*. London: University of London Press.

Caless, B. (2011) *Policing at the Top: The Roles, Values and Attitudes of Chief Police Officers*. Bristol: Policy Press.

Carlen, P. (ed.) (2002) *Women and Punishment: The Struggle for Justice*. Cullompton: Willan.

Carlen, P. and Worrall, A. (2004) *Analysing Women's Imprisonment*. Cullompton: Willan.

Carrabine, E. (2004) *Power, Discourse and Resistance: A Genealogy of the Strangeways Prison Riot*. Aldershot: Ashgate.

Carrabine, E. (2008) *Crime, Culture and the Media*. Cambridge: Polity Press.

Carter, E. (2011) *Laughter, Confessions and the Tape: Analysing Police Interviews*. London: Continuum.

Clarke, R.V. (2004) 'Technology, criminology and crime science', *European Journal on Criminal Policy and Research*, 10(1): 155–63.

Cohen, S. (1972) *Folk Devils and Moral Panics: The Creation of the Mods and Rockers*. Oxford: Martin Robertson.

Cohen, S. (2002) *Folk Devils and Moral Panics: The Creation of the Mods and Rockers* (3rd edn). Abingdon: Routledge.

Cornish, D.B. and Clarke, R.V. (eds) (1986) *The Reasoning Criminal: Rational Choice Perspectives on Criminal Offending*. New York: Springer-Verlag.

Corston, J. (2007) *The Corston Report: A Report by Baroness Jean Corston of a Review of Women with Particular Vulnerabilities in the Criminal Justice System*. London: Home Office.

Crewe, B. (2009) *The Prisoner Society: Power, Adaptation and Social Life in an English Prison*. Oxford: Oxford University Press.

Cromwell, P. (ed.) (2010) *In Their Own Words: Criminals on Crime* (5th edn). New York: Oxford University Press.

Cromwell, P. and Olson, J. (2003) *Breaking and Entering: Burglars on Burglary*. London: Wadworth.

Darwin, C. ([1859]1998) *The Origin of the Species*. Ware: Wordsworth.

Darwin, C. ([1871]2004) *The Descent of Man*. London: Penguin.

Denzin, N.K. (1970) *The Research Act in Sociology*. Chicago: Aldine.

Denzin, N.K. (1978) *The Research Act: A Theoretical Introduction to Sociological Methods*. New York: McGraw-Hill.

Ditton, J. (1998) 'Public support for town centre CCTV schemes: Myth or reality?', in C. Norris, J. Moran and G. Armstrong (eds) *Surveillance, Closed Circuit Television and Social Control*. Aldershot: Ashgate.

Ditton, J. and Farrall, S. (eds) (2000) *The Fear of Crime*. Aldershot: Ashgate.

Downes, D. and Rock, P. (1998) *Understanding Deviance*. Oxford: Oxford University Press.

Eaton, M. (1986) *Justice for Women? Family, Court and Social Control*. Milton Keynes: Open University Press.

Falco, D.L. and Freiburger, T.L. (2011) 'Public opinion and the death penalty: A qualitative approach', *The Qualitative Report*, 16(3): 830–47.

Farrell, G., Bowers, K. and Johnson, S. (2005) 'Cost-benefit analysis for crime science: Making cost-benefit analysis useful through a portfolio of outcomes', in M. Smith and N. Tilley (eds) *Crime Science: New Approaches to Preventing and Detecting Crime*. Cullompton: Willan.

Farrington, D. and Welsh, B. (2002) *Effects of Improved Street Lighting on Crime: A Systematic Review*, Home Office Research Study No. 251. London: HMSO.

Farrington, D.P., Coid, J.W., Harnett, L. et al. (2006) *Criminal Careers Up To Age 50 and Life Success Up To 48*, Home Office Research Study No. 299. London: Home Office.

Felson, M. (2002) *Crime and Everyday Life*, London: Sage.

Ferrero-Lombroso, G. (1911) *Criminal Man, According to the Classification of Cesare Lombroso, Briefly Summarised by His Daughter*. London: G.P. Putnam's Sons.

Fielding, N. (1982) 'Observational research on the national front', in M. Bulmer (ed.) *Social Research Ethics: An Examination of the Merits of Covert Participation Observation*. London: Macmillan.

Finney, A. (2006) *Domestic Violence, Sexual Assault and Stalking: Findings from the 2004–05 British Crime Survey*, Home Office Online Study 12/06. London: Home Office.

Fitzgerald, R. and Ellsworth, P. (1984) 'Due process v crime control: Death qualification and jury attitudes', *Law and Human Behavior*, 8: 31–51.

Foster, J., Newburn, T. and Souhami, A. (2005) *Assessing the Impact of the Stephen Lawrence Inquiry*, Home Office Research Study 294. London: Home Office.

Foucault, M. (1967) *Madness and Civilisation: A History of Insanity in the Age of Reason*. London: Tavistock.

Foucault, M. (1977) *Discipline and Punish: The Birth of the Prison*. Harmondsworth: Penguin.

Freud, S. (1961) *The Complete Works of Sigmund Freud* (vol. 16). London: Hogarth Press.

Fussey, P. (2011) 'An economy of choice? Terrorist decision-making and criminological rational choice theories reconsidered', *Security Journal*, 24(1): 85–99.

Gadd, D. (2000) 'Masculinities, violence and defended social subjects', *Theoretical Criminology*, 4(4): 429–49.

Gadd, D. (2002) 'Masculinities and violence against female partners', *Social and Legal Studies*, 11(1): 61–80.

Gadd, D. (2003) 'Reading between the lines: Subjectivity and men's violence', *Men and Masculinities*, 5(4): 333–54.

Gadd, D. (2006) 'The role of recognition in the desistance process: A case analysis of a former far-right activist', *Theoretical Criminology*, 10(2): 179–202.

Gadd, D. and Farrall, S. (2004) 'Criminal careers, desistance and subjectivity: Interpreting men's narrative of change', *Theoretical Criminology*, 8(2): 123–56.

Garland, D. (1996) 'The limits of the sovereign state: Strategies of crime control in contemporary society', *British Journal of Criminology*, 36(4): 445–71.

Gerbner, G., Gross, L., Jackson-Beeck, M. et al. (1976) *Violence Profile No. 7: Trends in Network Television Drama and Viewer Conceptions of Social Reality 1967–1975*, Annenberg School for Communication, University of Pennsylvania.

Giddens, A. (1997) *Sociology*. Cambridge: Polity Press.

Giddens, A. (2007) *Over to You, Mr Brown*. Cambridge: Polity Press.

Gilbert, N. (2008) *Researching Social Life*. London: Sage.

Girling, E., Loader, I. and Sparks, R. (1999) *Crime and Social Change in Middle England: Questions of Order in an English Town*. London: Routledge.

Glaser, B. and Strauss, A. (1967) *The Discovery of Grounded Theory: Strategies for Qualitative Research*. Chicago: Aldine.

Goldacre, B. (2009a) 'Bad science: Home Office research so feeble someone ought to be locked up', *The Guardian,* 18 July.

Goldacre, B. (2009b) *Bad Science*. London: Harper Perennial.

Griffith, A. (2010) *SPSS for Dummies*. London: John Wiley & Sons.

Groff, E. and Birks, D. (2008) 'Simulating crime prevention strategies: A look at the possibilities', *Policing: A Journal of Policy and Practice*, 2(2): 175–84.

Guerry, A.M. (1833) *Essai sur la statistique morale de la France*. Paris: Crochard.

Gunter, A. (2009) *Growing Up Bad? Road Culture, Badness and Black Youth Transitions in an East London Neighbourhood*. London: Tufnell Press.

Gutting, G. (2011) *Thinking the Impossible: French Philosophy Since 1960*. Oxford: Oxford University Press.

Haggerty, K. (2008) 'Book review: The novelty of crime science', *Policing & Society*, 17(1): 83–8.

Hale, C. (1996) 'Fear of crime: A review of the literature', *International Review of Victimology*, 4: 79–150.

Hales, G., Lewis, C. and Silverstone, D. (2006) *Gun Crime: The Market In and Use of Illegal Firearms*, Home Office Research Study 298. London: HMSO.

Hales, J., Nevill, C., Pudney, S. and Tipping, S. (2009) *Longitudinal Analysis of the Offending, Crime and Justice Survey 2003–06*, Home Office Research Report 19. London: HMSO.

Hall, N., Grieve, J. and Savage, S. (eds) (2009) *Policing and the Legacy of Lawrence*. Cullompton: Willan.

Hall, S., Critcher, C., Jefferson, T. et al. (1978) *Policing the Crisis: Mugging, the State and Law and Order*. London: Macmillan.

Harrison, J., Simpson, M., Harrison, O. and Martin, E. (2005) *Study Skills for Criminology*. London: Sage.

Hart, C. (1998) *Doing a Literature Review: Releasing the Social Science Research Imagination*. London: Sage.

Hassan, N. (2001) 'Letter from Gaza. An arsenal of believers: Talking to the "human bombs"', *The New Yorker*, 19 November, www.newyorker.com/archive/2001/11/19/011119fa_FACT1.

Heidensohn, F. (1968) 'The deviance of women: A critique and an enquiry', *British Journal of Sociology*, 19: 160–75.

Hirschi, T. (1969) *Causes of Delinquency*. Los Angeles: University of California Press.

HMCPSI (Her Majesty's Crown Prosecution Services Inspectorate) (2007) *Without Consent*. Home Office: HMIC.

Hobbes, T. ([1651] 2002) *Leviathan*. London: Penguin.

Hobbs, D. (1988) *Doing the Business: Entrepreneurship, the Working Class and Detectives in the East End of London*. Oxford: Oxford University Press.

Hobbs, D. (1995) *Bad Business*. Oxford: Oxford University Press.

Holdaway, S. (2009) *Black Police Associations: An Analysis of Race and Ethnicity within Constabularies*. Oxford: Oxford University Press.

Hollway, W. and Jefferson, T. (2000) *Doing Qualitative Research Differently: Free Association, Narrative and the Interview Method*. London: Sage.

Home Office (2010) *Crime in England and Wales 2009/10*. London: HMSO.

Hood, R. and Hoyle, C. (2008) *The Death Penalty: A Worldwide Perspective* (4th edn). Oxford: Oxford University Press.

Hopkins Burke, R. (ed.) (2004) *Hard Cop, Soft Cop: Dilemmas and Debates in Contemporary Policing*. Cullompton: Willan.

Hopkins Burke, R. (2009) *An Introduction to Criminological Theory* (3rd edn). Cullompton: Willan.

Hough, M. (1995) *Anxiety About Crime: Findings from the 1994 British Crime Survey*, Home Office Research Study No. 147. London: Home Office.

Hough, M. and Mayhew, P. (1983) *The British Crime Survey: First Report*, Home Office Research Study No. 76. London: Home Office.

Jansson, K. (2007) *British Crime Survey: Measuring Crime for 25 Years*. London: Home Office.

Jefferson, T. (1996) 'From "little fairy boy" to the "complete destroyer": Subjectivity and transformation in the life of Mike Tyson', in M. Mac an Ghaill (ed.) *Understanding Masculinities: Social Relations and Cultural Arenas*. Buckingham: Open University Press.

Jefferson, T. (1997) 'Masculinities and crimes', in M. Maguire, R. Morgan and R. Reiner (eds) *The Oxford Handbook of Criminology* (2nd edn). Oxford: Oxford University Press.

Jefferson, T. (1998) 'Muscle, "hard men" and "iron" Mike Tyson: Reflections on desire, anxiety and the embodiment of masculinity', *Body and Society*, 4(1): 77–98.

Jefferson, T. and Gadd, D. (2008) *Psychosocial Criminology*. London: Sage.

Jewkes, Y. (2004) *Media and Crime*. London: Sage.

Jewkes, Y. (2007) 'Introduction', in Y. Jewkes (ed.) *Handbook on Prisons*. Cullompton: Willan.

Johnson, N. (2008) 'Mathematics, physics, and crime', *Policing: A Journal of Policy and Practice*, 2(2): 160–6.

Jones, T. (2006) *Criminology*. Oxford: Oxford University Press.

Jones, T., McLean, M. and Young, J. (1986) *The Islington Crime Survey: Crime, Victimization, and Policing In Inner-city London*. Aldershot: Gower.

Kalven, H. and Zeisel, H. (1967) 'The American jury: Notes for an English controversy', *The Round Table*, 57(226): 158–65.

Katz, J. (1988) *The Seductions of Crime: Moral and Sensual Attractions in Doing Evil*. New York: Basic Books.

Kozinets, R.V. (2009) *Netnography: Doing Ethnographic Research Online*. London: Sage.

Laycock, G. (2005) 'Defining crime science', in M. Smith and N. Tilley (eds) *Crime Science: New Approaches to Preventing and Detecting Crime*. Cullompton: Willan.

Laycock, G. (2008) 'Special edition on crime science editorial: What is crime science?', *Policing: A Journal of Policy and Practice*, 2(2): 149–53.

Lees, S. (2002) *Carnal Knowledge: Rape on Trial*. London: Women's Press.

Levi, M., Maguire, M. and Brookman, F. (2007) 'Violent crime,', in M. Maguire, R. Morgan and R. Reiner (eds) *The Oxford Handbook of Criminology* (4th edn). Oxford: Oxford University Press.

Loftus, E. (1974) *Eyewitness Testimony*. Cambridge, MA: Harvard University Press.

Lombroso, C. ([1876]2006) *L'uomo delinquente* (*The Criminal Man*), trans. N.H. Rafter and M. Gibson. Durham: Duke University Press.

Lombroso, C. and Ferrero, W. (1895) *The Female Offender*. New York: Appleton.

Lyotard, J.F. (1984) *The Postmodern Condition*. Manchester: Manchester University Press.

Maguire, M. (2000) 'Researching "street criminals": A neglected art', in R. King and E. Wincup (eds) *Doing Research on Crime and Justice*. Oxford: Oxford University Press.

Maguire, M. (2002) 'Crime statistics: The "data explosion" and its implications', in M. Maguire, R. Morgan and R. Reiner (eds) *The Oxford Handbook of Criminology* (3rd edn). Oxford: Oxford University Press.

Martinson, R. (1974) 'What works? Questions and answers about prison reform', *Public Interest*, 55: 22–54.

Matthews, R. (1992) 'Replacing "broken windows": Crime, incivilities and urban change', in R. Matthews and J. Young (eds) *Issues in Realist Criminology*. London: Sage.

Matthews, R. (2009) *Doing Time: An Introduction to the Sociology of Imprisonment* (2nd edn). Basingstoke: Palgrave Macmillan.

May, T. (1997) *Social Research: Issues, Methods and Process*. Buckingham: Open University Press.

Mayhew, H. (1862) *London Labour and the London Poor*. London: Dover.

Messerschmitt, J. (1993) *Masculinities and Crime: Critique and Reconceptualization of Theory*. Lanham, MD: Rowman & Littlefield.

Miller, J. (2001) *One of the Guys: Girls, Gangs, and Gender*. New York: Oxford University Press.

Mills, C. Wright (1959) *The Sociological Imagination*. New York: Oxford University Press.

Ministry of Justice (2009) *Statistics on Women and the Criminal Justice System*. London: Ministry of Justice/Institute for Criminal Policy Research, School of Law, King's College London.

Murray, C. (1990) *The Emerging British Underclass*. London: Institute of Economic Affairs.

Murray, C. (2000) 'The British underclass', *The Sunday Times*, 13 February.

Neuman, W.L. and Wiegand, B. (2000) *Criminal Justice Research Methods: Qualitative and Quantitative Approaches*. Boston: Allyn & Bacon.

Newburn, T. (2007) *Criminology*. Cullompton: Willan.

Norris, C. and Armstrong, G. (1999) *The Maximum Surveillance Society*. Oxford: Berg.

Pakes, F. (2010) *Comparative Criminal Justice* (2nd edn). Cullompton: Willan.

Pallant, J. (2010) *SPSS Survival Manual: A Step by Step Guide to Data Analysis Using SPSS*. Milton Keynes: Open University Press.

Parsons, T. (1937) *The Structure of Social Action*. New York: McGraw-Hill.

Pease, K. (2008) 'How to behave like a scientist?', *Policing: A Journal of Policy and Practice*, 2(2): 154–9.

Peckham, A. (1985) *A Woman in Custody*. London: Fontana.

Pfol, S. (1985) *Images of Deviance and Social Control*. Long Grove, IL: Waveland.

Porter, M. (1994) '"Second hand ethnography": Some problems in analysing a feminist project', in A. Bryman and R.G. Burgess (eds) *Analysing Qualitative Data*. London: Routledge

Pratt, J. (2002) *Punishment and Civilisation: Penal Tolerance and Intolerance in Modern Society*. London: Sage.

Pratt, J. (2007) *Penal Populism.* Abingdon: Routledge.

Rake, K. (2005) *Whither Feminism*. London: Fawcett Society.

Rawlinson, P. and Fussey, P. (2010) 'Crossing borders: Migration and survival in the capital's informal marketplace', *Criminal Justice Matters*, 79(1): 6–7.

Reiner, R. (1991) *Chief Constables*. Oxford: Oxford University Press.

Reiner, R. (2000) *The Politics of the Police* (3rd edn). Oxford: Oxford University Press.

Reiner, R. (2007) *Law and Order: An Honest Citizen's Guide to Crime and Control*. Cambridge: Polity Press.

Ringrose, J. (2006) 'A new universal mean girl: Examining the discursive construction and social regulation of a new feminine pathology', *Feminism and Psychology*, 16(4): 405–24.

Rodeghier, M. (2010) *Surveys with Confidence: A Practical Guide to Survey Research Using SPSS.* Chicago: SPSS.

Roe, S. and Ashe, J. (2008) *Young People and Crime: Findings from the 2006 Offending, Crime and Justice Survey*. London: HMSO.

Rowe, M. (2004) *Policing, Race and Racism*. Cullompton: Willan.

Sacks, H. (1984) 'Note on methodology', in J.M. Atkinson and J. Heritage (eds) *Structures of Social Action: Studies in Conversation Analysis*. Cambridge: Cambridge University Press.

Senior, P., Crowther-Dowey, C. and Long, M. (2007) *Understanding Modernisation in Criminal Justice*. Milton Keynes: Open University Press.

Shaw, C. and McKay, H. (1942) *Juvenile Delinquency and Urban Areas*. Chicago: University of Chicago Press.

Silverstri, M. and Crowther-Dowey, C. (2008) *Gender and Crime*. London: Sage.

Smart, C. (1976) *Women, Crime and Criminology*. London: Routledge.

Smith, M. and Tilley, N. (2005a) 'Introduction', in M. Smith and N. Tilley (eds) *Crime Science: New Approaches to Preventing and Detecting Crime*. Cullompton: Willan.

Smith, M. and Tilley, N. (eds) (2005b) *Crime Science: New Approaches to Preventing and Detecting Crime*. Cullompton: Willan.

Smith, M. and Webb, B. (2005) 'Vehicle excise duty evasion in the UK', in M. Smith and N. Tilley (eds) *Crime Science: New Approaches to Preventing and Detecting Crime*. Cullompton: Willan.

Sparks, R. (1992) 'Reason and unreason in "left realism": Some problems in the constitution of the fear of crime', in R. Matthews and J. Young (eds) *Issues in Realist Criminology*. London: Sage.

Sparks, R., Bottoms, A. and Hay, W. (1996) *Prisons and the Problem of Order.* Oxford: Clarendon Press.

Sumner, C.S. (1994) *The Sociology of Deviance: An Obituary.* Buckingham: Open University Press.

Sutherland, E.H. (1937) *The Professional Thief*. Chicago: University of Chicago Press.

Sykes, G. (1958) *The Society of Captives*. Princeton, NJ: Princeton University Press.

Taylor, I., Walton, P. and Young, J. (1973) *The New Criminology*. London: Routledge & Kegan Paul.

Temkin, J. (2002) *Rape and the Legal Process* (2nd edn). Oxford Monographs on Criminal Law and Justice. Oxford: Oxford University Press.

The Guardian (2008) Just how expert are the expert witnesses?, 18 May, available from http://education.guardian.co.uk/egweekly/story/0,,2279458,00.html.

Thrasher, F.M. (1927) *The Gang: A Study of 1313 Gangs in Chicago*. Chicago: University of Chicago Press.

Tierney, J. (2005) *Criminology: Theory and Context* (2nd edn). Harlow: Pearson Longman.

Tilley, N. (ed.) (2005a) *Handbook of Crime Prevention and Community Safety*. Cullompton: Willan.

Tilley, N. (2005b) 'Driving down crime at motorway service areas', in M. Smith and N. Tilley (eds) *Crime Science: New Approaches to Preventing and Detecting Crime*. Cullompton: Willan.

Travers, M. (2001) *Qualitative Research through Case Studies*. London: Sage.

Tseloni, A. and Pease, K. (2003) 'Repeat personal victimisation: "Boosts or flags"', *British Journal of Criminology*, 43: 196–212.

Van Dijk, J.J.M., van Kesteren, J. and Smit, P. (2007) *Criminal Victimization in International Perspective: Key Findings from the 2004–2005 ICVS and EUICS*. The Hague: Boom.

Wacquant, L. (2002) 'Scrutinizing the street: Poverty, morality, and the pitfalls of urban ethnography', *American Journal of Sociology*, 107(6): 1468–532.

Wacquant, L. (2009) *Prisons of Poverty*. Minneapolis: University of Minnesota Press.

Walklate, S. (2004) *Gender, Crime and Criminal Justice* (2nd edn). Cullompton: Willan.

Webb, B., Smith, C., Brock, A. and Townsley, M. (2005) 'DNA fast-tracking', in M. Smith and N. Tilley (eds) *Crime Science: New Approaches to Preventing and Detecting Crime*. Cullompton: Willan.

Weber, M. (1964) *The Theory of Economic and Social Organization*. Glencoe: Free Press.

Webster, C. (2007) *Understanding Race and Crime*. Maidenhead: Open University Press.

Welsh, B. and Farrington, D. (2002) *Crime Prevention Effects of Closed Circuit Television: A Systematic Review*, Home Office Research Study 252. London: HMSO.

Whyte, W. (1955) *Street Corner Society* (2nd edn). Chicago: University of Chicago Press.

Wiles, P. (1999) 'The contribution of research to policy', speech given at the Centre for Criminal Justice Studies, AGM, November.

Wilson, J.Q. and Kelling, G.L. (1982) 'Broken windows', *The Atlantic*, 249(3): 29–38.

Winlow, S. (2001) *Badfellas: Crime, Tradition and New Masculinities*. Oxford: Berg.

Winlow, S. and Hall, S. (2006) *Violent Night: Urban Leisure and Contemporary Culture*. Oxford: Berg.

Wolfgang, M. (1972) 'Cesare Lombroso', in H. Mannheim (ed.) *Pioneers in Criminology*. Montclair, NJ: Patterson Smith.

Wortley, R. and Summers, L. (2005) 'Reducing prison disorder through situational prevention: The Glen Parva experience', in M. Smith and N. Tilley (eds) *Crime Science: New Approaches to Preventing and Detecting Crime*. Cullompton: Willan.

Wykes, M. and Welsh, K. (2008) *Violence, Gender and Justice*. London: Sage.

Young, J. (1987) 'The tasks facing a realist criminology', *Contemporary Crises*, 11: 337–56.

Young, J. (1994) 'Incessant chatter: Recent paradigms in criminology', in M. Maguire, R. Morgan and R. Reiner (eds) *The Oxford Handbook of Criminology*. Oxford: Clarendon Press.

Young, J. (2004) 'Voodoo criminology and the numbers game', in J. Ferrell, K. Hayward, W. Morrison and M. Presdee (eds) *Cultural Criminology Unleashed*. London: Glasshouse Press.

Zimring, F. and Hawkins, G. (1997) *Crime is Not the Problem: Lethal Violence in America*. Oxford: Oxford University Press.

INDEX